To Eileen Welsh:
an astute and empathetic observer of the
human condition, and an example to us all of
sustained commitment to others

LIVED DIVERSITIES

Space, place and identities in the multi-ethnic city

Charles Husband, Yunis Alam,
Jörg Hüttermann and Joanna Fomina

First published in Great Britain in 2016 by

Policy Press
University of Bristol
1-9 Old Park Hill
Bristol UK
BS2 8BB
t: +44 (0)117 331 5020
pp-info@bristol.ac.uk
www.policypress.co.uk

North America office:
Policy Press
c/o The University of Chicago Press
1427 East 60th Street
Chicago, IL 60637, USA
t: +1 773 702 7700
f: +1 773 702 9756
sales@press.uchicago.edu
www.press.uchicago.edu

© Policy Press 2016

British Library Cataloguing in Publication Data
A catalogue record for this book is available from the British Library

Library of Congress Cataloging-in-Publication Data
A catalog record for this book has been requested

ISBN 978-1-4473-1571-1 paperback

Cover design by Andrew Corbett
Front cover image: Panos Pictures
Printed and bound in Great Britain by CMP, Poole
Policy Press uses environmentally responsible print partners

Woodland
CARBON
www.woodlandcarbon.co.uk
CMP (UK) LTD

Contents

About the authors

Yunis Alam is a lecturer in the Division of Social Sciences and Criminal Justice Studies at the University of Bradford, UK. His teaching and research interests include ethnic relations and social cohesion, popular culture, post-colonial literature and ethnographic research.

Joanna Fomina is a researcher and policy analyst. Her research interests include migration and cultural diversity, Polish diaspora in the UK, civic participation of migrants, border management as well as democratisation in Eastern Europe. She has authored a number of articles, research reports and policy papers as well as a book on British multiculturalism.

Charles Husband is an interdisciplinary social scientist with a commitment to policy relevant research in the area of ethnic relations. He is professor emeritus in social analysis at the University of Bradford (UK), docent in sociology at the University of Helsinki (Finland) and visiting professor at the Sámi University College (Guovdageaidnu, Norway).

Jörg Hüttermann is a research fellow at the Max Planck Institute for the Study of Religious and Ethnic Diversity, Göttingen University, Germany. He has worked in recent years as a researcher at the Institute for Interdisciplinary Research on Conflict and Violence Research at Bielefeld University. His research has sought to illuminate the constructive potential of conflict for multi-ethnic societies.

Acknowledgements

This book is a product of a project that was carried out under the aegis of a grant from the Deutsche Forschungsgemeinschaft (DFG) (Germany) with Professor William Heitmeyer and Dr Jörg Hüttermann (project director), entitled 'Immigration, figuration, conflict. A comparative space analysis in Bradford and Duisberg'.

The data here could not have been generated without the willing cooperation of the very many people who were interviewed; and those who shared their experiences and views in casual conversation: and we recognise our indebtedness to them.

Other colleagues have been valued participants in a number of ways, and here we should mention Dr Tom Cockburn, Dr Nathan Manning, Professor Tom Moring, colleagues at the Helsinki Collegium for Advanced Study and particularly Ms Rūta Kazlauskaitė-Gürbüz for her invaluable insights and fieldwork.

The team of Yunis, Jörg, Joanna and Charlie have benefitted from their friends and colleagues in differing national contexts who have fed their enthusiasm and tenacity in bringing this monograph to completion.

We are very grateful to the team at Policy Press for their friendly and efficient support, in particular Laura Greaves, Laura Vickers, and Emily Watt, and to Alan Halfpenny and Liz Fawcett in their editorial staff who have so efficiently scanned our text and helped us to reduce the flaws in our script.

CHAPTER ONE

Introduction

Location, Location, Location. Indeed, yes. Where would we wish to live? Low-cost television has found, if not exactly a specific, tightly defined genre, then at least a theme that has wide televisual appeal, namely, our homes and where, and often how, we would wish them to be. Whether it is sending intrepid scouts into the rural idylls of Midsommershire in pursuit of *that* house for under £600,000 that will address the dearest aspirations of nice people in urban flight, or the opportunity to follow inspired and obsessed couples building their own architectural *Elysium* in making over a neglected property, or less financially well-resourced individuals buying properties at auction and converting them into properties that *we* feel comfortable in critically appraising, the message is clearly out there: houses and homes are a national fixation. Newsagents' shelves are heavily stocked with magazines that both nurture and reflect widespread individual aspirations regarding the quality of their homes and gardens. Home improvement provides a major market for weekend shopping in heavily utilised outlets. Whether it is a modest back-to-back in a working-class terrace or a detached mansion, individuals have a demonstrable capacity to make strong affiliations with the place where they live. A reflection of this will be apparent in the chapters that follow.

However, we must note that in this daily encounter with human dwellings, the location and amenities surrounding the property are as worthy of close inspection as the property itself. As a nation, we have a finely tuned repertoire of diagnostic categories whereby we are able to evaluate the desirable and undesirable characteristics of different locales. The person in the street does not need the sociological insights of Norbert Elias (Elias and Scotson, 1965) in order to talk fluently about the territorial demarcations that operate in the areas where they live. The boundaries between the desirable and the rough, between the established and the incomers, and between the respectable and disreputable are typically well-rehearsed social boundaries. The criteria that justify these certitudes are rehearsed and validated in exchanges of emotionally rich expressions of opinion, shared between in-group members as they record the most recent violation of their territorial dignity.

For all the frequently aired discussion of globalisation, for very many people, their place of residence is one of the key anchoring realities in their daily, locally grounded life. The linkage between house and home is not to be taken lightly. The physical structure of the property, the house or apartment, is merely the substantive focus for the investment of ego. The multiple routines of residence are wound round with the layered biographical remembrance of lives lived in this space. My bedroom, my kitchen, my study, my pocket-handkerchief front garden are all instances of the claimed affective relationship between personal identity and domestic territory. Unique individual efforts at self-expression are mapped onto the fabric of houses. Whether it is the ability of the teenager to have *their* choice of posters on the wall, or the ability of the parent to have *their* idea of a fully fitted kitchen, the physical fabric of a house is permeated by the aspirations of its occupants to find security and recognition there. The harrowing narratives of novelists who beautifully and sensitively craft stories relating the desperation of individuals to live in a house in which they have had no recognition of their unique personhood offer powerful, inverted, complementary accounts of the potency of these same dynamics between identity and home.

The biographical and affective ties between individual and home are not hermetically sealed within the walls of their house. The house provides one fulcrum around which individuals' daily lives are lived. The necessary quotidian routines of life result in encountering neighbours, shopkeepers and friends. A territorial penumbra of neighbourhood affiliations is hard to avoid. While it is possible to live *your* life despite the neighbourhood in which you live, it is not possible to effectively detach yourself from your neighbourhood. Its reputation has implications that are likely to impinge upon the value of your property, your comfort in providing your address in certain status-laden contexts and the negotiation of routine interactions with others who have their own resolution of the significance of the neighbourhood in their lives.

Coexistence in urban settings can relatively accurately be described in terms of a detailed account of the demography of the area. The proportion of residents, depicted by class, age, gender, ethnicity, health status and education, can be mapped onto different constructions of the spatial layout of a town. Such an account is invaluable in many contexts, but it lacks any grip on the lived experience of the place. Age may be a unit of time lived, but, in any meaningful sense, individuals construct their own experience of aging and develop their own style of living their age. Equally, ethnicity may be a category routinely deployed in government forms, but ethnicity is not a fixed property of an individual. Ethnic identities are powerfully shaped by deep historically embedded social imaginaries (Taylor, 2004) in which elements of the past relations between peoples are recorded as significant criteria of in-group definition, and they provide seemingly self-evident boundary markers to police the recognition and exclusion of others. Thus, in a post-colonial, once imperialist, society such as the UK, ethnicity is no mere convenient marker of interesting difference between citizens; it is a powerful means of coding a complex web of conceptions of superiority/inferiority, entitlement/disenfranchisement and closeness/distance. When you add to this cognitive and affective repertoire the insidious ideological certainties of 'race', then the racialisation (Rattansi, 2005) of popular understandings of social differentiation becomes a potent means of ossifying and energising social distinctions. At the heart of this book is a need to recognise the significance of the many ways in which social policy and political discourse have racialised the experience, and conception, of coexistence in multi-ethnic urban settings.

The urban environment has a strong affinity with notions of the development of civilisation; its scale and density of population provide a basis for the specialisation of human capacities, complemented by symbiotic cooperation. From the Greek civic state to the large contemporary megalopolis, the urban environment has been a crucible in which conceptions of the politics of coexistence have been nurtured and contested. Equally, the acquired histories of the realities of urban life have provided a substantive basis for anxieties about the viability of different political conceptions of urban life, and of the administrative means of managing the physical challenges of scale that they present. There is a long tradition of social-scientific exploration of city dynamics, and of life within them. A significant element within the very extensive literature on urban life has been the exploration of the reality of coexistence in multi-ethnic urban contexts.

There is nothing particularly modern about ethnic diversity in cities. The great cities of antiquity typically extensively reflected the geographic reach of the empires within which they had been constructed. However, in the 20th century, the development of the disciplines of the social sciences coincided with major transitions in human mobility: the movement of African-Americans from the rural South in the US; the movement of peoples following the First and Second World Wars in Europe; and the movement of ex-colonial citizens from their homelands to the cities of their colonial masters. Throughout the 20th century, major civil disturbances based upon the tensions and conflicts experienced by minority groups living within the exclusionary politics of major cities have erupted, and social scientists have sought, and have been expected, to provide insight into the causes of these fractures in urban life. All too often, the political elite required accounts of multicultural urban systems that would be congenial to their hegemonic interests, and the social sciences have been appropriately critiqued for their pathologisation of minority group cultures and refusal to engage with fundamental issues of inequality.

Multi-ethnic urban experience in Europe and elsewhere over the last seven decades has provided a recurrent source of anxiety to political leaderships in Europe, as national debates around immigration and settlement have recurrently nurtured xenophobic anti-immigrant sentiments that have been out of kilter with the *de facto* change in the ethnic demography of their cities and towns. National xenophobic and racist immigration policies have been paralleled by local civic attempts to make sense of the reality of ethnic diversity developing within their jurisdiction. This is a political and policy misalignment that has exacerbated the dynamics of life in multi-ethnic urban areas, and that continues to impede a positive response to the challenges and possibilities of our multi-ethnic cities. The title of Rex and Moore's (1967) landmark analysis, *Race, community and conflict*, was all too prescient in anticipating a dominant framing of the conceptualisation of the challenge of ethnic diversity in British cities. This perspective was centrally embedded in governmental policies of 'social cohesion' and 'counter-terrorism', both of which were premised upon a depiction of Muslim inner-city populations as fundamentally severed from British society, and as a significant threat to British cultural integrity and security (Husband and Alam, 2011). Thus, framed by a persistent conflict model of disaffected and inadequately assimilated minority groups destabilising urban life, there has developed over the last decades a body of social-scientific research that has interrogated minority group culture and family life in order to locate the inherent pathologies in their way of life that have rendered them a dysfunctional and threatening presence in our urban landscape. At the same time, as we shall see traced through the arguments in the chapters that follow, there has emerged an extensive and diverse body of research literature that has critically sought to examine the multiple complexities of coexistence in multi-ethnic urban communities. Fusing urban geography, urban sociology, anthropology, cultural studies and social psychology, this research literature has provided nuanced, and not always comfortable, insights into the intersecting forces that shape daily multi-ethnic coexistence.

Perhaps before proceeding further, it might be useful to pause to reflect upon the use of the term 'coexistence' here. All terms in social science, as in language generally, carry with them a baggage of previous usage and of familiar applicability. The term is used here quite deliberately because it speaks directly of *co*existence, namely, a capacity to live together. However, we bring to the demography of cohabitation of a town or neighbourhood normative expectations about how we *should* live together. (An issue addressed at the end of the book as we reflect upon what our response to data and the analysis presented here might be.) Thus, for example, the *Oxford English dictionary* includes the phrase 'be together in harmony' in its definition of 'coexist'. Therefore, here, when we speak of multicultural coexistence, we also wish to invoke the reality of a negotiably viable capacity to live together with a degree of mutual respect. The word 'civility' should be seen as a companion to the practice of coexistence invoked here (see Fyfe et al, 2006; see also the final chapter of this book).

There is nothing in the concept, or reality, of coexistence invoked in our use of the term here that does not allow for the simultaneous presence of banal tensions and conflicts of interest as individuals, families and communities negotiate their capacity to live together within sustained routines of sharing space and place. However, the key issue that we wish to raise is the possibility and reality of a viable and enduring coexistence within a shared urban context. This may include routines of mutual recognition and dialogue, as well as patterns of non-confrontational mutual distancing. The question that flows though this text is: *what do we expect of people who share life in specific neighbourhoods?* Do we demand that they engage in an extensive, inclusive interpersonal network of social activities in which everyone is respected and acknowledged as a valued neighbour? If so, large swathes of bourgeois urban Britain would fall well outside of this ambition, as individualised lives exist within cocoons of motorised sociability that have little to do with fellow residents in the street, or even the neighbourhood. It is the capacity for civil interaction based upon values of mutual respect that underpins the notion of coexistence that we are employing throughout this text. Perhaps the bottom line is a capacity for civil coexistence, even in the presence of well-rehearsed, structurally determined inter-group tensions.

The discussion of multicultural coexistence that follows throughout this text is framed by its location within a specific urban context, where the particular demography of an inner-city neighbourhood provides the intersection of space, place, identities and opportunity, which are interpreted within a history of the area that has quite different collective trajectories for the specific demographic groups living there. Thus, perhaps, again, we should make explicit the implications of this chosen approach. We are aware of the debates about 'disembedding' (Giddens, 1991: 21–8) and 'globalisation' (Robertson, 1992; Albrow,

1997; Dürrschmitt, 1997; O'Byrne, 1997), which have suggested a reduced relevance of local contexts in societies marked by globalisation. At the beginning, it seemed that locality would be fully absorbed by the related time–space compression (see Harvey, 1990). However, Robertson (1995), in his chapter on 'glocalisation', made clear that the relevance of the local was not reduced to nothing, but instead re-embedded into a new global circumstance. Since then, an overlapping consensus has been established within the social sciences, which says that locality and globality do not exclude each other, but, rather, are intertwined.

Within that extended field of consensus, there are still scholars who are more enthusiastic about the idea of a reduced but persisting relevance of locality and others who are less so. To mention some positions, Helmuth Berking (2006) criticises the 'globocentrism' ('*Globozentrismus*') of globalisation theory and opts for analysing the uniqueness if not singularity of each local context. On the other hand, Ash Amin (2008: 6; see also Amin, 2012: 59–82) argues that 'urban public space has become one component, arguably of secondary importance, in a variegated field of civic and political formation'. Appadurai's position is even more de-spacialised (see, eg, 2005: 178–97): for example, at first sight, his understanding of neighbourhood seems to preserve what classical urban sociology understands as spatial. However, he then states that neighbourhood can be merely 'imagined' and thus disembedded from an urban reality independently existing from what urbanites apprehend (eg as opportunity structure).

As will become apparent in the data and analysis that follows, we are happy to place our analysis within the frame of an urban sociology that happily recognises *both*: the transnational basis of many lived identities *and* the concrete structural realities of a specific neighbourhood within a particular northern city. In setting out the historical context of the development of Manningham, and of the growth of specific class-based and ethnic populations within it, we are seeking to place the existential experience of the people whose lives we are seeking to reflect within a quite concrete locality, where demography and access to economic and social resources are embedded in quite distinct histories.

We hope that the research presented in the following pages will provide a further contribution to the body of literature on multi-ethnic coexistence, and on the dynamics of neighbourhood realities in shaping this. Drawing upon a range of disciplinary competences and experience, we hope to provide some insights into the dynamics of everyday life in an inner-city area that has been extensively depicted as being archetypically problematic.

The research agenda

This book arises from a prolonged period of involvement by the authors in carrying out research on ethnic relations in the UK and elsewhere. The research reported here set out to explore the contemporary experience of banal multi-ethnic coexistence in a specific inner-city area of Bradford in the north of England. Ethnic diversity in Bradford has a long history, but since the early 1960s, it has been the arrival and settlement of migrants from South Asia, and particularly Pakistan, that has given Bradford its specific demography. In the context of post-11 September 2011 and the 'War on Terror', cities like Bradford acquired a prominence in the national political neurosis around the Islamic presence in Britain. The fact that, as we shall see later, Bradford also had a prior history as a locale for South Asian dissent and civil disruption served to enhance the city's visibility in the emerging policy furore around social cohesion and counter-terrorism. The area of Bradford that forms the focus of this analysis is Manningham, which has acquired in some quarters an entrenched reputation as a problematic multi-ethnic inner-city area. As the project developed, it transpired that one facet of the analysis offered below is the juxtaposition of this reputation with the lived reality of life there.

Chapter Two provides a descriptive account of the history of Manningham in order that the accounts of contemporary life there can be placed in an appropriately historicised context. One of the themes in our story is, in fact, the significance of people's understanding of the history of the area within which they live, and of the history of their families' and communities' trajectory of settlement there. As Chapter Two describes both the history and physical properties of Manningham, what emerges is a picture of a once highly desirable area of Victorian development, but one in which commerce and domestic dwelling, elegant villas and very modest working-class housing were closely interwoven. The description of the housing stock and the streetscape of Manningham provides the reader with a concrete sense of the terrain in which the contemporary everyday interactions of the residents now take place.

Chapter Three builds upon this descriptive account of Manningham by providing a more detailed discussion of its current streetscape. Drawing upon tens of hours of observation while walking the streets of Manningham, this chapter employs contemporary theorisations of the streetscape in order to develop an understanding of the significance of the physical environment of the area for the residents' identification with the area.[1] Merging description with the introduction of appropriate theory, this chapter challenges some of the stereotypical expectations of life in Bradford that might be derived from an uncritical acceptance of some of the dominant stereotypes of the area. Such a mismatch between reputation and reality is by no means unique to Manningham, and its recurrence constitutes a significant element in the political problematic of understanding the substantive challenges and opportunities that inner-city areas might present to local and national government. This chapter builds upon Chapter Two's sense of the flux of peoples through the area by again underlining the balance between change and continuity as it is reflected in the physical fabric of Manningham.

Chapter Four provides an opportune and concrete challenge to any lazy association of Bradford and Manningham with South Asian communities. By providing an account of the Polish communities in Bradford and Manningham, this chapter explores a particular history of migration and settlement. This chapter strongly underscores the significance of people's construction of their unique understanding of their trajectory of migration and settlement. The accounts that were developed to provide coherence for a community establishing itself in post-war Bradford are shown to have a continuing relevance for perceptions of contemporary Polish immigration into the area. This chapter, drawing upon 60 qualitative interviews carried out by Dr Joanna Fomina with a cohort of established Polish residents and a cohort of bilingual recent Polish migrants, strongly demonstrates the necessary recognition of the internal distinctions made within minority ethnic communities. Just as in Chapter Two, one of the clear messages here is a necessary rejection of any simplistic usage of ethnic labels to account for the observable behaviour in the area. The very rich diversity within ethnic communities makes such essentialist usages of ethnic labels in popular discussion, and more particularly in policy debates, entirely fallacious. This chapter illuminates our understanding of the power of the stories that people tell themselves in order to make sense of their collective history of migration and settlement. The impact of these shared imaginaries upon the experience of the settlement of recent Polish migrants into Manningham provides one way of grasping the impact of past collective experiences upon current in-group dynamics. This account of the internal dynamics of the Polish population in Bradford and Manningham provides a valuable comparative perspective

---

[1] A description of the methods employed in collecting the data for each chapter can be found in the Appendix.

for the examination of the multi-ethnic interaction that follows in Chapter Five.

Chapter Five provides accounts of individuals' perceptions of their everyday life in Manningham based upon qualitative interviews with majority and minority ethnic residents of Manningham and innumerable conversations with individuals in the area and beyond. In the space available in this book, some of the major themes emerging from this data are presented. The diversity of residents, and the significance of their individual biographic understanding of their location within the life of Manningham, makes the data presented here powerfully reveal the strong role of individual values and experiences in shaping their interaction with the area. Echoing some of the issues from Chapters Two and Three, the data in this chapter reveal the complex ways in which the reputation of Manningham may impact upon individuals' perception of their life there. Again, the diversity within ethnic populations is apparent in rendering any simplistic account of inter-ethnic behaviour unsustainable. The data provide a clear linkage between the subjective concerns of individuals and the physical topography of the area sketched in previous chapters, as individual aspirations and collective identities are mapped onto the streetscape of Manningham. This chapter challenges something of the apparently benign picture of Manningham that emerged from the descriptive account in Chapter Three. In particular, the gendered nature of interaction on the street raises some pointed questions about the role of males in employing the street for expressive performances of territorial behaviours.

Chapter Six was not a planned element of this book, but emerged as an irresistible topic that very powerfully augmented many of the points made elsewhere in our analysis. In starting the fieldwork, there was an awareness of the significance of the car and urban myths about the driving habits of young Asian men that had sensitised us to the potential significance of the car as a potent element in inter-ethnic dynamics. As the research developed, the interviews carried out by Dr Yunis Alam provided an increasingly rich account of the role of the car in the lives of individuals in Bradford. At one level, this chapter provides a brief insight into the intensive investment of individuals into a particular interest (in this case, their cars) to the extent that it comes to constitute the basis for a very strong subcultural identification among its practitioners. This chapter is redolent of untrammelled enthusiasms, and of networks of sharing, which constitute an example of an invisible vitality within a community like Manningham. It points to the importance of identifying and acknowledging the potential of such enthusiasms for enriching lives in urban contexts that may appear to others to be without charm. This chapter also necessarily notes the unfortunate capacity of the car to provide a particularly potent means of inter-ethnic irritation on the streetscape of an urban area.

In the concluding chapter (Chapter Seven), we draw out some of the themes that emerge across the following chapters and then pause to ask a quiet: 'So what?' The data assembled do much to challenge the simplistic notions of inner-city ethnicity that have been articulated in government policy and in the confident assertions of certain cultural commentators. The essentialising language of government statements about the role of Islam in British minority ethnic communities is mocked by the diversity of lives lived in Manningham, both within and between specific ethnic communities. Furthermore, the daily viability of life on the streets of Manningham, with its low-key capacity of individuals to rub along together, exposes the political agendas behind the neurotic pessimism regarding British multicultural competence. Manningham is not a fairytale place of joyous multi-ethnic coexistence, but it is a working example of people's ability to identify with an area that has a markedly diverse demography, and to make lives together there.

This reality then raises the question of what model we have in play when we speak about improving inter-ethnic relations. If we wish to go beyond the insights provided in the chapters that follow and move towards advancing a policy framework for facilitating equitable coexistence in a society that is unquestionably multi-ethnic, then it is necessary to explore the principles that we need to make explicit and the values that we need to invoke. The latter part of the final chapter provides a brief attempt to address this challenge and sketches a model that will need further development elsewhere in subsequent writing.

CHAPTER TWO

Bradford and Manningham: historical context and current dynamics

Bradford as a city context

The city of Bradford has a proud history as a major engine of 19th-century manufacturing that made it one of the wealthiest cities in the country. It expanded in the 19th century as a centre of textile manufacturing and, like many cities of its kind at the time, its expansion was rapid. As technological innovation moved textile production from small hillside village communities into the concentration of factories, embedded in the hub of canals and railways that made them viable, then so, too, the face of Bradford changed. Large aspects of Bradford's contemporary physical fabric owe much to this period of radical transformation.

Historically, Bradford is mentioned in the Domesday Book of 1086. Nestling in Bradford Dale, it was well supplied with water but surrounded by steep-sided hills that made it unsuitable for agricultural development. Fieldhouse (1978) suggests that this topography had an impact in determining the character of the developing community, noting that in the 17th century:

> In country districts, away from the large towns, the inhabitants were usually small farmers who turned to cloth making as a useful sideline, especially on wet days. In Bradford because there was so little arable land, the order was reversed and the people came to rely more on their looms and spindles than on husbandry. (Fieldhouse, 1978: 47)

Manufacture and industry, then, has a long association with the developing wealth of Bradford, and the opening of the Bradford Canal in 1774, linking Bradford to the Leeds–Liverpool canal, and hence to both coasts, did much to provide a critical infrastructural element to the rapid expansion of Bradford in the latter part of that century. As the Industrial Revolution gathered momentum, Bradford was blessed with a propitious mix of natural resources, including coal, iron and local stone for building mills and houses. The technological innovations in the cloth and wool industries provided the impetus that radically changed the demography of the North West and Bradford, as power looms and new combing machines effectively put an end to the home-based industry by the middle of the 19th century.

The development of the textile industry in Bradford was reflected in the burgeoning growth of mills and the complementary terraced housing for their workforce. The speed of this development was echoed in the attendant social misery of many of the workforce, who worked in exploitative conditions and lived in unsanitary accommodation. Taylor and Gibson (2010:3) note that, 'By 1810 at least six textile mills had been built in Bradford, but the town had still not expanded much beyond its boundaries of 1700.' But they then record that:

> In little more than half a century, two thirds of Manningham township was transformed from an area of thinly populated countryside, with a small, nucleated but churchless village roughly at its centre, into a mixed residential suburb hedged and encroached upon by industrial corridors and crowned by Manningham Mills. (Taylor and Gibson, 2010: 3–5)

Of the wider Bradford, Fieldhouse (1978: 141) notes that during the first half of the 19th century, the population grew from 13,264 to 103,771. He adds that the influx of Irish immigrants into Bradford following the potato famine of 1845/46 produced a significant Irish population in the town, who, anticipating more recent scenarios, were preponderantly crowded into a few areas of the town, and who attracted considerable hostility from the resident population of Bradford.

Throughout the second half of the 19th century and into the 20th century, Bradford saw itself develop into a highly prosperous city, with its wealth founded in the textile industry and particularly in the manufacture of worsted yarns. The extensive wealth generated through this manufacturing became expressed in the many large, and handsome, stone-built mills and the development of a wide range of housing. For the wealthy textile barons and their senior personnel, Bradford acquired a range of large, splendid free-standing houses and elegant terraced villas, which often included gated carriage drives (see Taylor and Gibson, 2010: ch 3). For those in the lower echelons of employment, housing ranged from comfortable terraced housing to cramped and overcrowded back-to-back terraces. The civic buildings of Bradford also became an overt expression of the self-regard and confidence of Victorian Bradford, with the construction of such expansive architectural statements as the City Hall, St. Georges Hall and Cartwright Hall, which was itself set in a beautiful public park, Lister Park, which was a splendid local nod in favour of the ethos of rational recreation for the working classes (Bailey, 1987). Despite the ravages of a 'modernisation' of the city centre during the 1960s–70s, the streetscape of contemporary Bradford continues to reflect the architectural heritage of its Victorian economic zenith.

Regrettably, the 20th century proved to be less kind to Bradford and the heavy reliance on textile manufacturing as the economic engine of the city's wealth proved to be its undoing. Without the economic diversity of its affluent neighbour, Leeds, Bradford found itself vulnerable to the globalisation of trade in post-war Britain, and by the 1970s, the pressure from international competition had ripped the heart out of the local economy. In recent decades, Bradford has found itself struggling to find a means of economic reconstruction in a broader national economy that has seen the widespread loss of unskilled and semi-skilled jobs and the decline of many national manufacturing industries. Cruelly exposed by the dramatic economic vitality of Leeds, which has become the major commercial hub of the region, Bradford has suffered an economic decline that has proved somewhat resistant to concerted efforts to change its fortunes. Along with other ex-textile towns in North West England, Bradford has come to be associated with economic deprivation and the wider 'crisis of British multiculturalism' (see, eg, Lentin and Titley, 2011).

In the 2011 census, the Bradford District population was reported to have increased by 11.0% since the 2001 census to 522,452, of whom, 22% are aged under 14 – only two other local authorities have a larger percentage in this age bracket. Almost one fifth (19.6%) of the population are aged between 16 and 29, making Bradford a population with a significant proportion of young people who will be seeking to enter the labour market in the coming decades. The ethnic diversity of Bradford is apparent in the census data, with: 106,614 (20.41%) being of Pakistani origin; 9,893 (1.89%) being of Bangladeshi origin; 9,267 (1.78%) being of one of the 'black' ethnic categories, including those of Caribbean heritage; and the continuing presence of the Irish population being reflected in the 15,715 (3.0%) people recorded as 'white Irish'. Interestingly, the number of people born in European Union (EU) accession states has increased by 10,000 since 2001, with the number of people born in Poland increasing by nearly 5,000, reflecting the movement of East Europeans into the region following their states' entry into the EU. Given the analysis that is to follow, it is worth noting that 24.7% of the Bradford District population are recorded as being Muslim (an increase of 8% since 2001), 0.98% as Sikh, 0.93% as Hindu, 0.19% as Buddhist and 0.06% as Jewish; 239,843 (45.91%) are recorded as being Christian. The unemployment rate in 2011 was reported as being 5.8%, which was higher than the regional figure of 4.8% and the figure for England as a whole of 4.4%. Linked to a lower-than-average economic activity rate in Bradford District (the lowest in West Yorkshire), these unemployment figures reflect the current economic circumstances of contemporary Bradford.

Migration into Bradford

As already suggested, the history of Bradford is not exceptional in that it has grown over the centuries through an influx of labour to meet the changing face of economic production. As Fieldhouse (1978) noted, the population of Bradford expanded rapidly in the 19th century as the successive waves of technological innovation created new modes of production and ever-more concentrated forms of manufacturing in the textile industry. While much of the early expansion of Bradford saw local labour drawn from the adjacent countryside into the town, with the demise of domestic production, James (1990) reports that by the mid-19th century, immigrants into Bradford were being attracted from around the country and beyond:

> The 1851 census showed that immigrants came from every county in England, though some parts of the country provided more than others.... Of those from further afield over 4000 came from Lancashire, and there were large groups from the former wool textile centres of East Anglia and the South-West counties. There was a small but influential community of Scots, but the major long distance immigrant groups were the Irish and the Germans. (James, 1990: 81)

This overseas migrant flow provided a strong reminder that migration is seldom a homogeneous process and that different levels of social capital and skill sets are reflected in quite different experiences of migration and settlement.

Echoing Fieldhouse (1978), James (1990: 84) notes that the 19th-century Irish immigrants, being predominantly from rural, peasant backgrounds, were uneducated and unskilled in Ireland, and found that they consequently 'Lived in the worst slums and generally had the least popular, most ill-paid jobs'. Being both Irish and Catholic, and carrying the burden of well-established English racist conceptions of their character (Curtis, 1971), they faced the additional burdens of prejudice and social ostracism and ended up living in ethnic concentrations, where, anticipating the experience of the post-Second World War Polish community, the Catholic Church became a central force in providing the social and economic infrastructure that shaped their collective survival and identity.

The experience of German migration into Bradford was different, both in terms of the profile of the immigrants and in the reception they received. In the early 19th century, there was an influx of German merchants into Bradford as the rapid expansion of the Bradford worsted industry seemed likely to eclipse the standing of its neighbouring trade in Leeds. Fieldhouse (1978: 125) reports that, 'In 1822 Bradford had 5 worsted merchants and Leeds 24, but by 1861 Leeds had only 17 and Bradford 157, over a third of whom were foreigners, mostly German'. The success of this entrepreneurial migration is underlined by James (1990: 32), who reports that, 'As late as 1902, 21 out of 36 yarn merchants and 31 out of 63 piece merchants were of German origin.' This migration was not only German, but also largely Jewish, and resulted in the formation of a significant German/Jewish community in Bradford.

Unlike the Irish immigrants into Bradford, this bourgeois German community was well accepted in the town and they became important both culturally and through their philanthropy, which included building and maintaining several hospitals and establishing a benevolent fund for the aged and infirm within the town. The area still called 'Little Germany' in Bradford continues to bear witness to their presence in the continuing architectural splendour of the warehouses that they built. Furthermore, one of Britain's most iconic 'English' composers, Delius, is a Bradford-born son of a German merchant. As James (1990: 32) notes of this immigrant community who possessed substantial economic and cultural capital: 'They were civilized, sophisticated and wealthy, wearing their foreignness and religion lightly.' (The easy allocation of the sobriquet 'civilised' to this professional and affluent migrant group tellingly reveals the class and national stereotypes that underpinned the perception of migrant communities.) Yet, their positive contribution to Bradford and their successful integration into the civic life of the city proved insufficient to protect this 'cultured' community from the rabid anti-German sentiments engendered by the First World War, and their presence in the city suffered a quick and noticeable decline.

A further period of significant migration into Bradford came after the Second World War, when immigrants from the Ukraine, Poland, Yugoslavia and Italy came to the city. Many of these people were 'displaced persons', and on being granted the status of 'European Voluntary Workers' (EVWs), were part of a rare British experience of planned migration where EVWs were sent to work in particular towns in order to meet the needs of industry, a proportion being sent to Bradford to work in the textile industry. Similarly, Polish servicemen who did not wish to return home were found employment in Britain as members of the 'Polish Resettlement Corps'. Thus, James (1990: 176) reports that, by 1987, 'there were 4,000 people of Polish origin living in the town, 3,700 from the Ukraine, 1,500 from Italy, 1,200 from Yugoslavia, and 500 each from Estonia, Hungary, Latvia and Byelorussia'. The experience of the Polish community settling in Bradford will be discussed in more detail in Chapter Four.

The entry of migrant workers into Bradford from the British Commonwealth came as a local expression of the major movement of labour into post-war Britain, where the need for labour following the repositioning of the indigenous labour force within the changing infrastructure of British employment resulted in the deliberate recruitment of labour from the Commonwealth (Deakin et al, 1970). Thus it was that the first wave of South Asian migrant labour came to Bradford to work in the textile industries, along with smaller numbers of 'West Indians' who came to work in transport and elsewhere. Published in 1966, the following description of the early settlement of Bradford's Pakistanis provides a quick insight into some of the key determinants of the ways in which this population has developed over subsequent years:

> The large preponderance of Pakistanis, who as a group have several special characteristics, has important social consequences. They have come largely from the area around Mirpur on the Kashmir frontier, as a result of the fighting and disturbance caused by the dam project. Most people associated with the immigrants estimate, in fact, that around 80 per cent of the Pakistanis come from this relatively small area, and frequently consider this group, which has a high level of illiteracy (in any language) to be both introverted and generally backward. This group provides the majority of the unskilled employees in some sections of the textile industry, particularly nightshift wool-combing, and has a reputation locally for amassing money by working long

hours and living cheaply in poor conditions of multiple occupancy. (Lelohe, 1966: 30)

The first phase of immigration was of single men, who took up multi-occupation in cheap accommodation near to the mills in which they worked. Nationally, this influx of migrant workers throughout the 1960s was associated with extensive racial hostility, which regrettably became a key populist discourse within party-political competition for the electorate's support. The introduction of anti-immigration legislation became the focus of inter-party competition, as they sought to be seen to be willing to address this populist racism (Solomos, 2003). Ironically, the rush to limit immigration, encapsulated in the draconian Immigration Act 1968, created a rush for entry prior to the introduction of restrictions, which again ratcheted up anti-immigrant sentiments. The heavy restrictions upon primary immigration for employment also meant that for the Pakistani communities in Britain, the notion of cyclical migration, with a flow in and out of family members, became replaced by an acceptance of permanent settlement and a shift to family reunification by the bringing in of wives and children.

In cities like Bradford, as this process of family formation accelerated, then so, too, the dynamics of community infrastructure changed. Instead of single men living in multi-occupation dwellings, the demand for family homes increased. Equally, as families came from specific areas of Pakistan, then so, too, the internal differentiation of the community changed to reflect differences in shared communal languages, and in their adherence to specific sub-variations of Islam. Thus, the second generation of young Muslims of Pakistani heritage in Bradford grew up within areas that had strong internal social linkages, whilst, at the same time, they grew up as Bradfordians. One concrete expression of this process was a movement away from men attending a mosque common to them all, as Bradford saw the proliferation of mosques within specific communities that had a much more finite sense of their membership, both in terms of ethnic identity and faith-based allegiances. At the same time, because of the concentration of this population within limited segments of the labour and housing market, there was a concentration of Pakistani children in certain schools, which placed novel demands on the educational system. Thus, the physical fabric of the streetscape started to change as buildings were converted into mosques or madrasas and as shops developed to serve the ethnic tastes and needs of the local community. As we shall see later, Manningham was one such area.

Crucially, the development of the Pakistani communities in Bradford took place throughout a continuing and evolving politics of 'race relations' (Solomos, 2003). The feedback loop of anti-immigrant sentiment being taken up and amplified by politicians was classically expressed in the late 1960s through the virulent politics of Powellism, and the linkage between strong immigration control and accompanying legislation to counter racial discrimination became the dominant characteristic of British policy over the next three decades (Husband, 2003). The politics of 'popular capitalism' (Jessop et al, 1988) that characterised Thatcherism saw the creation of a divisive politics in which, anticipating events of the last decade, racialised politics became integral to the construction of what Hillyard and Percy-Smith (1988) called the 'coercive state'. Inner-city minority communities became a contentious element in the social pariah category of the 'enemy within' in a New Right discourse that contained a cultural construction of racism at its core (Gordon and Klug, 1986; Levitas, 1986; Seidal, 1986). The communities of British-born Pakistanis that were developing in Bradford learnt to negotiate their Britishness from within a continuing politics of race that was constantly evoked around a spiral of themes, including the threat of immigration, inner-city violence and the cultural threat of emerging minority/British communities. The arrival of 13 years of Labour government saw a significant continuation of many of the tropes of Thatcherite politics (Back et al, 2002).

As we have seen earlier, in recent years, the arrival of new migrant populations from Eastern Europe has continued this long history of the changing demography of the population of Bradford. Change has been a continual process, partially driven by the arrival of new immigrant communities, but also by the continuous changes within different communities as generational changes in social, cultural and economic capital have changed the dynamics within each community and provided new lines of commonality and tension between them. Generational differences in the class profile of the post-war East European communities, and of the Pakistani communities, are a striking example of this process.

Manningham

Manningham is located close to the centre of Bradford, a city in the north of England. As we have seen, the city's former economic success was dependent to a large extent upon the textile industry, which began to lose its economic prowess in the 1970s. Despite the decline of its industrial spine, Manningham remains a traditionally working-class area that, today, has a sizeable majority of Pakistanis, who first started moving into the neighbourhood upon their arrival to the UK in the late 1950s and 1960s. Before that, Manningham became home to Poles, Ukrainians and other European migrants. Today, with new arrivals from Eastern Europe, Manningham has established its credentials as a zone of diversity and transition: a place where new communities, often with relatively little social, cultural, economic and political capital, can become established and, in some cases, within a generation, become integral as citizens and residents of the neighbourhood.

Manningham, like other inner-city neighbourhoods and zones, has a racialised aspect to its character that has developed alongside the growth of its constituent populations and their resulting generations. In the 1960s and 1970s, the first generation of Asian communities, who were still becoming 'integrated' and were yet to be comfortable and confident as citizens, remained, as the stereotype goes, passive and accepting of more discrimination and oppression than people of the current generation are likely to imagine, let alone tolerate. By the 1980s, however, there was a growing second generation that was British born and, as such, had a more textured understanding of rights and expectations. This second generation, Bradford born and educated, had a real sense that this was their home and, because of that, they had certain rights (for comparable transitions in Marxloh in Germany, see Huttermann, 2003). Whether or not they were actually granted those rights in practice was at one level irrelevant; knowing that they had rights led to a desire to set up infrastructures and support mechanisms that would help realise these rights, no matter how long it took.

This was a period where the success of Black Power and the 'civil rights' struggle in the US, and the impact of feminism there and in Europe, had already significantly shaped the emergence of a new widespread sensibility that Taylor (1992) has described as the emergence of a new 'politics of difference'. This was a transition from a world view based on a claim to post-Second World War universal individual rights, to a new assertive demand for the respect of collective identities and their attendant rights. This was a transition from a demand to be given equal recognition and to be treated the same, to a demand to have one's difference from others fully recognised and to have one's universal rights expressed in relation to the particularity of one's needs.

With the emergence of a new, British-born generation of South Asians, who had their own sense of mixed, fluid and adaptive ethnic and cultural identities, came organisations like the Asian Youth Movement, which aimed to emulate some of the North American strategies, and, in some cases, ideological lenses, through which social change, in particular, 'race' equality, could be fostered. Thus, for example, an interview with one of the founding members of the Asian Youth Movement reported that they had the slogan 'We're here to stay and we're here to fight'. Of this slogan, he said:

> 'But the statement "here to stay" was that we're not going anywhere. Our parents came here, they've no thought of going back: we certainly didn't have any thought of going back – so "We are here to stay." And, we recognised that we had to fight for our rights as young black people.' (A6)[2]

This generation, having grown up with the political heritage of North American political struggle as part of their cultural capital, developed their trajectories of resistance to the marginalisation and exploitation that their parents had largely tolerated. In the opposition between the peaceful protest of Martin Luther King's civil rights movement and the militant politics of the Black Panthers (Cleaver, 1969; Seale, 1970; see also Humphrey and John, 1971), with their core creed of 'self-defence', minority ethnic communities in Britain had found a repertoire of discourse and practice that addressed their experience of marginalisation through racism in the context of living in Britain. The African-Caribbean communities in Britain had found a new militancy in opposing their experience of racism and oppressive policing, focused around the 'Sus Laws' (section 4 of the Vagrancy Act 1824; see Dabydeen and Gilmore, 2007). The radicalisation of British 'race relations' throughout the 1970s followed a dual trajectory of ever increasing anti-immigrant legislation, and accompanying shifts in public hostility, paralleled by the passage of anti-discriminatory 'Race Relations Acts' (Husband, 2003). Throughout this period, policing and the abusive role of law in the suppression of the rights and legitimate aspirations of 'black' citizens in Britain made inner-city minority ethnic communities the locus of bitter struggles that echoed those of a more virulent nature in the US. It is shocking to reread Humphry's (1972) *Police power and black people*, the Centre for Contemporary Cultural Studies' (CCCS, 1982) *The empire strikes back*, Gordon's (1983) *White law* and Hall et al's (1978) *Policing the crisis*, which give a cumulative picture of the extensively racist nature of British society in that period. The Brixton 'uprising' of 1981 and subsequent civil disorders in the 1980s created a period of national self-scrutiny and political reflection that sought to address the means of moving from conflict and contention in a multi-ethnic Britain characterised by coexistence, underpinned by a commitment to the recognition of difference framed by anti-

---

[2] Letters/numbers after quotes are coded identifiers of the interviewees.

discrimination legislation (see, eg, Scarman, 1981; Joshua et al, 1983; Benyon, 1984; Benyon and Solomos, 1987). The tortuous oppositional play of the ideologies of racism and nationalism against those of equality and a politics of difference continued to eddy through the national political and local everyday negotiation of models of multiculturalism in opposition to populist racism and xeno-nationalism throughout the 1970/80s. This formed the political backdrop to the emergent forms of self-assurance and self-assertiveness that were simultaneously developing within the different minority ethnic communities in Britain (Goulbourne, 1990a; Centre for Contemporary Cultural Studies, 1982).

This same climate of resistance and mobilisation was present in the Bradford Asian community and became a national source of attention with the arrest of the 'Bradford 12' in 1981. Their subsequent acquittal provided a powerful legitimacy to community resistance, both in Bradford and nationally:

> In June 1982, after a 9-week trial, 12 Asian men, known as the Bradford 12, were acquitted of charges of making explosive devices with the intent to cause damage to property and persons.
>
> Less than a year earlier on 11 July 1981, the 12 young men had been arrested after a police [sic] found 38 milk bottles filled with petrol in a raid. The men, who were all members of the United Black Youth League, were involved in community and anti-racist activism. The group argued that they made petrol bombs for the purpose of self-defence against skinhead gangs.
>
> Tariq Ali, one of the 12, claimed that many attacks against the Asian community in Bradford – which numbered up to 45,000 – often went unreported and many considered them as a 'way of life'. Four days before the arrest there were two arson attacks on homes perpetrated by three men – one of whom was a National Front member – who were only charged with conspiracy to assault.[3]

The successful defence of the Bradford 12 based around their core assertion that 'self-defence is no offence' was a powerful testimony to the change away from political acquiescence to racism and marginalisation within significant sections of the younger Bradfordian

---

[3] Quote from: www.runnymedetrust.org/histories/race-equality/53/bradford-12-acquitted

Pakistani population. In many ways, it marked a clear assertion by this generation of their British, as opposed to immigrant, status. It was a critical element in the formation of a collective history by the emergent 'Brasian' population of Bradford (Ali et al, 2006). (Perhaps the proven legitimacy of this positive self-regard, and assertive stance, in the face of majority hostility may have provided one existential basis for the species of young Asian machismo found among segments of Bradford's Pakistani population that will be explored in Chapter Five.)

While Bradford may have been perceived as a city let down, or even led astray, by the claimed failed policies of British multiculturalism, it is also a place that can concretely extol the social enhancements that cultural diversity brings. For example, at a commercial level, the 'curry trail' and the Asian Film Festival are examples of a civic celebration of Bradford's diversity that positively affirms its multi-ethnic character, and that provide points of self-affirmation for segments of its 'Brasian' (Ali et al, 2006) population. Nevertheless, even today, it also remains tied to a series of events spanning the last four decades that have formed the basis of its broader biographical self, which is acutely defined with an 'ethnic' component. The controversial school 'bussing' policies of the 1970s were soon followed by the 'Halal school meals' debate, and by the nationally contentious Honeyford Affair (see Halstead, 1988; McLoughlin, 2006), which centred on a school in Manningham. In the late 1980s, there came the Rushdie Affair following the publication of *The satanic verses* (see Appiganesi and Maitland, 1989; Akhtar, 1989; Ruthven, 1991; Samad, 1992; Lane, 2006; Nasta, 2002), which signalled a turning point in the history of British ethnic relations. As McLoughlin (2006: 130) notes:

> During the 1980s discussions of 'Islam' and 'Muslims' in Britain were often subsumed under the categories of ethnicity, 'race' or culture. All that began to change of course when on 14 January 1989 members of the Bradford Council for Mosques burned a copy of Salman Rushdie's novel *The Satanic Verses*.

Since then, there have been at least two sets of disturbances/'riots' (1995 and 2001) focused within Manningham, which were largely defined by the presence of a 'problematic young male Muslim youth'. This male is defined through a three-faceted identity: British (by birth), Pakistani (by heritage) and Muslim (by faith). Both events were heavily represented, and, to some extent, constructed, through the lenses of local, national and, in the case of the 2001 events, international media.

Subsequently, the events led to research and reports, with the former event eliciting a document entitled the 'Bradford Commission report' (1996), which set about exploring a range of factors that contributed to the rioting and aimed to offer means by which the likelihood of future events of a similar nature would be reduced. The report also covered the management and policing of the 1995 riot, including the purported events that triggered it. The disturbances of 2001 across the North, however, yielded a number of wider-ranging documents with a much deeper and longer-term impact at the levels of policy and rhetoric (Community Cohesion Independent Review, 2001; see also Burnley Task Force, 2001; Ouseley, 2001; Oldham Independent Panel Review, 2001). For the Independent Review Team, one of the key causes of the disturbances was linked with ethnic and cultural segregation. Although written in a subtle code where little reference is actually made to ethnicity, it seems obvious that communities with different religious and cultural values are key actors within the statement:

> Whilst the physical segregation of housing estates and inner city areas came as no surprise, the team was particularly struck by the depth of polarisation of our towns and cities. The extent to which these physical divisions were compounded by so many other aspects of our daily lives, was very evident. Separate educational arrangements, community and voluntary bodies, employment, *places of worship*, *language*, social and *cultural* networks, means that many communities operate on the basis of a series of parallel lives. (Independent Review Team, 2001: 9, emphases added)

Clearly, the places of worship, languages and cultural networks that could be problematised are those that are not, in essence, mainstream British. Nevertheless, while it is self-evident that some degree of segregation does exist in places like Bradford, there is strong data to suggest that ethnic and cultural markers come a close second/third place to those more closely related to social class and/or wealth. In other words, the communities at the heart of the social cohesion narrative that developed after the 2001 disturbances were invariably poor or working class but it was their ethnic character that became the focus of attention. This was consistent with the neoliberal ideology that framed both Conservative and Labour governments, and that produced a policy discourse in which class had been largely extinguished from the political lexicon.

The reports that followed the 2001 disturbances enabled policymakers, academics, politicians and other figures of established authority to suggest that social cohesion, however it was to be defined, was both under threat and in need of repair. Meanwhile, the voices of those who had taken part in the violence was, as usual, absent, or, if at all heard, was framed in the language of the growing discourse of what often appeared to be irreconcilable difference. For the most part, however, questions were nevertheless asked of those who had apparent insight into the motives of the rioters. As Amin (2003: 462) notes, the rioters had, in effect, become another folk devil:'The media gathered snippets of fact and fiction to demonize them as drug dealers or addicts, petty criminals, school dropouts, car-cruisers, perpetrators of gratuitous attacks on elderly whites, beyond the control of their community, disloyal subjects, Islamic militants'. Much of this labelling, even after 10 years − after a whole generation has developed − remains strong and woven into the imagery of parts of Bradford's character, and of what elements of its population do.

While the riotous activity itself had an overtly Pakistani character in terms of the ethnic background of the participants, for some, there was also a correlation between ethnicity and *motivations* underlying residential choice. As a result, the argument went, the existence of segregated communities fed into levels of dissatisfaction, as well as perceptions of difference.

The riots somehow encapsulated this difference and irreconcilability between communities, which were defined according to their distinct ethnicities; class, income and wealth seemed largely absent from the process of analysis or the accompanying political policy debate. For some commentators and academics: Pakistanis rioted because they were not fully integrated; they were not fully integrated partly because they chose to remain segregated; and they were segregated because of their Pakistani-ness. All this and more was explored and debated, often in the absence of meaningful engagement with those who took part in the riots, as well as without providing a nuanced account of the structural modes of exclusion that were a background to these events (for critiques of the emergence of the post-riot policy of social cohesion, see Cheong et al, 2007; Husband and Alam, 2011; for a rare account that draws upon interviews with convicted rioters and their families, see Bujra and Pearce, 2011).

The rioting of young Pakistanis − and in the 1980s, of white and black youth − ought to be seen in a broader historical and political context where social change is all but captured in moments of unrest and violence that, for some, form an unspoken but powerful protest (for a historical context of riot, see, eg, Fogelson, 1971; Kettle and Hodges, 1982). At first sight, the disturbances of 2001 (and, similarly, those in Tottenham and elsewhere of 2011) seem to suggest a nihilistic tendency: destruction for the sake of it. A closer scrutiny accounting for structural inequality, environmental and economic underdevelopment, along with the politics of racialised cities and towns suggest that the rioters – although far from organised around a set of political ideals – may well have been, in a somewhat inarticulate and apparently thoughtless manner, expressing some form of social and/or political protest. After the 2011 riots elsewhere in Britain, there has been research which suggests that many of those involved, and caught, were simply there for the thrill of the experience. However, it remains apparent that discrimination was one of the long-standing factors that led to the build-up of anger preceding the 2001 riots (Hussain and Bagguley, 2005). In turn, the rioters 'expressed a demand to own and mould these towns of racialized space allocation on their own terms.... It is the rejection of a racialized coding of British civic and public culture that has made these riots so politically charged' (Amin, 2003: 462). Amin (2003) argues that the rioting was, in some ways, a corollary of citizenship. In order to riot, a certain amount of investment in and attachment to place has to be a precondition.

As outlined elsewhere (Alam, 2006; Husband and Alam, 2011), it is clear that there is a maturing of British Pakistani consciousness whereby, for many, identity is, as it is for all of us, a hybrid beast, but it remains heavily influenced by environment and culture. In other words, British Pakistanis are aware of their Britishness and, as such, even rioting, for the rioters, was an extension or manifestation of their identity. Put simply, and somewhat conversely, one reason why the rioting happened was because it could: had the rioters not had a sense of affinity or belonging – in spite of discriminations and inequalities – they may not have had the confidence and capacity to engage in such social and political activity. Again, as Amin (2003: 462) notes: 'Their acts were the claims of full British subjects, without qualification and freed from the politics of community and consensus practices by their community leaders'. Anticipating some of the argument from the conclusion, we would argue that the second and third generation of young Bradfordians of Pakistani heritage have rejected a politics of multiculturalism premised upon their generous *toleration* by the majority; rather, as British citizens, they are prepared to assert their legitimate rights. This is a claim that resonates all the more harshly with majority sensibilities given the effective quiescence of assertive class-based identity politics in recent British political history.

While the purpose here is not to focus on the disturbances per se, the research on which this book is based did focus upon Manningham, the epicentre of those disturbances. The shock of Pakistani youth revolt, and the destruction it caused, has continued to have a role in shaping the perception of both Manningham as an area and the Pakistani population as a presence in the city. This sense of 'dangerous difference' is at the heart of Islamophobia in general (Husband and Alam, 2011: ch 4), and of the distorted perception of Bradford's Pakistani communities in particular. The language of social cohesion, and its fusion with the politics of fear that is British counter-terrorism rhetoric and practice (see Husband and Alam, 2011), has provided a powerful and highly visible discourse of *self-segregation and living parallel lives* that has made the demographic characteristics of the Muslim communities in our cities a major area of policy, and popular, concern. Additionally, in the national development of the CONTEST counter-terrorism policies in Britain following the London bombings of 7 July 2005, it was the Muslim communities of Britain's inner-city populations who were identified as the threat to security and the target of intervention. Doubly marginalised as being committed to self-segregation and as being the location for the next wave of 'home-grown bombers', Britain's Muslim population had every right to feel themselves to be the target of abusive government incursions into their everyday lives. The possession of a self-conscious *British identity* among Bradford's Muslim populations fed their sense of outrage at being so labelled and targeted.

Not unusually, there is some degree of clustering among Bradford's minority ethnic groups that can be a source of empowerment and positivity as it can yield and enhance 'social and cultural relations, and provide social support, a sense of belonging and well developed community infrastructures' (Phillips et al, 2002: 10; see also Phillips, 2006). Furthermore, many of the positive features of South Asian communities appeared to dovetail with the attributes that were purported to produce stronger social cohesion promoted by the government soon after the 2001 riots. However, for central government policy in the post-riot and post-7 July 2005 London bombings period, a de facto clustering of Muslim residents in inner-city areas became defined as problematic 'self-segregation' (Cantle, 2001; Ouseley, 2001; Carling, 2008). Indeed, in Carling's discussion of internal migration trends and dynamics within the city of Bradford, a discussion that depends heavily on statistical data, there is a not-too-subtle interjection of 'motive'. Granted, speculative though some of Carling's argument appears to be, it nevertheless places the practice and process of *self-segregation* within the cultural spaces of the city's minority ethnic culture. In other words, it is argued that Muslims self-segregate (Carling, 2008: 560) – and thus form zones like Manningham – because they want to.

Muslim self-segregation, therefore, is an important and ongoing aspect of the city's narrative in relation to cohesion and ethnic relations. It is also worth reminding ourselves that when attending to the concern around the British Muslim pathology of insularity, Bradford is not alone in terms of how its population has been geographically located, often according to ethnic heritage. Analysis of data from the 2001 census informs us that:

> People from religious minorities also tended to be clustered in relatively small areas: Muslims made up a majority of the population in parts of Birmingham; Hindus formed the majority in some areas of Leicester; Jews made up almost half the population in one part of Salford; and Sikhs made up more than a third of the local population in parts of Ealing and Birmingham. (Dobbs et al, 2006: xvii)

At the same time, even an acknowledgement of 'ethnic clustering' itself does a disservice to reality. As Dorling (2009: 64) notes:

> Of the 35 districts in Britain that had one ward at the last Census with fewer than 50% White residents, only one of them was in Yorkshire and Humberside. That one district is Bradford, and even there it's a minority white ward – called 'University' ward – which had 25% white residents, hardly a separation. During the year before the Census, more white residents came to that ward from other parts of the UK than left it and more black and Asian residents left the ward than came to it: so it is becoming more mixed from migration, not a separate ghetto.

So it is now that Manningham exists as a distinct inner-city ward of Bradford, with a particular history and current demography. The 2011 census has revealed contemporary Manningham as being a highly diverse terrain with a wide variety of persons of differing ethnicities resident within it. The largest proportion by some margin is that represented by those of Pakistani heritage, who constitute 60% of the population; the British white population constitutes only 10% of the whole. The next largest communities are the Bangladeshis, with 9%, and the 'Other white' (who will include recent East European migrants), at 5%. With a total population of 19,983, Manningham is a largely South Asian ward, but also a very ethnically mixed one. Given this demography, it is not therefore surprising that Manningham is preponderantly Muslim (75%), with 13% being Christian; no other faith reaches 1% of the population. Manningham is also a distinctly youthful area, with 55% being aged under 30 and 25% being aged between 16 and 29. A significant proportion of the population are in owner-occupation (46%), 23% are in social housing and 6% are in council housing; a further 22% are in various forms of private rental. This pattern of housing tenure may be relevant when we consider the nature of the streetscape of Manningham in Chapter Three. Finally, it is worth noting that the gender split in Manningham in the 2011 census is 51.5% male and 48.5% female; thus suggesting that it is some way removed from being an area characterised by a high proportion of single males, which might have been more typical of its earlier experience as a zone of transition.

In its current formation, Manningham can be seen as an inner-city ward with a very diverse ethnic population and with significant levels of owner-occupation and dwelling in social housing, much of it from housing associations. This latter fact may also have much to contribute to our understanding of the apparently good quality of the housing stock as perceived when travelling through the area. The sedimented history of Manningham – as a place with clear associations with distinctive features of the conflict and struggle of minority ethnic communities, and particularly the Pakistani community, with their experience of marginalisation and racism – acts as a shared social imaginary that may inform contemporary residents' views of their attachment to the area.

The housing stock

Given the centrality of the discourse of *self-segregation and living in parallel cultures* in the development of government policies around Muslim communities in inner-city Britain, it is necessary and appropriate before completing this chapter to give some consideration to the dynamics of housing preference and to note some highly relevant research data on the circumstances in Bradford. The formal and informal housing policies of the 1950s, 1960s and 1970s have had an acute impact on residential patterns, not just in Bradford, but across cities and towns that became home especially to the former New Commonwealth migrants arriving in Britain after the Second World War. Referring to the experiences of African-Caribbeans, Dilip Hiro (1973: 64–5) notes:

three out of four accommodation bureaux practised racial discrimination.... Avoidance of black clients was what ... two out of three estate agents were found to be practising. The estate agents' stock responses to the black enquirers were: 'No property available'; 'Mortgages will be difficult to get' ... hypocritical subterfuges were often used in lieu of open discrimination.

The ways in which housing patterns have formed, then, also have a historical and complex narrative partly underlined by racism and race thinking. While there is also sufficient support for theses in which minority ethnic groups, especially early on in their settlement/immigrant experience, tend to live in the same neighbourhoods in order to maximise levels of mutual support and to develop necessary infrastructure, the impact of various forms of race discrimination ought not to be taken for granted or situated as a now-irrelevant aspect of history. However, after the 2001 disturbances, the fallout of which also coalesced with the aftershocks of the attacks of 11 September 2001 in the US, the continuing impact of history appears to have been sidelined or ignored altogether, to the extent that 'race' as a political idea and as a marker of identity that still has an impact on life chances is currently barely mentioned. Academic forays into promoting the 'post-racial society' sit happily with governmental ambitions to strip out key elements of the accumulated policies directed at countering racial discrimination: a process carried out under their populist rubric of cutting through excessive 'red-tape'. (This is a rhetoric that, incidentally, has attached to it a strong anti-European [European Commission] focus, and thus provides an affective and ideologically compatible xenophobic sentiment.) However, any inclination to accept the demise of racisms and racial discrimination in contemporary Britain can be dispelled nationally by monitoring the output of the Runnymede Trust, and locally through the attentive sustained observations of JustWestYorkshire.

With reference to segregation, the focus has shifted from a complex understanding, accounting for a range of factors (class, wealth, discrimination, un/employment, etc), to more simplistic descriptions, where the onus has been placed on something that is peculiar to a particular community: certain communities have become segregated because they want to be. Indeed, discussions focusing on the motivations underlying minority ethnic residential choice have been shaped through inference and assertion rather than evidence (see Carling, 2008; for a counter to the existence of 'ethnic' self-segregation, see Simpson et al, 2009).

Housing is not a simple feature of an ability to buy access into the housing market; it is also fundamentally determined by the nature of the housing stock. In this context, the profile of the housing stock in Britain has changed dramatically over the last few decades. As Pearce and Milne (2010: 9–11) have noted, as a result of government policy and of the Thatcherite 'right to buy' policies of the early 1980s:

> The national stock of council homes in England was halved between 1979 and 2004 ... by 2004 the social housing sector totalled 19 per cent of all households (4 million households), of which 11 per cent were council homes and the rest belonged to housing associations.

The reduction in the availability of council housing had an inevitable consequence upon access to it, and access was increasingly defined through a 'points system' based upon 'need'. Consequently, the residents in council housing increasingly became among the most disadvantaged in Britain (Hills, 2007) and the status of council estates became associated with stereotypes of a marginal and welfare-dependent residue of the working class. As Campbell (1993: 319, cited in Pearce and Milne, 2010: 10) evocatively phrased it:

> The word that embraced everything feared and loathed by the new orthodoxy about class and crime was estate: what was once the emblem of respectability, what once invoked the dignity and glamour of a powerful social constituency, part of the body politic, but which now described only the edge of class and the end of city. 'Estate' evoked rookery, slum, ghetto – without the exotic energy of urbanity.

The demise of the council estate as a 'normal' route into housing for people unable to buy has put a considerable strain on the social housing sector sustained by housing associations, and in Bradford, such housing has been an essential element of the housing supply. The pressure within the housing market has been exacerbated by the economic decline of a large part of Bradford's labour supply over the last three to four decades, which has produced a population with large numbers of white unemployed and underemployed people, and a difficult labour market for minority ethnic labour. As Finney and Simpson (2009) have shown, Bradford's Muslim populations have experienced internal processes of economic transition, with the growth of a newly affluent sector, many of whom have chosen to move out from Manningham and other inner-city areas. (Thus, for example, in a conversation with a taxi driver in March 2011, he reported that he had put all three of his children through university and all had professional jobs, and that he had moved from Manningham to a predominantly white area on the edge of the town.) As Phillips et al (2010: 13) noted, in 2001, housing tenure in Manningham/Girlington was '51% owner-occupation, 28% social rental, and 21% private rental'. Owner-occupation in Bradford as whole was 72%. Furthermore, referring to 2007 data, Phillips et al (2007: 221) noted that '80% of British Muslims in Bradford … live within some of the poorest urban areas in these cities'. However, the same study notes that 10% of the Muslims in Bradford live in the outer urban suburbs (Phillips et al, 2007: 222).

The issue of the relation of housing stock to the needs of different communities in Bradford is not new. Ratcliffe (1996) noted the issue of overcrowding in Pakistani and Bangladeshi communities and reported concern with the state of repair of much of the housing stock occupied by these communities. Additionally, the intra-ethnic diversity of the Bradfordian Asian populations has raised questions about the challenge of addressing the housing needs of the Asian elderly, who are disadvantaged in a number of ways in relation to access to appropriate housing stock (see, eg, Ahmad and Walker, 1997).

Thus, housing and access to the housing stock preferred by specific segments of the population defined by age, wealth, gender and ethnicity has become a key variable in shaping the social and political dynamics of Bradford. In recent years, we have seen a growing concern with the rights and experiences of the marginalised white working class (Dench et al, 2006; Sveinsson, 2009). Under 13 years of the Labour government's 'third way', Blairism saw a transition in British politics that resulted in a Labour Party essentially developing its policies in order to woo the British middle class. While urban malaise and aspects of poverty remained active elements in the policy framework, the white working class rightly concluded that neither the Labour Party nor the Conservative Party had *their* interests at heart. The collapse of the traditional locations of working-class mass labour in textiles and heavy industry was paralleled by a political evisceration of *class* from the discourse of British politics. Made marginal in British national politics, the working class have reciprocally come to regard party politics as irrelevant to their concerns and best interests, and have chosen to opt out of local and national elections in significant numbers, thus closing the loop in rendering themselves political irrelevant in electoral terms across large swathes of British politics. It is this bitter cycle of neglect that has made it possible for Garner (2009: 47) to report the sense of 'abandonment, loss and resentment' that he found in white working-class communities across England, which feeds the 'logic of unfairness we have picked up as a pattern, relating your own, deserving yet unrewarded experience with that of an undeserving neighbour'. As Garner (2009: 46) also notes, housing allocation is 'easy to represent as a site of unfairness, particularly when it can be identified with new migrants, and even more easily when those new migrants are black and Muslim'.

Thus, in the context of Bradford and Manningham, we have a specific expression of the national fragmentation of life chances by class, ethnicity, gender and age. One location where this fragmentation is explicitly made concrete is through the housing market and the demographies of civility that become established around particular patterns of residential opportunity. In Manningham, it is clear that the cheaper cost of housing has facilitated access to home ownership, and that a substantial provision of social housing has made viable housing available to many who could not afford to buy a house of their own. It is important, however, to note that local demographics are shaped not only by powerful forces of market provision of housing opportunities, but also by the ways in which individuals and families make their own choices within this determining framework.

Housing preferences

In Phillips et al's (2007) study of the housing preferences of Asian communities in Leeds and Bradford, they noted that the benefits of residential clustering were widely recognised. In the context of the negative discourse of 'the self-segregation' of South Asian communities, the analysis provided by Phillips et al shows the pragmatic rationale underlying such sentiments. They reported that:

> For the most part, interviewees recognized the continuing importance of 'community spaces', which were seen to engender feelings of familiarity, security and support. These give access to amenities, facilitate religious and cultural observance and, importantly, enhance a sense of belonging. Just over 70% of households in inner Leeds and Bradford had other people they regarded as family (including close family acquaintances referred to as aunts, uncles, cousins etc.) living within walking distance. (Phillips et al, 2007: 224)

This is an image of urban coexistence that is echoed in Alam's (2006) account of the strength of commitment to neighbourhood identities (including their ethnic complexity) that he found in an ethnographic study of young Muslim men in Bradford. The picture of close neighbourliness that comes from Phillips et al's (2007) account is, of course, deeply redolent of the traditional image of white working-class communities, now so often celebrated with a nostalgic sense of loss. That such social cohesion should be problematic when expressed in the lived experience of South Asian, British citizens, when defined as unhelpful *bonding social capital*, is a reflection of the racialised constructions of the world that are so deeply infused in British political discourse.

As Finney and Simpson (2009), among others, have shown, this image of a closely knit community is, of course, not a static phenomenon, and there are other interests and forces that are creating movement away from such communities. Indeed, as Phillips et al (2007) show in their study, the very closeness of a community can be intrusive for some members of the community, including some of the younger generation, whose aspirations may include a vision of a more independent lifestyle. As they observe:

> while the pull of the inner-city cluster is strong for many some of the younger interviewees in particular felt ambivalent or negative about the lifestyle of the close knit community, the opportunities it affords and the problems it may bring. (Phillips et al, 2007: 225)

They noted, for example, that for younger women who had been born in Britain, the support offered by such communities was heavily compromised by the level of surveillance that they felt from within their own community, and from the restraints on developing their preferred use of their domestic space: 'Some women thus regarded spatial relocation as desirable and empowering, bringing them (and their daughters) greater independence when entertaining and socializing, undertaking paid work or entering higher education' (Phillips et al, 2007: 226).

If gender is one factor that is shaping the current transitions in the demography of Bradford's South Asian populations, another is class. The emergence of a new, more affluent, and, for some, *very* affluent, segment within these communities has produced class-based preferences for moving from Manningham and other inner-city areas to more salubrious suburban areas. Aspirations that are based on class are held in common with the majority white population. Preferences for 'good schools', better housing, a good environment, suitable amenities and 'respectable' neighbours are not ethnically specific (see, eg, Alam, 2011). Phillips et al (2007) note that the very great majority of their interviewees who had moved to the suburbs of Bradford cited class considerations as a significant factor. They also noted that two thirds of their sample would, in principle, be happy to live in areas where there was a greater mix of British Asian and white families – 'so long as they felt safe' (Phillips et al, 2007: 227). In fact, Phillips et al (2007) report that a resistance to moving to all white areas was based upon fears of harassment, racism and isolation.

As with the majority white populations, a concern about personal safety and living in an area where you can feel secure ranked high among the concerns of Phillips et al's (2007) British Asian respondents; but, for them, there was the very real reality of racism, and its multiple forms of expression, which affected their housing choice. Fear of racial harassment and violence shaped their perceptions of some of the majority white areas of Bradford and informed their preference for avoiding white areas completely. However, additionally, Phillips et al (2007) report the existence of discriminatory behaviour by estate agents and housing providers as further limiting the housing choices of Bradford's Asian population (for a further account of discriminatory features of the Bradford housing market, see also Phillips, 2006). Thus, we can see that the current demography of Bradford and Manningham has to be seen within the nuanced framework of the role of patterns of immigration in relation to available opportunities for work, the available housing stock and access to it, as well as individual and collective housing preferences.

Conclusion

From the preceding, it can be seen that the mixed ethnic population of Manningham cannot be seen purely from the perspective of the statistical profile provided by census data. Manningham, as an area within Bradford, has its own distinctive history, which includes a long history of different flows of migration. The association of Manningham with a high proportion of Muslim residents over the last six decades has attached to it accretions of ethnic conflict associated with schooling, faith, contested change in the streetscapes and riot. Since the attacks of 11 September 2001 in the US and the bombings of 7 July 2005, the significance of the 'Muslim' presence in Manningham has added a further potent discourse of counter-terrorism and anxious social cohesion that has permeated the salience of this history for the popular understanding of the present. As we shall see in the chapters that follow, Manningham has become an area in which the streetscape, in many ways, asserts the predominance of the Pakistani/Muslim presence in the area. It may be an area that has acquired negative associations over the years for many who live outside of the area; however, as we shall see, for those who live in the area, it has social and physical properties that make it a desirable locale for a wide variety of persons.

CHAPTER THREE

Walking Manningham: streetscapes, soundscapes and the semiotics of the physical environment

Part One: An initial descriptive account

As we saw in Chapter Two earlier, Manningham is an area of inner-city urban Bradford that has a long history, with a mixed range of housing stock. The success of Victorian industrial expansion laid down the particular mix of substantial bourgeois mansions and large terraced houses alongside the modest, and even minimal, terraced and back-to-back terraced housing for the large population of workers who were the engine of this economic revolution. This same economic transformation also attracted waves of migrant workers to service the demand for labour, which not only changed the demography of the area, but also significantly changed its perceived character among residents and those living outside of Manningham. The reputational biography of Manningham, as discussed earlier, has provided a significant social framework within which its residents have learned to coexist and, in many cases, thrive. In this chapter, we will begin to enter into our contemporary analysis of Manningham by, first, *descriptively* exploring the physical properties of the area and then, second, discussing the contemporary significance of this *streetscape* for its residents.

Given the language of *parallel lives* and the heated national discourse around the dangers of the Muslim inner cities of the North, it might reasonably be assumed that walking through this area has all the characteristics of walking through a North American ghetto. The reality is quite the contrary. After tens of hours of walking through these streets, what remains striking is the mismatch of the reality with what it would be reasonable to assume that a stranger who knew this neighbourhood only by reputation and through the media might have anticipated. The prevailing sense of the terraced streets is of quiet domestication: of housing that is cared for and valued as home. The great majority of the housing is in good external repair. The paintwork is not dilapidated and the curtains, and often contemporary vertical blinds, are in good shape. Perhaps, this is a consequence to some extent of the extensive presence of housing association stock across the area, where the care of the fabric of the buildings will be externally regulated. However, the areas of owner-occupied terracing show very much the same sense of pride. In regard to the Pakistani population of Manningham, it has been put to me on a number of occasions by Pakistani interviewees that with the decrease in the transmission of remittances back to relatives in Pakistan, the consequently larger element of disposable income available for domestic use has found one outlet in the care and pride expressed in individuals' own houses. One expression of this is the proliferation of iron railings, often with gold spiked tops, to mark off the individual's domestic territory at the front, and often the back, of their houses.

In the great majority of cases, the front gardens, often not more than a metre deep fronting the house, are not full of the rubbish and residue of collapsed social norms that stereotypical images of inner cities have often invoked. True, they are not usually bijou testimonies to the art of gardening: some are concreted over, some are carefully laid with stone slabs and, indeed, some do have flowers. A few are set aside for growing vegetables, not perhaps a traditional 'English' usage for such a space, but they are tended and tidy. Very, very few such front gardens have the old mattresses, broken furniture and garbage that the stereotype of urban decline would suggest. This applies to the housing that is from housing association stock, as well as to the owner-occupied housing. Equally, the back lanes behind the houses are routinely free of rubbish and litter. The back lane of the street where this writer lived for almost 10 years was entirely clear on the occasions I visited it – not something that could have been said when I lived there 12 years ago. This is an area that has an air of self-respect and an apparent norm of tidiness.

It is possible that this personal expression of pride and ownership of the exterior extension of the home has been facilitated by the parallel process of government policies that have aimed at promoting economic improvement and civic pride in the depressed areas of Britain. Programmes such as the New Deal for Communities (from 1998), Sure Start (from 1999) and the National Strategy for Neighbourhood Renewal (from 2001), in different ways, all sought to have an impact upon the most deprived local authorities, and Bradford benefited from this.

The National Strategy for Neighbourhood Renewal was launched in 2001 with the aspiration that 'within 10 to 20 years no-one should be seriously disadvantaged by where they live' and with two long-term goals:

in all the poorest neighbourhoods to have common goals of lower worklessness and crime, and better health, skills, housing and physical environment ... [and] to narrow the gap on these measures between the most deprived neighbourhoods and the rest of the country. (Cited in DCLG, 2010: 6)

There is some evidence that these initiatives have had a positive effect (see, eg, Tunstall and Coulter, 2006; Power, 2009; DCLG, 2010). However, there is no evidence of a guaranteed 'permanent fix' and the indications are that such initiatives are highly dependent upon a sustained commitment to pursue such investment at the local level. We cannot fail to acknowledge the possible relevance of such initiatives, along with very many other factors, in shaping the current physical fabric of this area. There is cumulative evidence that the physical condition of an urban area has a strong impact upon individual residents' sense of pride and attachment to it and, reciprocally, the likelihood of them investing their own energies and resources in keeping their neighbourhood tidy. As Pearce and Milne (2010: 33) found in their study of two disadvantaged working-class estates in Bradford:

The way estates look has a huge effect on residents' sense of self respect and morale. 'You're embarrassed to bring people on the estate sometimes because of the old fencing, debris and rubbish. It's not inviting', a woman from Scholemoor told us. Closed shops and empty, boarded-up houses depressed people. Housing repairs were often not of good quality. Some of the most frequent complaints on both estates concerned the state of gardens, for example rubbish and furniture thrown in them, and broken fencing making it dangerous for young children to play.

The comparison between Pearce and Milne's (2010) description of the physical fabric of these two predominantly white working-class estates and the physical fabric of the terraces and streets of Manningham is quite striking. A modest indication of the impact of investment in their area is apparent in Phillips et al's (2010: 26) report that:

A number of settled Asian residents living in inner Bradford appreciated the improvements that had been made through housing and regeneration, although some young Asian women who have lived in the area for most of their lives were unhappy with what they perceived to be poor housing conditions (often owner-occupied), overcrowding and uneven regeneration. Asian men made fewer comments in this regard.

The children's playgrounds and small parks dotted around this area are also well tended and tidy; and, what is more, they are used. Litter on the playgrounds and in the streets is not a significant feature of the area, including such major shopping areas as Oak Lane and White Abbey Road. Additionally, graffiti is, again, to some extent, counter-intuitively, noticeably absent from this inner-city area. From experience in other cities, it had been expected that graffiti would be a major feature of the social landscape of this area. Quite simply, it is not. Routinely armed with a small camera, finding some graffiti became a reprehensible source of gratification. What graffiti there is appears to be individual in nature, rather than a visible means of marking 'gang' territory – again, another connotative association the outsider may be likely to make. There are areas of derelict land and boarded-up buildings within the Manningham area that would be regarded as utterly unacceptable in a suburban middle-class area, and while they are by no means the dominant feature of the area, their presence does signal something of the economic straits within which the area operates.

The housing stock in this area varies dramatically. There are short rows of 18th- and early 19th-century cottages that have become surrounded by the 19th-century working-class terraces put up to house the rapidly expanding labour force servicing the textile industry. There are large town houses that would have been the homes of the late 19th-century bourgeois that are now very largely multi-occupied; although some remain as private residences. Additionally, there are late 20th-century housing complexes built to house the aged, and there is the dramatic and dominant presence of Lister Mills, a huge 19th-century mill refurbished by the development company Northern Splash into high-quality apartments for the predominantly young and relatively affluent. It would be hard to suggest that there has been any pre-planned vision that shaped this urban diversity. It has been an ad hoc accretion of individual developments over a long period of time that has produced a remarkably diverse housing stock within a relatively small area. There are Victorian houses, for example, that were originally built for the city's affluent middle classes as domestic residences, which by the 1970s, were converted to be used as office space and, in some cases, multi-occupancy dwelling. Additionally, over the last decade or so, the city's growing middle-class Pakistani population have bought some of the properties for the express purpose of family residence. Thus, it is this diversity of housing stock, and its predominantly well-maintained external appearance, that gives this area a physical presence that sits uncomfortably with the stereotypical conception of battered and dilapidated buildings scarred by the overflow of old furniture and rubbish onto their frontages that is so powerfully evoked by stereotypical notions of multi-ethnic inner-city areas.

This is very predominantly a 'South Asian' area and for those not routinely familiar with Bradford, the site of some members of the local population in their 'traditional' dress might make the locality seem exotic. However, there is nothing exotic about the universal banality of people sitting on their front steps chatting, or taking in the sun. However, the combination of the locale, which has a pre-existing, externally constructed identity, with the non-European dress of some of the inhabitants may allow the ethnocentric observer to read this as a 'different space'. Walking the streets, however, one gets a sense of this being an area that people comfortably inhabit. *Their* cars line the streets, *their* children go to the neighbourhood schools, including Muslim schools, and they play in the neighbourhood's small recreational parks, and they shop in the local shops that provide a wide range of foodstuffs and consumer goods that might be appropriate to a South Asian neighbourhood.

The 'Muslim' identity of this area is signalled by the range of mosques, madrasas and schools that are distributed throughout it. As the photographs in the following pages richly demonstrate, the strength of this signalling system differs quite widely. Some mosques look 'like mosques should look', with cupolas and minarets, and others are converted cinemas or large buildings with only a limited amount of external signage to mark the distinctive transition in their form of usage. Similarly, Muslim schools may be 19th-century stone-built old school structures that have acquired new ownership, and madrasas may be a wide variety of buildings that have had quite different prior usage.

The economic activity in the area is marked by the existence of the 'Asian' shops, especially along Oak Lane and White Abbey Road, by the corner shops dispersed throughout the area, and by the scattering of garage workshops in terraces and backstreets. Walking up Oak Lane (a major shopping street in Manningham, discussed at more length later) during the day, one is struck by the relative absence of people. This is not an area marked by the hustle and bustle of an 'ethnic' shopping experience much beloved of Sunday supplement guides for the 'in touch' cognoscenti. On an average working day, looking down the length of Oak Lane, (perhaps 400 yards) one might see between five and 20 people going about their business: popping in to buy groceries or taking the opportunity to have an ice cream in one of the relatively new dessert parlours. In essence, in terms of the physical fabric, this is an area of contradictions held together by the meaningful use that the inhabitants of the area make of it.

The symbolic landscape of this urban environment: problematising the taken-for-granted streetscape

While a significant core of our work rests upon interview data, it is impossible to explore the negotiation of identities within the urban context without drawing upon the very extensive, relatively recent literature on the power of the symbolic landscape in constituting a potent presence in shaping the experience of identity in context. The possibility of taking the physical environment as a socially inert material given has been undermined by a great body of contemporary analysis. Harvey (1996, 2000), for example, opened up a capacity for seeing 'structured permanences' as being as much a social phenomenon as a physical one, and space and place as being located within a contested and dynamic set of forces. Over recent years, the tensions between essentially structural analyses of the formation of the urban environment and more semiotic accounts of the subjective experience of inhabiting these spaces has been a feature of the academic literature (Westwood and Williams, 1997). The 'cultural turn' in the social sciences in general has found a rich and fruitful terrain in informing the interrogation of the urban environment as a contested and socially constructed environment of symbolic systems and complexly shifting identities. So extensive and visible has this development been, that Soja (1997: 21) felt impelled to assert that:

> I have recently become uneasy over what I perceive to be a growing over-privileging of what has been called, often with reference to the work of Michel de Certeau, the 'view from below' – studies of the local, the body, the streetscape, psycho-geographies of intimacy, erotic subjectivities, the micro-worlds of everyday life – at the expense of understanding the structuring of the city as a whole, the more macro-view of urbanism, the political economy of the urban process.

Furthermore, in pressing home his argument, Soja notes the 'romancing' of agency that comes from those who would critique macro-analyses, and their identification with the unconstrained liberty of the free-wheeling flâneur. Thus, he argues that:

> A primary tactic in fostering these often reductionist critiques of macro-level theorizing has been a kind of epistemological privileging of the experience of the flaneur, the street-wandering free agent of everyday life, the ultimate progenitor of the view from below. (Soja, 1997: 21)

The lines of analytic contestation are clearly drawn here. In this analysis, we would argue that the tension between structural accounts of the city and more recent accounts of the subjective terrain of the locality do not have to be parallel and opposed discourses that are inherently incapable of finding points of articulation that are mutually beneficial. However, even a modest scrutiny of academic production about the urban context provides ample evidence of the separation of these approaches: through the editorial position of specific journals and the intellectual and political preference of individual scholars.

In our argument here, we will pragmatically privilege one approach over the other within specific moments in the developing argument; however, we would hope that the cumulative argument will benefit equally from both approaches. The location of Bradford within the global shift of labour markets and their impact upon the textile trade, and the impact upon Bradford of the radical transformation of labour and capital under Thatcherism, are macro-forces that cannot be ignored. Additionally, the globalised realities of terrorism and the Europe-wide policies of securitisation have had a dramatic impact upon the multi-ethnic dynamics of Bradford (Husband and Alam, 2011). Equally, in the domain of policy, the neglect of the working class in New Labour policymaking and the various tranches of urban programmes aimed at ameliorating the multiple disadvantages in inner-city Britain came armed with moral agendas of blame, as well as blocks of targeted funding (Levitas, 2005). Any attempt to account for the current dynamics in contemporary Bradford/Manningham that did not frame the individual experience of life there within a multilayered macro-account would provide a story told out of time and place – and evacuated of politics.

Equally, the rich insights into the negotiation of identities in multi-ethnic urban contexts provided by sensitive ethnographic accounts of lived experience, as 'viewed from below', have been a major contribution to our understanding of the contemporary city (Back, 1996; Eade, 1997; Herbert, 2008). The placing of salient identities into specific locales, and the exploration of the mesh of constraints and possibilities that render choices so situationally contingent and meaningful (Alexander, 2000), provides a necessary understanding of the exercise of agency in situ. Furthermore, the symbolic environment of the *streetscape*, with its layering of multiple meanings through signage and architectural features, has been revealed to show the power of the social encoded into the material environment of the city.

Human and cultural geography has developed a repertoire of conceptual tools to open up for scrutiny the processes of identity formation and their relationship to space and place. Building on the insights of De Certeau (1984), there has been an increasing focus upon the making of the physical environment through the process of living within it. Even walking in an urban context has been rendered a postmodern experience of considerable complexity. As Middleton (2010: 575) asserts in the abstract to her paper on urban walking: 'Walking is positioned and understood as a socio-technical assemblage that enables specific attention to be drawn to the embodied, material and technological relations and their significance for engaging with everyday urban movements on foot.'

As Secor (2004) illustrates in speaking of the 'city walker', the physical world is a relational process between material realities and lived practices:

> City walkers traverse interlacing 'grids of difference' and find themselves taking up particular subject positions in relation to the various (religiously, ethnically, or class-based) communities and spaces that organize their spatial trajectories. As their footsteps narrate urban stories – fixing, assembling, traversing, and transforming urban boundaries – urban travellers become active participants in the production of difference, identity and citizenship. (Secor, 2004: 358)

If De Certeau (1984) pointed to the flux and disorder of everyday life, we have also been encouraged to recognise the means whereby human beings have developed routines as a way of managing the continuous challenge of our rich social and physical environment. As Bourdieu's concept of 'habitus' seeks to demonstrate, within any specific environment (*social field*), individuals tend to develop a stable *habitus*: a learned mesh of habits and feelings that render manageable the daily negotiation of life. What is being recognised here is the relatively recent academic emphasis upon problematising and making salient the nature of the spatial configuration of locale as a critical element within this social field. As Clayton (2009: 483) puts it: 'Accordingly, the spatial, itself a product of competing discourses, practices and power relations, has the capacity to constitute, constrain and mediate social distinctions, including race'.

A product of living through the acquired routines of a local specific habitus is that individuals can develop unthinking practices that envelop them in a social world of familiarity and relative safety. Whether in terms of class, gender or ethnicity, they shop where they feel comfortable and are not likely to be treated as an unwelcome and unfamiliar intrusion. Of course, such routines ensure that their relative insularity remains in place since *they* have excluded themselves from violating the social norms that are reproduced in the shops they avoid. Similar behaviours contribute to the reproduction of social spaces in the neighbourhood as having a sense of being comfortable or unwelcoming or dangerous (see, eg, Ruddick, 1996; on the implications of 'geographies of belonging', see Clayton, 2009: 491). As we will see later in Chapter Five, the intersection of gender and ethnicity in Manningham is a significant determinant of the possible ownership of the street as a comfortably inclusive, defended or hostile place. While speaking of inter-ethnic encounters in the city of Leicester, Clayton (2009: 490) notes that: 'To speak of the everyday urban environment is not just a reference to the physical and sensory experience of the city, but also to its symbolic properties.'

These symbolic properties are woven into the fabric of space and place, as contemporary urban geographers and socio-linguistic scholars have revealed in ever-increasing detail (Westwood and Williams, 1997; Berg and Vuolteenaho, 2009; Gorter et al, 2012). As we have already noted, the locale of Manningham has a quite particular association with immigrant settlement. This association itself has revealed how such symbolic attachments are labile and subject to change over time. An area of the city that was developed through the burgeoning economic expansion of the 19th-century textile industry became associated with post-war Polish settlement and then with an expanding South Asian population and, more latterly, with 'riot' and Muslim 'self-segregation'.

Toponymy and contested space

Seen through the lens of contemporary urban geography, nothing in the urban environment can be taken as a self-evident given with a fixed social meaning. As Rose-Redwood et al (2010: 455) argue at length in their review of the development of '*the critical turn*' in toponymic scholarship (ie the study of the semiotics of place names and the politics of naming), this has radically changed toponymic research from the days when it viewed 'place names as transparent signifiers that designated places as "objects" or "artefacts" within a predefined geographical space'. Rose-Redwood et al (2010) note the considerable literature that explores the naming of places as a process, shaped through often contested hegemonic practices that contribute to the production of racialised, gendered and commodified landscapes (see, eg, Berg and Vuolteenaho, 2009). An exploration of the cultural politics of naming reveals the less than innocent content of the processes of naming, whereby street names and signage become sites of struggle over legitimacy and visibility for contesting identities within a locale. Thus, for example, commemorative street naming may lay down a received version of history that reads differently to different audiences (Azaryahu, 1996). More generally, Rose-Redwood and Alderman (2011:3) warn of the dangers of neglecting *banal naming practices*, with the consequence of failing to register their cumulative subliminal power to create a terrain of meaning that is incontestable precisely because it is so mundane. Alderman (2008) has pointed to the power of place naming as both a form of symbolic capital and symbolic resistance. Thus, in the middle of Manningham, in areas of high Muslim residence, we have streets that unequivocally reiterate the Christian heritage embedded in the area, with names such as St Paul's Road and St Mary's Road. Street naming in Quebec (see Gade, 2003), for example, has clearly been an active element in the contested identity politics that has operated there. However, at present, there is no apparent evidence of popular, or even elite, Pakistani and Muslim pressure in Bradford to free them from the banally present street signage landscape they inhabit. However, it is noteworthy (and something we will explore further later) that in the major recent reconstruction of Lister Park, which was a Victorian investment in 'rational recreation' on the edge of Manningham and Heaton, the planners inserted a Mughal garden (Husband and Alam, 2012). This is at least a modest indication of the formal response to changing the physical identity of the area in recognition of its changed demography.

Signscapes and evoked identities: transnational and local

As we move through any urban environment, we are confronted with multiple forms of visual information, for example, advertising hoardings that seek, through the arcane professional practices of the advertising industry, to find a link with us that will dispose us towards consuming this product or taking that holiday. As pedestrians, we are largely unaware of the proliferation of road traffic signs, which as a driver, we would be registering almost subliminally. Yet another ubiquitous visual presence is signage above shops, and in their windows, which inform us of the trade that they would wish to engage with us. Not only do they tell us whether this is a butcher or a greengrocer, but they often give us an indication of the ethnicity of the owner, through their name or, for example, through a direct reference to being a *halal* butcher, or perhaps through the language used in the signage. Shop signs are a significant part of the visual ecology of a neighbourhood and can cumulatively contribute to its sense of dominant ethnic identity. Where specific identities have been politically repressed through the exclusion of a community language from shop signage, this has been a site of struggle that has seen sometimes radical transformations in the language of shop signs following changed political circumstances (Gade, 2003). Ubiquitous in their presence, and subtle in their impact, shop signs are a means of negotiating identities and suggesting affinities with potential customers.

Hall and Datta (2010: 71), in a detailed and illuminating analysis of shop signs in Walworth Road, London, provide this synopsis of the significance of the semiotic linkage of signs with a diverse passing population:

> The distribution and valuation of capital through visual signscapes on the Walworth road, and its possibilities of exchange is not objective, but actors on the street are able to quickly learn the 'rules of the game' (Bordieu, 2002) that are implicitly agreed upon. As visual forms of cultural capital, they can be translated into social capital through the development of a social network base of valued customers and therefore exchanged for economic capital through their patronage. A key feature of these signages is that they are contingent upon the particular context of Walworth Road where they are read, interpreted and translated through a particular combination of social, cultural and economic capital vested in both entrepreneurs and clients.

In an analysis that is redolent of the poetics of postmodern cultural studies, Hall and Datta (2010) are concerned to demonstrate the trans-local dynamics in play as different individuals engage with the content of the local signage, mediated through their own situated identities in a borough of London, while simultaneously possessing biographic linkages to places of recent or distant migration. So, too, will we explore the semiotic possibilities of the signage found in Manningham at some length in Part Two of this chapter. It is noteworthy that in their study of Walworth Road, Hall and Datta (2010) reported that there were over 20 different countries represented in the nationalities of the proprietors of the shops in that street. In Oak Lane and elsewhere in Manningham, that degree of diversity will not be found and, hence, there is the possibility that a much more delimited sense of the identities in play will be found in our data, with the consequence of providing a basis for the perception of the area to be predominantly 'Asian' in character and ownership.

Manningham/Girlington soundscapes: the elusive auditory world of difference

If we again return to the stereotypical expectations of the multicultural inner-city urban streetscape, we might expect there to be a distinctive buzz of noise: the mingled call of street traders, the burst of staccato raised voices and the bursting through into the public space of individual choices of music. Sound is no longer an absent element of the reading of the urban environment. Following on from Schafer's (1969, 1977, 1993) groundbreaking examination of the nature of our banal *soundscapes*, we have come as social scientists to *hear* our auditory environment: to deconstruct its formation and query its impact. The analysis of our acoustic ecology has become a significant facet of our competence in revealing individuals' encounters with their physical environment (see, eg, Bull, 2000, 2008; Bull and Back, 2003). Thus, in the context of Manningham, it is interesting to explore the distinctive *keynote sounds* and *soundmarks* that distinguish this locale. (This will be carried out in further detail later, where the linkage of soundscape and streetscape in specific neighbourhoods within this area will be explored in more detail to provide a more textual and richer analysis.) However, at this point, it has to be noted that Manningham, even Oak Lane, does not have the distinctive sound of street vendors, of crowded cafes spilling out onto the street or of noisy groups energetically disputing the business of the day that may be stereotypically associated with inner-city multiculturalism. The dominant keynote sound in some areas is that of the traffic passing through the arterial roads; an occasional element within this being the loud eruption into the public domain of an individual driver's taste for music through their loud sound systems and boom box. Sometimes, this can be non-negotiably intrusive. If there is a distinctive *soundmark* in this area, it is the Muslim call to prayer, which in particular locales, can be heard coming from a distinctive mosque, where the visual and aural presence of Islam are co-present, and in others, from a building that has little external appearance as a place of worship. Unlike the case in other European and British cities, Bradford has seen no significant resistance to the building of mosques (Husband, 1994b; McLoughlin, 2005), and the religious architectural, and aural, signature of Manningham is one of the defining features of the area. (The absence of the vituperative politicised public resistance to mosques and the call to prayer [*Adhaan*] that has been apparent in some other European countries does not mean that there were no residents who found such unfamiliar insertions into their neighbourhood streetscape personally irritating and culturally unacceptable, but is does signal a significant absence in the politics of Muslim–non-Muslim relations in Bradford as compared with comparable urban contexts elsewhere.)

The culinary signature of Manningham

Among other things, within Manningham, Oak Lane came through the 1970s and 1980s to acquire a very distinctive identity as the location for a 'good curry'. It became a recognised epicentre of the Bradford curry scene, which later became part of the civic packaging of Bradford as the national curry centre with the establishment of the '*curry trail*'. Located within Manningham, Oak Lane became a place to celebrate culinary difference by customers, many of whom would, in travelling into the area, regard the surrounding terraces through a racialised lens as being an alien space occupied by 'pakis'. At the same time, on another outer-edge of Manningham, Lumb Lane became '*the front line*' in 1980s' inter-ethnic territorial posturing. In a way resonant of other liminal inter-ethnic locales, Manningham also became identified as the 'red light district' of Bradford, until the sex trade was unambiguously driven out by younger male members of the Pakistani Muslim community in an explicit display of control over *their* territory. Thus, a community that had experienced considerable racial stereotyping and denigration as inferior were instrumental in denying the 'respectable' majority white population access to illicit and illegal sex on 'their turf'. Furthermore, while issues of territory and morality were being fought out over a number of years, the *Sweet Centre* on Lumb Lane remained throughout the 1980 and 1990s a highly favoured curry house to be visited by the discerning and, more importantly, 'culturally au fait' white client. (The personal pride individual members of the white community may take in knowing where to find the *authentic* Bradford curry continues to be a significant factor in the intersection of *intercultural* dynamics with the food trade in Bradford.)

The positively valued quality of the 'different' cuisine may perhaps be given an added zest by the implicit alienness of the locale in which the restaurant is sited. The 'reputation' of neighbourhoods, and of particular streets within them, is a salient element of the symbolic terrain of any urban space, and certainly in Manningham, particular areas have had quite distinct symbolic relevance within the negotiated, and contested, understandings of territory and of the performative scripts that are likely to be played out there – by whom, in relation to whom and with what explicit agenda.

The culinary footprint of Manningham extends beyond the possibilities of consuming a 'good curry' and is expressed in concrete terms through the many possibilities of buying 'ethnic foodstuffs' in the supermarkets and corner shops. Walking down Oak Lane, the fruit and vegetables displayed on the shopfront stalls evoke the familiar 'homeland' fruits and vegetables to some, and the exotically unusual opportunities for practising a 'different' culinary repertoire for others. Browsing through the stacked shelving of the 'Asian' supermarkets provides an exposure to a world of multiple choices of pulses and tinned foods that speak loudly of a distinctive culinary tradition. The size of the packaging for spices and rice and pulses underlies the message of a cuisine with a different sense of priorities, and of a domestic pattern of consumption that is different to the one traditionally practised by the majority white populations of Bradford. For decades, Oak Lane had a Polish corner delicatessen that serviced the needs of that community; however, its closure has now been superseded by the opening of other Polish food shops and a café/restaurant on Manningham Lane to address the needs of the new Polish migrant population, and to again assert the ethnic diversity of the area.

Identity/identities? Hybrid identities and the city

> The dynamic possibilities of urban identities are clear, but the ability to 'become anybody' is restricted by the strength of community boundaries (Valkins, 2003), the nature of intercultural encounters as well as prevailing inequalities, racisms and power relations. (Clayton, 2009: 491)

This quotation points to the tension between the imaginative possibilities scripted into much postmodern writing about hybridity and the endless flux of 'liquid' identities under late capitalism, and the lived realities of negotiating identities within specific milieus and particular locales, framed as they are by the many structural expressions of power in society. In looking at the 'messiness' of identities, Noble (2009: 876) points to the need to recognise 'different kinds of recognition that revolve around legitimacy and competence, temporality and situatedness that relate to the contingencies of participation in a specific domain or setting'.

In a paper arguing against the easy emphasis upon ethnicity or gender in looking at situated identities, Noble is pointing to the need to recognise the contingent negotiation of possible identities within specific settings. Thus, the possibility of hybridity remains real, but the practical possibility of realising a specific identity becomes highly contingent upon the forces present in a specific context that render some identities more readily salient than others, and requires that the legitimacy of performing that identity is contextually supported. Additionally, the individual's own competence in performing that identity in that context at that time also becomes relevant.

This points us in the direction of remaining sensitive to Goffman's (1969, 1972) opening out for scrutiny the complexity of impression management in specific contexts. This makes salient not only the attributed identity cued by, for example, age, gender, sexual preference, ethnicity and class, but also the individual's competence in knowing and enacting the appropriate behavioural repertoire. The easy and familiar greeting on the street is such a script. The symbolic power of the handshake and the greeting *As-Salamu Alaykum* lies not in the difficulty in anyone performing the act, but in the performance being recognised as legitimate for the person performing in that specific context. In Bradford, majority white men do not typically shake hands upon meeting, and, consequently, this simple social ritual upon the streets of Bradford between Muslim men, young or old, serves to make salient their difference to the majority population, while simultaneously acting as a ritual reassertion of an affiliation between those sharing the performance. A white non-Muslim male may be perfectly capable of enacting this ritual upon meeting a Pakistani person on the street, but the reading of his performance would raise exactly those issues of legitimacy and context identified by Noble earlier.

Similarly, Hall and Datta (2010) emphasise the interaction of the concrete features of the situated characteristics of the locality with the active negotiation of multiple identities. This, they argue, may lead an individual to find emotive and cognitive resonances with their unique *trans-local* profile. As Smith (2005: 239) has argued: 'Contemporary transnational migration is highly differentiated by class, gender, generation, region, religion, and political and economic circumstances of migration within the same migrating "nationality", even within a single transnational city'.

This internal differentiation within apparently similar ethnic migratory populations has significant implications for the distribution of the social, cultural and economic capitals that Hall and Datta (2010) have noted to be central to the individual's ability to engage successfully and creatively with their location in a British urban setting. Thus, the essentialised language of Muslim communities living *parallel lives* in *parallel cultures*, which was discussed in Chapter One, provides a homogenising perspective that pre-empts any possibility of adequately understanding the negotiation of lives that take place in British multi-ethnic urban locales. In the case of Manningham, the very considerable internal divisions within the Muslim communities, defined by region of origin, faith group, language, class, gender and generation, make the necessity of engaging with this huge diversity of experience an absolute imperative. For Bradford's Polish community, too, the internal differentiation created by point of exit from Poland, education, class and gender has been sufficient to create quite distinct social cleavages within the 'Polish community'. (This will be developed in some depth in Chapter Four.) This diversity of experience and consciousness provides the basis for individuals to negotiate their own unique forms of hybrid trans-local identity. However, as Clayton (2009) pointed out earlier, the constraints of economic, cultural and social capitals that attend this unique trajectory also place limits on the viability of potential forms of identity as a basis for negotiating life in a specific context. Thus, as Smith (2005: 238) robustly points out:

> the unbridled celebration of the 'hybridity' of transnational subjects serves to erase the fact that no matter how much spatial mobility or border crossing may characterize transnational actors' household, community, and place-making practices, the actors are still classed, raced and gendered bodies in motion in specific historical contexts, within certain political formations and spaces.

Summary of Part One

Social science has provided us with a rich repertoire of concepts that have opened up for our comprehension the everyday significances of the physical environment within which individuals negotiate their life in urban neighbourhoods. We have sketched earlier something of the ways in which this literature illuminates our understanding of the daily dynamics of living in Manningham. The multiple mechanisms that provide a semiotic language of the streetscape have been provisionally outlined and their potential has been framed within an understanding of the implications of housing policy and of the demographic dynamics of Bradford. In the second part of this chapter, we will move on to develop further the insights that this approach can offer us in developing an understanding of everyday interaction in a multi-ethnic neighbourhood by drawing more concretely on ethnographic evidence.

Part Two: Everyday encounters with the physical world

Introduction: stereotypical expectations and perceived reality?

Walking the streets of Manningham as an alert observer within the context of this project, it is necessary to be explicitly aware of the conceptual baggage and prior assumptions that you might be carrying with you, and one pervasive perceptual frame is shaped by an awareness of what people who had never been to this area, but only knew it by reputation, may expect. As outlined in Chapter Two, Manningham has been very heavily associated with the popular imagery of a problematic inner-city Britain: portrayed as a classic instance of an inner-city area dominated by migrants, and specifically being an area of Muslim settlement. Associated with inner-city riot and with the dangerous possibility of 'radicalised' Muslim youth and their potential as the next wave of 'home-grown bombers', this would be no generic multicultural site of benign cosmopolitanism. Framed by the language of Muslim 'self-segregation' and the assertion that they are determinedly pursuing living within 'parallel cultures', this is an area that is redolent of perceived difference. As we saw in Chapter Two, the language of the ghetto, in political and local parlance, has been applied to this area, and that brings with it the possibility of invoking a strong stereotype of the physical and social conditions that would be routinely associated with such an inner-city area.

Inner-city 'ghetto' or domestic neighbourhoods?

Let us make that stereotype concrete. This should be an area in which the majority white population is a distinct minority. It should be an area of strangeness as the local milieu reflects a dominant minority culture, and it should be an area suffused with a palpable sense of danger and threat to the majority visitor. If this is 'the ghetto', it should be characterised by the vigorous street life that we see in cinematic representations of streets, with local people 'hanging out' in dilapidated neighbourhoods and where roaming dogs scavenge among the litter and detritus of overcrowded housing. This should be an area of 'alien' vitality, marginality and decay, with graffiti marking out gang territory and youths clustering on street corners. This is very much the mediated imagery that is invoked by labelling an area a ghetto. (For a scathing critique of the misuse of the concept of the ghetto in the contemporary European setting, see Waquant, 2008.)

Indeed, an awareness of such a potential stereotypical conception of Manningham was a recurrently present sensibility when carrying out the fieldwork in this area; most concretely, when the perceived reality was so strongly at odds with such a set of expectations. Some elements of the stereotype are concretely present, such as the dominant presence on the streets being people of an 'Asian' appearance, while other elements were very strongly countered by the reality – as we shall see.

The housing stock and built environment

It is in walking the streets of Manningham that one is most immediately struck by the misfit of the stereotype with the observed reality. The predominant sense one has of the housing stock in this area is that this is an area where houses are well tended. If one steps across the road from the Carlisle Road Business Centre and enters into the terraced streets leading away from that arterial road, it is impossible not to be struck by the sense of domestic pride in their houses that the people in this area demonstrate. The houses are in good repair, the paintwork on the windows and doors is in good condition, the windows are clean, and the curtaining and blinds are neat.

Similarly, if you walk around Oak Lane and wander through the streets of terraced housing in that area, there is again a sense of ownership of this housing stock, of care being taken in its upkeep.

This is no area of slum dwellings or rank urban malaise. Even if you walk up St Paul's Road, which has a large stock of large, multi-occupied Victorian terraced houses, where you might expect some degree of neglect, the streetscape is one of tidiness, and viewed up its full length, it has the appearance of quiet respectability. Indeed, the following image – comprising a road, pavement, cars, housing, the church and especially the greenery – could quite easily be mistaken as a scene depicting an archetypically leafy, middle-class area.

In walking around the streets, there is a cumulative sense of tidiness and a collective pride in the way in which houses and the streets

themselves are maintained. There is an almost total absence of the piles of broken and rejected furniture, old mattresses and the ad hoc assemblage of packaging that is so often associated with inner-city

decay. Indeed, even walking along the back streets and alleys behind these houses, there is a very noticeable absence of rubbish and litter. Together with a notable absence of the leakage of domestic rubbish into the public gaze, one overarching meaning/interpretation is that of domesticity, calm and – if one chooses to read the image in such a way – well-embedded ownership of the neighbourhoods.

The back lanes are predominantly tidy, sometimes with cars parked, but in the great majority of cases, they echo the domestic respectability

that is apparent at the more visible frontage of these houses. On only a few occasions has discarded furniture been found in the small gardens typically fronting these terraced houses. Indeed, these proximal 'defensive zones' in the front of the houses are routinely tidy and free of any unsightly content. Many of them are concreted over, or have stone slabs laid in the place of gardens, but they are nonetheless tidy. Some do have plants established in them, and a few, such as in St Mary's Road, where there is a more generous amount of available space, have been shaped into attractive communal gardens due to the initiative of local residents.

In case this account should seem too devoid of inner-city decay, it has to be said that there are derelict buildings in this area, including large 19th-century public buildings like the former children's hospital on St Mary's Road, which is currently boarded up and represents a substantial eyesore. There are also the occasional patches of derelict land, reminding the visitor that this is not a bourgeois suburb, despite some of the elegant housing stock, where such excrescences would not be tolerated. This part of Bradford, like many other areas within the city, developed with a close intermingling of domestic accommodation with industrial premises, mills and workshops, and it is predominantly the now-defunct industrial buildings that present a challenge in maintaining

the area's visual integrity. This is so despite the frequent, and creative, reuse of many of these buildings.

Signalling difference?

In the majority of cases, there is nothing about the content of the house frontage that would indicate the probable ethnicity of the occupants. However, in a few instances, onions, spinach and white radish and other vegetables – 'continental' and British – are being grown in this space, which is a practice that would not be regarded as typical of the majority white working class. Over a decade ago, it might have been possible to speculate about the possible ownership of a house by noting the choice of colours used to paint the window frames, doors and downpipes from the guttering. In this area, there was an unspoken white working-class normative expectation about what colours were appropriate for the external decoration of one's house. A small 'c' conservative palette of greens, browns, blues and white seemed to predominate, and in that context, purples, bright greens, yellows and mauve were noticeably aberrant, signalling the probable 'Asian' identity of the occupants. In walking around this area after an absence of over 10 years, there had been an expectation that this same visual expression of 'difference' would be readily observable. This was not so. The possible reasons for this may be an accommodation to the majority ethnic normative repertoire, partially driven by the number of Bradford-born younger occupants, and the extensive presence of housing association properties, where the choice of colour would be in the hands of the owners and would be expressed across a number of houses in a street.

One feature of the housing stock that had the capacity to signal the likely ethnicity of the occupants was the proliferation of iron fencing around the often very small front garden space. In pre-war England, such iron fencing was often a feature of urban terraces, but this metal was stripped from the urban scene as the iron was reclaimed (requisitioned) for the war effort, never to be replaced. However, around Manningham now, these domestic claims to territory have become a highly visible feature of the area in recent years. Typically painted black, and often with gold fleur-de-lis deterrent spikes on top, they not only mark out individual houses, but also give a distinct visual character to a street, or large sections of one. Seen in the two-storey terraces in the area, these fences give a distinctive presence to the housing and underline the claims to proprietorial pride and territorial sensibilities.

However, these decorative and defensive flourishes are in no way limited to the terraced streets of the area, for within this area, there are also very substantial Victorian piles that are now adorned with

more elaborate ironwork that echoes the same aesthetic, and the larger affluence of the occupant.

Neither is this demonstrative largesse limited to Manningham, for in the areas of new South Asian settlement in the more affluent periphery of the city centre, there can be found the same expressive ironwork. Thus, it can be argued that as a form of cultural expression that is particularly, though not exclusively, associated with the South Asian populations of Bradford, this metal fencing provides a non-intrusive, but nonetheless salient, marker of ethnic difference. It is part of the banal streetscape to which locals may be habituated, but which the occasional visitor my find striking in its declaration of a culturally different presence.

Challenging the expected inner-city physical fabric

If, as has been suggested earlier, the imagery of a multi-ethnic ghetto has been associated with constructions of Manningham in the popular press and political rhetoric, then a walk around this area produces some remarkably counter-intuitive experiences. Because of the historical transitions that have formed the current built environment of the area, there are to be found almost randomly scattered through the area buildings that loudly shout a different form of identity to that which would be spontaneously invoked by this stereotypical framing of the area. Thus, for example, in the heart of Manningham, one turns a corner and facing you, in Skinner Lane, there is a row of beautifully preserved 19th-century cottages that have a longer prior history. Taylor and Gibson (2010: 18) report numbers 11, 13 and 15 as having been originally a single farmhouse that was subdivided into three dwellings in the late 18th or early 19th century, when they were used for domestic textile manufacturing.

They are now, by any conception of contemporary housing preferences, delightful 'period' houses that should have no place in anyone's imagined ghetto. Similarly, as a continuing statement of the 19th-century wealth associated with the textile industry in Bradford, there are to be found throughout Manningham the classic villas and substantial houses that were built for what Taylor and Gibson (2010: 28, 36) describe as 'the pioneering new rich' and the 'succession of middle orders', respectively. Some of these, like Blenheim Mount and Manningham Villas, which are set back from the arterial Manningham Lane, are now largely multi-occupied, and on close inspection, some show some signs of the distressed economy of their occupants. However, elsewhere, elite housing from the 19th century still provides spacious

accommodation for their new affluent occupants, and as comfortable and spacious family homes, offer a direct challenge to the idea of this area as being defined by inner-city poverty and overcrowding. As we shall see in Chapters Five and Six, the acquisition of wealth cannot be simply linked to a wish to exit from Manningham. For many, there is no incompatibility in having considerable disposable income and choosing to continue to live in Manningham as the preferred location for self and family.

Speaking of the quality of the textile buildings that were erected in Bradford from the mid-19th century onwards, Taylor and Gibson (2010: 86) note that:

> The same quality and craftsmanship is found in Manningham's smaller buildings, ranging from the villas of the wealthy industrialists and merchants to the terraces and back to backs lived in by the thousands of workers who helped to make the city prosperous. The smooth ashlar stone of some of the best terraces, the carved details, the durability and the quality of the building materials all lift Manningham out of the ordinary. Even the humble back to backs were substantially built and above the housing standards in many contemporary cities.

It is this heritage that underpins the distinctive visual streetscape of much of contemporary Manningham. The broad streets of three-storey housing in, for example, St Paul's Road, the distinctive character of Southfield Square, Peel Square and Hanover Square, and the robust terrace houses with their little additional finishes of stone lintels or other minor architectural flourishes laid down the essential architectural fabric of much of this area, which has responded well to the current care, and perhaps affection, that is apparent in walking through this townscape at present.

Standing as a major statement of the continuing presence of Bradford's 19th-century textile wealth, Lister Mills (also known as Manningham Mills), described as 'an extraordinary statement of industrial ambition' (Taylor and Gibson, 2010: 86), continues to dominate the Bradford skyline from the centre of Manningham. Taylor and Gibson (2010: 59) describe it in these terms:

> When complete (in 1888) the new Manningham Mills was the largest silk-spinning and weaving mill in Great Britain, employing as many as 11,000 at its height. Its visual impact is hard to over-emphasise. With its colossal chimney, it was and is a prominent and architecturally lavish eye-catcher, seemingly intended by Lister to be as much a visual asset to

the residential neighbourhood as the Park which bore his name. From a distance it appears monstrous yet coherent, while at close quarters it seems endless but impressive with startling variations in scale and repetitive but well proportioned detailing to the various elevations.

Lister Mills was an engine that created the demand for labour that then generated much of the housing in the area. Recently, completely refurbished as apartment accommodation by Northern Splash, a highly regarded development company, Lister Mills now stands as a de facto gated community for relatively affluent young couples and individuals who are able to drive into the underground car park and, from there, enter the building lobby, to their dwelling. Occupied by an ethnically mixed clientele, the new apartments, predominantly for singles and couples, but with penthouse apartments on the roof, offer accommodation of high quality in a remarkable listed building that offers unique views over much of Bradford. Placed in another locale in another city, the rental that could be charged for this distinctive form of inner-city accommodation would be astronomical.

The reality is that the area of Manningham contains some striking housing that would be usually associated with a different form of self-segregation, namely, pristine white bourgeois enclaves. The housing stock of this area is very varied and services a diverse housing market, which includes those on social benefits, affluent white cosmopolitans

and a significant number of highly affluent South Asian families who have a preference for living in this area rather than moving out to more 'respectable', but less *simpatico*, neighbourhoods.

Another major feature of this area that again does not at all fit with the imagery of a deprived inner-city area is the recently restored Lister Park. As described earlier in Chapter Two, Lister Park was a major presence in Victorian Bradford and was a local expression of the Victorian ideology of 'rational recreation' (Bailey, 1987). Now, following a major restoration, this large public park, with the striking Cartwright Hall, gallery and museum at its heart, is a resource for the whole community, and, as we shall see later, offers a site for social interaction for people in the neighbourhood, and for those from distant parts of Bradford. With its beautifully tended flower beds, Mughal garden, boating lake, bowling greens and expansive grassed areas, the visual statement of ordered and civil leisure provided by Lister Park is a direct challenge to the routine stereotype of inner-city malaise.

Mughal Gardens

These gardens have been modelled on the fabled Mughal gardens of Northern India and Pakistan. Most of the Mughal Emperors, (Mughal rule over the Indian sub-continent extended mainly from the 16th to the 19th centuries) were not only great patrons of art and architecture but also lovers of nature, particularly all forms of flora.

Mughal Emperors commissioned a number of beautiful gardens including the Shalimar gardens in Srinagar, Kashmir and the gardens of the legendary Taj Mahal in Agra.

Formal Mughal gardens are a geometric ordering of nature. The avenue of trees, pathways, flowering plants, tumbling water cascades and graceful fountains are a wonderful example of fusion between Muslim and Hindu styles. The very picture of tranquility, Mughal gardens usually provided a majestic setting for a mausoleum or a palace.

The Mughal gardens of Lister Park too follow this tradition, since they link in a number of ways with Cartwright Hall Art Gallery. The gardens use the same mellow Ashlar sandstone as Cartwright Hall. The objects in the permanent collections of Cartwright Hall also encompass different cultures, including many fine works of art that come from the Indian cub-continent.

Signage and the streetscape

This is an 'Asian' area: signage and linguistic inclusion

Passing through Manningham, whether on foot or by car, there is one aspect of the streetscape that would signal that you are in an area that is, in British terms, 'multi-ethnic', and that is the signage above shops. Particularly along the main arterial and shopping streets of Oak Lane, White Abbey Road, Carlisle Road and Manningham Lane, there is very ample evidence of the ethnic identity of the proprietors. These major arteries of the area signal the predominance of the 'Asian' presence – and not just an Asian identity, there is also specific signage signalling the Muslim nature of some of the properties. Signage, pointing out that this is a Muslim bookshop or that this is a *halal* butcher, indicates the religious identities that are the primary target of these shops.

Again, in looking at this signage, one of the important observations lies in noting not just what is present, but rather what is not. It is important to note the language and the written script that this signage employs. It is very predominantly written in English, sometimes with an Urdu script in a less prominent, supplementary position. In addition, it is often the case that an anglicised form of Urdu is used: if the text in English says 'Khan's Jeweller's', so too – phonetically/literarily – will the text, using Urdu characters, spell out the same noun, be that 'Jeweller's', 'Chemist', 'Insurance' or even 'Fashion'. Nevertheless, the higher visibility of the English text suggests that the message of this streetscape is that the English-speaking majority population is not excluded from easy engagement with the commercial possibilities of this area. Furthermore, just as importantly, they are not symbolically excluded by being refused information about the nature of the businesses being carried on here. The significance of the linguistic landscape in defining the perceived accessibility to and ownership of an area is no small feature of an urban streetscape (Gorter et al, 2012). Even for those who have no intention of visiting a *halal* butcher, or patronising an 'Asian' gold jewellery shop, they are not required to peer into the shop window in order to know what is on offer. If this is compared with the sense of exclusion and bewilderment that an English tourist can experience in a 'foreign' city, then we have some sense of the latent inclusion of the majority population in the streetscape of this area. However, occasionally, signage – such as in the example here, relating to a mosque – does not employ English (but then may have an adjacent sign giving the same information in English).

Thus, overall, the signage of this area reflects the predominant ethnic identity of the area, while simultaneously enabling the majority English

resident, or passing visitor, to feel comfortable in the recognisable familiarity of what these shops are offering the potential customer. Indeed, the very presence of English as the principal communicative text becomes an unusual, if rarely acknowledged, phenomenon that perhaps indirectly suggests a common ownership of the language itself, which, in turn, may also serve as a marker of belonging and citizenship. Of course, it might also be the case that it makes economic sense to be able to communicate the nature of your wares to your potential consumers, since many members of the younger Pakistani community are not literate in Urdu, and white customers still constitute a relevant element of the client population.

Shop frontages and window displays

While the signage over the shops in this area provide an immediate and, perhaps for many residents, an unobtrusive assertion of the cultural profile of the area, the contents of the shop windows themselves, and the fruit and vegetables displayed on tables in front of shops on Oak Lane, also have a distinct cultural content. There is nothing 'un-English' about having stalls outside your shop that take the goods outside for the passing trade to be tempted by, and the intending customer to have the pleasure of an anticipatory browse. This is, in fact, a routine feature of the nostalgically informed 'picture postcard' image of small-town Britain.

However, the nature and origin of some of the fruit and vegetables displayed outside these greengrocers points to the presence of a culinary tradition that is outside the routine of 'traditional' Yorkshire cuisine. However, it is worth mentioning that the South Asian greengrocers in Manningham do have a steady trickle of white and other non-South Asian customers who will try and experiment, and routinely use, a whole host of fruit and vegetables that, in the 1970s and 1980s, were almost solely imported into the UK for the growing British South Asian population. Today, then, it is not uncommon for Bitter Gourds/Karela, Lady Fingers/Okra/Bhindi, Paalak and even Methi/Fenugreek to be consumed by an increasingly diverse clientele, which is itself becoming expanded through the arrival of new migrant communities and their cuisines (eg including a noticeable growth in Middle Eastern/Persian and Eastern European foodstuffs). At the same time, much of this fare – at one time, solely available through the city's South Asian retailing sector – is now also available through major supermarket chains, which also reflects a recognition of, and commercial interest in, a changing population and its tastes.

As noted, such 'exotic' fruit and vegetables are not uniquely of interest to the local South Asian populations alone. For many of the majority ethnic population of Manningham, and beyond, the goods available in these shops are a necessary part of their self-definition as a cosmopolitan citizen of Bradford. It is unlikely, and, indeed, obviously not the case,

that only the members of the Pakistani communities look forward with eager anticipation to the arrival of this season's small, yellow-skinned, kidney-shaped 'Honey' mangoes – to be bought, by those lacking restraint, by the box. Looking in the windows of the gold merchants would also be a reminder that the cultural tastes being serviced here are primarily those from the South Asian communities. The multiple bangles and the expansive spread of filigree gold necklaces speak of a cultural use of gold in jewellery that has a distinctive heritage, and that services a culturally shaped demand that is reproduced in Manningham, and in wider Bradford. Furthermore, in a similar vein, the rich colours and the expansive flourish of fabric in the shops selling saris and *salwaar kameez* speak eloquently of the enduring tradition of a dress style that is found in the Bradford South Asian communities. Additionally, of course, the many food outlets, from curry houses to ice cream parlours, directly signal the South Asian identity of the ownership and the cultural origins of the foodstuffs on offer.

Complementing this range of South Asian culturally derived enterprises, there is, of course, a just as expansive range that has a white and European heritage: DIY stores, 'motor factors', hairdressers and what at times appears to be an overpowering fast food sector, offering everything from fried chicken, burgers and pizzas to fish and chips. Furthermore, it is within this facet of lived culture that syncretism operates: the Pakistani version of fish and chips is not the same as the traditional indigenous variant. The fish, the potatoes, the frying and serving equipment, and even the design of the outlet may be identical, but the distinction lies in one compromise within the frying itself. Unable to use the more traditional beef dripping or lard as frying substance, the fish and chip shops of Manningham, and elsewhere, have little choice but to use vegetable oil or some other *halal* option. Examples such as this demonstrate the syncretic compromises that are not necessarily filled with tension, or, indeed, signal the destruction of something that purports to be authentic, but which rather may create new cultural practices and acceptable options for all. (Although, fish and chips, like curries, can carry a heavy cultural load, and there are certainly those who regard dripping as the only authentic medium for cooking them.)

Culture, as ever, evolves and, as noted earlier, Manningham's 'immigrant' identity is not exclusively defined by the presence of South Asian commerce, as the recent addition to the established Polish community of Bradford has visually reasserted the Polish presence in the area through the development of a few new commercial outlets.

Thus, the repertoire of retail activity within this area very strongly underscores the visual signage in asserting that this is an area that is not only multicultural, but predominantly South Asian. This is a perception that could only be reinforced by a casual observation of the balance of 'white' and South Asian persons on the street. For if the major shopping streets of Manningham are taken as an index of diversity in terms of the demography of identities represented on the streets, then this would most certainly be seen as a multi-ethnic area, with a predominant South Asian presence. The visual cues here come not only from personal physiognomic characteristics of skin colour and facial appearance, but also very strongly from the fact that many of the South Asian residents, male and female, wear 'traditional' clothing. Males in *salwaar kameez* and the bright colours of some of the females' clothing make their presence particularly visible when judged against the normative expectations of 'English' dress codes. Additionally, given the centrality of the issue of the veil across Europe, and the fusion of the *niqab*, *burqa* and headscarf as definitive signs of Muslim difference, the presence of women in dark clothing representing an expression of Muslim modesty can be seen by the Orientalist eye as an *assertion* of Muslim identity. For some of the majority white ethnic population living in this area, this variety, and visibility, of dress is part of the cosmopolitanism that makes the area so attractive to them. For others, it has merely become a banal aspect of the reality of their daily environment; while for those with xenophobic or racist sentiments, this visible sartorial presentation of difference can be a continuing source of resentment at the usurpation of the urban environment that they believe should be uniquely theirs.

However, it is not the case that this area is entirely South Asian in its 'un-Englishness'. For many years, there was a Polish shop on the top-right corner of Oak Lane that serviced the Polish families, and their descendants, who had lived in Manningham and wider Bradford since the end of the Second World War. Now, following the recent influx of Polish workers after Poland's accession to the European Union (EU), a new infrastructure of Polish commercial enterprises has reappeared (as described in Chapter Four).

Street signs and toponymy

The street-naming practices that have given Manningham its ubiquitous and banal 'British' cultural capital are exactly the same as would be found in any urban area with a similar developmental history. As we have seen, the hegemonic status of Christianity is reflected in the dusting of saints' names over the area. Some merely acknowledge the past local geography, which has now become incorporated into the centre of a major city. Places such as Southfield Square and Quarry Lane are merely barely credible echoes of past physical truths. Park View Road similarly holds no profound secrets as to the mystery of its naming. Streets such as Wellesley Terrace, Marlborough Road and Blenheim Road provide typical instances of the celebration of historic 'British' heroes in the commemorative naming of streets; a symbolic gesture that will be as wasted upon large parts of the current majority ethnic white population as much as upon the minority ethnic populations of today. More mundanely, Apsley Crescent was so named because it was part of an 1852 development by the Apsley Land Society. The German 19th-century migratory presence in Bradford is also reflected in some of the street names from the latter 19th and earlier 20th century and in the more recent naming of Hamme Strasse. There is even a distinctly Yorkshire presence in some of the street language where, for example, 'royd' is used, as in Bolton Royd and High Royd.

In sum, the dominant impact of the toponymy of the street names in this area is to very heavily assert the normalcy of a mono-ethnic British/English/Yorkshire historical and cultural perspective, with a few strategic acknowledgements of a prior migrant presence.

In this context a relatively recent, and highly visible, innovation within the physical fabric of the area has been the explicit civic acknowledgement of the power of the physical environment in symbolically acknowledging the demography of the area through the construction of the Mughal garden in Lister Park. This was both a toponymic and an architectural assertion of the legitimacy of the presence of the South Asian communities in Bradford. The creation of a Mughal garden within the extant Victorian landscape and architecture of Lister Park was a deliberate initiative by Bradford Council to introduce a physical presence within the park that would acknowledge the changed demography of its surrounding streets. In their initial proposal submitted to the Heritage Lottery Fund, the council asserted that 'The inclusion of a Mughal garden within the proposals for Lister Park is fundamental to creating harmony between the cultural exhibits in Cartwright Hall, the park and the culturally diverse community in Manningham and the wider area of Bradford'.[4]

Through a process of wide public consultation, and with the collaborative efforts of a number of local authority departments, a Mughal garden was incorporated into the heart of Lister Park in a way that complemented the existing Victorian physical fabric of Cartwright Hall and the adjacent gardens, while, at the same time, providing an explicit recognition of a non-European cultural heritage through the incorporation of a highly visible water feature in a prominent location within the park (for a fuller account of the background to, and success of, this initiative, see Husband and Alam, 2012).

The physical representation of places of faith

As we saw in Chapter Two, the area of Manningham developed in the 19th century, with a robust Christian presence marked by the building of churches that represented the differing sectors of Christian worship: Catholic, Anglican and Protestant. These buildings, and many of their associated buildings in the form of community halls and school buildings, continue to serve as an enduring remembrance of

---

[4] Proposal 17 document is no longer publicly accessible but a copy was made available by the relevant office holder of Bradford Council during the fieldwork/empirical research phases.

that period of Christian assertiveness, and of the dominant place of the Christian faith in shaping the weekly routine of many residents of the area. Taylor and Gibson (2010: 65), for example, report that St Luke's Church was built by public subscription in 1880 to alleviate the overcrowding at the nearby St Paul's Church: a physical statement of the size of the Anglican congregation and of their commitment to their faith. They also report that St John's Wesleyan Methodist Chapel, completed in 1879, and having all the outward appearance of an elegant Anglican parish church, was able to accommodate 1,000 worshippers. Given the parlous state of church attendances in Anglican churches in Manningham today, it is hard to truly appreciate the power of faith in everyday life in this area a century ago – unless, of course, you go to watch the congregation leaving Friday prayers from the mosques in the area. The visible sign of religious devotion now made manifest by the Bradford Muslim communities would once have been normative for the majority Christian populations. Today, the comparative size of the exit from Sunday services in Manningham Christian places of worship, compared with that from the larger mosques, acts as a telling statement of Christianity's diminished role in the performative life of the majority population. As has been argued elsewhere (Husband and Alam, 2011), it may be that Christianity still continues to operate as a very profound social imaginary (Taylor, 2004) within British nationalism, but as the basis for routine religious observance, it has suffered a dramatic decline over the last half-century. Nevertheless, it is still the case that the streetscape of Manningham is marked by the presence of church buildings. Church spires erupt over buildings and at the end of streets, and for those who may pause to read them, the foundation plaques on buildings throughout the area reveal their prior Christian heritage. In a number of instances, these buildings have now been taken over for Muslim usage, that is, not only by South Asian persons, but specifically in connection with the expression and practice of the Muslim faith.

Perhaps one of the strongest physical representations of Islam in the streetscape of this area is the presence of mosques. Across Europe, the building of mosques has been associated with often-impassioned resistance from the local populace and from local authorities. This has not been the case in Bradford (Husband, 1994b). Mosques exist across the city and Manningham has its own share. Many look like mosques should look to the Western gaze, and have resonance with that undertow of Orientalist imagery that has been encrypted in the European and British consciousness. They stand as a very explicit statement of a perceived non-European, as well as non-Christian, presence in the midst of streetscapes that, in terms of their dominant architecture, are redolent of the working-class North. This area may have the possibility of becoming cosmopolitan, and it may have its share of contentedly cosmopolitan residents, but the dominant signature of the physical fabric shouts 'up North'. Consequently, these mosques do not sit in a neutral semiotic visual space; they articulate themselves in relation to another assertive identity.

Some mosques and madrasas occupy buildings that once had very different usage. One mosque occupies an old cinema, some are terraced houses and one madrasa now occupies a one-time pub, the Belle View on Manningham Lane, which had a reputation for hard drinking and, in the late 20th century, offered 'unsophisticated' striptease.

The use of houses and other buildings as madrasas has provided a new life for buildings that might otherwise have fallen into disrepair, but this practice has also spread the 'Muslim' visual footprint across Manningham. Importantly, it should be noted that these buildings are not only physical statements of a Muslim presence, but also the foci for activities where Muslim people will gather and depart at specific times. Given that, for many, there will be an increased likelihood that they will wear appropriate dress (*salwaar kameez*, and there also appears to be an increase in the wearing of a Middle Eastern/traditional Islamic-type garment called the 'juba' among males) when attending, then these buildings also become locales for the visible concentration of a collective expression of difference through clothing preferences – even though there is a fairly normative practice of mixing Eastern and Western dress cultures. Still, the exit from Friday prayers is made all the more visually distinctive to the non-Muslim eye because of these elements of performed identity. If there had been resentment at the

transition in ownership and usage of these buildings, then it might be assumed that the physical presence of the new users would not have lessened the sense of grievance at the changing 'character' of the area. However, if such sentiments were felt by individual members of the majority ethnic community, then, unlike in other European cities, they

did not become translated into significant political opposition to the building of mosques in Bradford. It is a recent phenomenon worthy of report that the last synagogue in Bradford would have closed had not the Muslim communities came forward to pay for its restoration because the Jewish community could not afford the cost of replacing the roof.

The relative absence of graffiti

If we pursue the framework of relating the reality of the physical streetscape of Manningham to the expectations that would routinely be created by the trope of the inner-city 'ghetto', then we should certainly expect to find a florid marking of the surfaces of the area with graffiti. This is very definitely not so. It was a most striking absence, which, if nothing else, revealed that the stereotype was alive and well in the, now-suburban, cognitive structures of this fieldworker. The absence of graffiti was so extensive that there was almost a sense of fieldworkers' gratification when instances of graffiti were found. These examples appear to be the tags of individuals rather than any marking of territory by gangs.

It is apparent that much of this graffiti would appear to fit with the *zero-tolerance* model of protecting the urban infrastructure in that it occurs on the side of buildings exposed to waste ground or in back lanes, namely, it occurs on surfaces in areas that appear to be 'unclaimed' and that have no immediately visible ownership and form of social policing. The absence of graffiti, along with the relative absence of litter, in this area is a phenomenon that adds significantly to the sense of an area that has been 'domesticated', that is, owned by its residents and having some sense of a collective *amour propre*. To what extent the city authorities have played a significant role in enabling this perception,

through an invasive commitment to keeping the area clear of rubbish and litter, is open to question; although it is almost certainly significant.

The soundscape

The area of Manningham is, as we already noted earlier and in Chapter Two, very heterogeneous in terms of the built environment and in terms of the social usage of the spaces within it. There are working-class terraces, many of them cul de sacs, where through traffic, both vehicular and pedestrian, is limited. There are small enclaves of modern housing, some dedicated to housing older people that have a designed closure, and there are busy arterial roads that service traffic and are foci for shopping. Interspersed in this, there are community centres, small garage businesses and backstreet workshops. Each of these areas generates its own soundscape. In the centre of Lister Park in the summer, among the *keynote sounds* (the sounds that may not be consciously registered, but which 'outline' the character of the people living there) will be the sound of birds, of children's voices and of the background hum of the traffic along Manningham Lane. The soundscape of the main shopping streets of Oak Lane, Manningham Lane and White Abbey Road will not be characterised by the competitive cry of the retailers seeking to attract their customers, nor by the vibrant exchanges of their customers. This is not the Chinese or Arab quarter of Singapore, nor even a lively farmers market. The keynote sound on these streets is predominantly that of the traffic passing through. No longer do the factory sirens and hooters marking the end of shifts define the day as significant *sound signals* (salient sounds that are listened to consciously), as they once would have done. Probably, the dominant sound signals are the chirping of the pedestrian crossings signalling when it is safe to cross and the blare of car horns telling pedestrians and other drivers that the occupant of this vehicle has absolute primacy in this space. All these are sounds that might reasonably be expected to be found in any area of Bradford, but one *soundmark* (a sound that is unique to this area) is the call to prayer from the mosques in the area. While not exactly unique to Manningham within the larger area of Bradford, this sound is nonetheless a very distinctive sound signature of the area and provides an aural complement to the other signs which signal that this as a predominantly South Asian and Muslim area. Again, in many European cities, there has been heated opposition to the call to prayer, but in this area, it is now a largely uncontested part of the daily experience of life.

Having mentioned the ubiquitous presence of traffic as a keynote sound, it must be noted that the car is a platform from which, for many pedestrians, unwelcome sound signals emanate in the form of loud music. The preference among a section of youth, and it must be said, in this area, South Asian youth, to have loud sound systems on board as a significant element of their presentation of self results in the streets of the area being assailed with loud music and the beat from boom boxes. As a contentious point of intersection of self-expression, a specific subcultural practice, and perceived intolerable anti-social behaviour, this phenomenon of car sound systems has a distinctive place in the soundscape of the area. (This will be explored in greater sophistication in Chapter Five.) A related auditory feature of car culture is the fetish of the exhaust system and its capacity to make a lot of noise. This, too, has contributed significantly to the content of the soundscape of this area. As we shall see in more detail in Chapter Five, the problematic association of young Asian men with the motor car in both the majority and South Asian communities means that this auditory contribution to the environment of the area is likely to have an added salience due to its 'racialised' connotations. This is not just noise, this is *their* noise and it is *in my face*.

Conclusion

To walk through Manningham is to enter into a terrain that is most certainly both multicultural and predominantly South Asian. It is also to enter into a built environment that still wears its 19th-century heritage very visibly in its everyday contemporary appearance. Very often, the uses to which these buildings have been put have changed, but the architectural style and the stone used to build it still give a distinct sense of being a Northern industrial town in its origins. Bradfordians have a strong sense of their local identity, and while typically having a strong affiliation to their neighbourhood, they additionally have a clear sense of their shared Bradfordian identity. This is true of the South Asian populations as much as of the majority ethnic community (Alam, 2006). Consequently, how the streetscapes of Manningham are read will depend very much upon the biography and consciousness of the particular individual. For many members of the Muslim South Asian population of Manningham, this is a familiar place of safety that provides the infrastructure for maintaining important elements of their own cultural practice. For some majority (white) residents, this is a space of diversity that provides them with a context for practising a cosmopolitanism that they value; for some others, it is a place in which they feel a self-conscious minority. For a visitor from an affluent Southern white enclave, they might find the apparent *Northern-ness* and *Asian-ness* equally alien, and their fusion disturbing.

However, what this chapter has revealed is that there are distinctive features of this urban environment that constitute a specific semiotic environment. While this area can justifiably be defined as having a predominantly South Asian and Muslim population, this chapter has also indicated some of the ways in which this presence is cumulatively reproduced in the streetscapes of the area. At the same time, this chapter has refuted the stereotypical expectations that this area should manifest the typical characteristics of an inner-city ghetto. For individuals in the UK and overseas who only know the area through the media, the description presented here must seem improbable, as it would to many Bradfordians who have actively avoided contact with the area precisely because of its reputation. The account presented here provides a more detailed and nuanced understanding of the physical context within which people make sense of their lives in Manningham.

CHAPTER FOUR

Migratory waves and negotiated identities: the Polish population of Bradford

As indicated in Chapter Two, the Polish population in Bradford has a substantial history going back to the end of the Second World War. In the context of the cumulative argument being developed in this book, this chapter seeks to provide a fulsome account of the contemporary social dynamics within this population, framed within their particular history and trajectories of migration. Some of the background data about this community could easily have been presented in Chapter Two, where the history of diversity in Bradford was sketched, but it has been retained for presentation here in order that this chapter may have its own internal coherence. The story that emerges here provides a powerful comparative account of the internal diversity within communities that is a significant element of the account of the Bradfordian Pakistani communities. It speaks of the power of collective constructions of a past history in shaping current attitudes towards fellow community members, and again reveals the relevance of intersectional identities shaping both individuals' experience of their environment, and their response to it.

Despite the attention given to the recent arrival of Poles in Britain following Poland's entry into the European Union (EU) in 2004, Polish migration into Britain has an extensive history, with significant immigration in the 19th century followed by another flow after the First World War. Contemporary understandings of the presence of Poles in Britain are shaped by the extensive entry of Poles following the end of the Second World War, by a further influx in the 1980s following the suppression of the Solidarity Movement and by the recent arrival of young economic migrants following the opening of the British labour market to citizens of the new EU member states. Garapich (2008b) indicates that within the Polish population, this historical patterning of migration flows is echoed in popular narratives of settlement that make distinctions between these three cohorts in terms of their shared identity and characteristics. These narratives, in turn, have implications for the ways in which members of these different migration cohorts have related to life in Britain, and to each other. This chapter focuses on the trajectories of inter- and intra-group dynamics and the process of identity formation with regard to two cohorts: the settled post-war community and recent, post-2004 Polish migrants.

Polish migration into Britain

The settlement of Poles in the post-war years was of former members of the Polish army who found themselves outside of Poland at the end of the war, former Polish prisoners of war who had been liberated by the allies (including those who had been drafted to German work camps) and displaced persons from the allied occupied territories (Zubrzycki, 1956; Sword, 1996). The settlement of this flow of migrants varied with their status. The displaced persons recruited into the European Voluntary Worker Scheme (EVWS) were regarded by the British government as migrant labour subject to regulation, which deprived them of significant freedoms and rights. Their contracts stipulated that they would:

> enter Great Britain for an initial period of twelve months subject to good behaviour and to specific conditions that they undertake only employment selected by the Ministry of Labour and National Service, on the clear understanding that they will only be able to change their employment with the consent of that department. (Cited in Kay and Miles, 1992: 197)

Those recruited into the EVWS were sent to specific locations around Britain to work in agriculture, coal mining, textiles, health and other industries, and were housed in hostels where different nationalities would be mixed. Often, qualifications were ignored and people were significantly down-skilled in the labour they were allocated. These conditions, coupled with the short-term contracts that made them vulnerable to the pressures implicit in the 'good behaviour' clause, meant that a large number of them left Britain during the 1950s. Given the argument to be developed later, it is significant that although EVWS workers were treated as disposable migrant labour, they were simultaneously given 'political status' by the International Refugee Organisation. The numbers recruited into the EVWS were, however, far outnumbered by the Polish ex-servicemen who settled in Britain during this period. Estimates vary, but a figure over 200,000 would seem to be a reasonable estimate of the number of Poles settling in post-war Britain. Of these, perhaps 5,000 settled in Bradford.

The resettlement of Polish ex-servicemen was a complex undertaking involving a number of state institutions, including the War Office, Ministry of Education, Ministry of Health, Ministry of Labour and the Home Office, as well as the voluntary sector. Also, under the Polish Settlement Act, a number of institutions aimed at meeting particular needs of Poles were established. The Committee for Education of Poles in Great Britain dealt with child and adult education. The Central Polish Resettlement Office ensured that Poles located on the territory of the UK who wanted to emigrate to other countries would have means to do so (Zubrzycki, 1956). Poles wishing to become British citizens could apply for naturalisation. Yet, not all Poles wished to do so, as many felt betrayed by the allies, who had made a deal with their enemy – the Soviet Union – as well as not wanting to renounce their Polish citizenship (even if the country they remembered did not exist anymore).

The Poles settling in Britain during this period could reasonably see themselves as the 'victims of Stalin and Hitler' in the cataclysmic events that had overtaken their country in the 20th century (Lane, 2004), and, consequently, the population that settled in Britain at this time had a raw sense of themselves as exiles forced by political circumstances to live elsewhere. It could also be argued that settlement in Britain contained something of a cruel irony, as, for many, Britain had betrayed Poland in the Soviet land grab that was legitimised through the Treaty of Yalta (Stachura, 2004). However, this was a country where they did successfully settle. Their standing with the native population was enhanced by both their reputation as brave allies and by a general understanding of their political refugee status in the context of an increasingly robust Cold War mentality in which communism was a common threat. The predominance of single men in this initial settler population also promoted a significant amount of marriage outside of the Polish population, which acted as an aid to integration; although it must be noted that a good deal of this inter-ethnic marriage took place with other migrant populations, including Italians and Ukrainians, for, among other things, the EVWS had deliberately recruited single women into the labour force.

The arrival of a new influx of labour to serve the expanding postwar economy came in the 1960s from Britain's ex-colonies. These British Commonwealth immigrants came predominantly from the Caribbean, and from India, Pakistan and Bangladesh (Deakin et al, 1970), and changed the dynamics of British ethnic relations. While they were British and Commonwealth citizens and had rights that would have been envied by the European Voluntary Workers, in the

British context, they had a significant disadvantage: their colour. Deeply embedded within British culture, there was a symbolic lexicon of colour as stigma (Miles and Phizacklea, 1984; Husband, 1994a), which had a long history in the British exploitation and denigration of people of colour through slavery, in the British Empire and, later, in the British Commonwealth.

The Polish population in Britain had the cumulative virtues of being white, Christian and European, and thus when compared with these new arrivals, the settling Polish communities had positive credentials, and advantageously for them, the growing politics of 'race relations' in 1960s' and 1970s' Britain was focused upon the issue of Commonwealth immigration (Solomos, 2003). The Polish communities were thus marginalised within this new political discourse. As later demographic evidence was to reveal, the permeability of the boundaries between the Polish community and the majority British population was considerable, and out-marriage was to have a significant effect upon the dynamics within this Polish population.

Starting from the early 1960s, following the Khrushchev thaw, contacts between Poles in the UK and their relatives back in Poland intensified. Some short-term visits from Polish relatives resulted in their settlement in the UK. The imposition of martial law on the 13 December 1981 in Poland barred Poles abroad, including in the UK, from going back to Poland. Thus, in a way, they also became political migrants. However, 1980s' migration from Poland gained a truly political edge after the Polish regime decided in 1982 to give the possibility of emigration to all 'undesirables', political opposition activists, the interned and individuals with a criminal past; in other words, to all who posed a threat to the regime. With the exception of the 'undesirables', the general tendency in the first half of the 1980s was to close borders. However, the situation changed in 1986 when migration dynamics grew considerably, and peaked in 1988/89 when passports, at least for tourist visits, were easy to obtain, and thus considerable numbers of Poles emigrated under the pretext of visiting a relative abroad or for the purpose of spending holidays in Italy (Stola, 2001). Although the decisions to leave the country were political as well as economic, the political climate in the country reaffirmed for the resident British Polish population the oppressive nature of the political regime operating in Poland. This both legitimated the existing narratives of exile operating within this community and allowed the new immigrants to be embraced within that narrative as 'political' migrants. However, for some within the settled Polish community, the long existence of these immigrants within a communist regime also provided a basis for suspicion regarding their true character.

For contemporary Bradford, the much more significant development came with the most recent wave of migration in the last decade and more. The flow into Britain was part of a much larger European diaspora of Poles seeking a better life outside of Poland (Triandafyllidou, 2006). Although the flow of Poles into Britain in significant numbers pre-dated the British government opening up the labour market to EU citizens in 2004, the formal entry of Poland into the EU was marked by an extensive transition in the flow of Poles into Britain. The numbers are difficult to calculate with accuracy but modest estimates put the number at 521,000 in 2010 (ONS, 2011). The estimate of the number entering Bradford ranged from 7,000 to 10,000, which was a very significant addition to the existing Polish population of the city. (As noted in Chapter Two, the 'official' growth of the Polish population recorded in the 2011 census was near to 5,000 persons.) These newcomers are not a homogeneous group, differing in education and qualifications, past employment experience, competence in English, and age. There are also differences in their aspirations. Some wish to settle permanently in Britain, some see themselves staying for a number of years and some see themselves as short-term labour migrants. These differences have significant implications for the individual's experience of entry into the British labour market and for their relationship with the extant Polish community. A survey of 500 Poles in Britain carried out in 2006 (Eade et al, 2006) reported that 22% of the respondents identified themselves as seasonal workers and 33% stated that they intended to stay for less than two years, with only 15% claiming to wish to settle permanently. The much higher evidence of an intention to settle in Britain found in the sample that is the basis of this analysis reflects the fact that the sample were all bilingual, and, consequently, likely to be better educated than those migrants who spoke no English, and that the Bradford labour market has no place for the seasonal agricultural labour that has been such a large part of the experience of Polish migrants in counties like Norfolk. This new cohort of Poles in Bradford are internally diverse and their relationship with the existing Polish community shows a pattern of complex interaction resulting from the diversity within both the new and the settled Polish population. Before moving on to examine this relationship, it is appropriate to pause to examine some relevant features of the context.

Migration and identity

Garapich (2008: 736) notes that 'the liberalisation of migrant restrictions in the UK began before the enlargement (of the EU member states) in 2004', and argues strongly for the significant role of the 'migration industry' in facilitating that process. He cites Cohen's (1997: 163) definition: 'despite the rigorous official control of immigration, there has been an extensive and rapid development of a "migration industry" comprising private lawyers, travel agents, recruiters, organizers, fixers and brokers who sustain links with origin and destination countries'.

While noting that ethnic networks have a long history of facilitating migration, Garapich is keen to emphasise the unrecognised role of the immigration industry in providing a highly developed and efficient means of aiding migration, which complements existing non-governmental organisation (NGO) and community activity, while notably lowering the risks of migrating (Garapich, 2008: 738). For, as he argues, not only does the migration industry aid entry into Britain, but, just as importantly, it facilitates processes of settlement. In his words: 'what the Polish case in the last few years offers is a unique insight into how the creation of a migration industry, along with the evolution of immigration law, has stimulated emancipation, incorporation, and new identity formation' (Garapich, 2008: 740). Prior to the accession of Poland to the EU and the opening of the UK labour market to Poles, a large part of this migration industry was engaged in enabling Poles to acquire resident work visas, often as self-employed business persons. Much of this hovered on the edge of illegality, and it was not without its element of criminality and the exploitation of migrants. However, the existence of such an extensive infrastructure for enabling the legalisation of residence in the UK was a significant element in the emergence of a large Polish migrant population in the UK.

With the legalisation of entry following 2004, much of the migration industry infrastructure was still relevant in such areas as facilitating the transfer of funds back to Poland, providing assistance in dealing with the British tax system and local authorities, and enabling people to find work. Garapich emphasises the role of the extensive media infrastructure that had developed to address the needs of the Polish population in Britain; this was something underlined by the work of Fomina in this study, whose research presented an account of the extensive and diverse media that serviced the established and newly migrant Polish populations. In a forthright and unambiguous manner that might distress many who have worked within the voluntary sector, Garapich offers a robust assertion of the critical role of this commercial migration industry's contribution to the settlement of Poles in Britain over the last decade or so. He argues that:

> this construction of a new set of institutionalized networks, commercial advocacies and mutual connectedness did not emerge out of some abstract sense of common heritage, duty towards extended kinship group, cultural affiliation or essentialist definitions of national identity or shared common set of values. Rather, it was the migrants inclusion in the labour market which created the niche for agents to ease incorporation and spread information assisting fuller integration. To put it briefly, in the case of Polish migrants, no voluntary NGO could have facilitated migrant's entry into their host society better than the media and the underlying migration industry have done. In fact, traditional Polish ethnic associations and institutions, especially the Polish Catholic Church, have been rather slow in reacting to and assisting newcomers. (Garapich, 2008: 744)

Garapich is nothing if not positive about the role of the market-oriented, Polish migration industry in enabling the migrant Polish population to negotiate their relationship to the economic, social and political realities of life in the UK. Rather optimistically, he announces that:

> Market-oriented activities of Polish migrants, embodied in the proliferation and complexity of the migration industry, have resulted in the removal of vast numbers of Polish migrants from insecurity, taking them from a state of marginality into a visible public and political sphere. (Garapich, 2008: 748)

This is, however, a perspective that we might fruitfully compare to the much more modest nature of the migration industry that was available at the time of the post-war settlement of Poles in the UK, and of the arrival of South Asian migrants in Britain from the 1960s.

The legal status of post-war Polish entry into the UK was not problematic, and, as we have seen, their settlement was one of the few instances of state-planned settlement in the history of immigration into Britain. However, until the formal accession of Poland into the EU, much of the entry of Polish migration into the UK in recent history was ambiguously legal. Thus, as Garapich (2008: 747) notes, 'illegality in this period impeded not only job prospects but also their ability to forge ties, institutionalize their presence, join trade unions, and establish strong economic bases'.

He further suggests that this experience of legal marginality may have been partially responsible for the observed levels of mistrust found *between* Polish migrants in London during this period (Duvell, 2004). However, following the legalisation of Polish migration into the UK after EU accession, Garapich suggests that such restraints on social cohesion within the Polish communities will have eased. However, as we shall see later, the data from the Bradford study suggest that freedom from such exclusionary pressures has far from produced a burgeoning Polish communitarian collective warmth. Indeed, elsewhere, Garapich (2008b) provides reasons why there may, in fact, be quite significant historically rooted reasons why this may not be so.

He argues that Poland is a country with a long history of migration, and that within that history, there has developed a strong 'emigration ideology' that makes a potent distinction between political and economic migration: the former being virtuous and the latter being, to varying degrees, deplorable. The history of political migration consolidated over the 19th century and carried through the 20th was associated with nationalism and political exile. Additionally, Garapich (2008b) argues, this dichotomy was paralleled by an associated class differential between the gentry and educated who fought for independence, while the peasants and working class merely left the fatherland to seek a better life abroad. Thus, the post-Second World War settlers constituted a virtuous continuation of the long history of political migrants who were exiled in the pursuit of keeping the faith with a true Poland, free of communism. The first generation were the true exiles and the subsequent generations of this post-war UK Polish population were encouraged to see themselves as an exilic fragment of Polish society who had the role of maintaining a version of Polish identity and patriotism uncorrupted by communism. To press home this point, Garapich (2007) cites Janowski (2004: 18):

> The mythical notion of a Poland held in trust until the fall of Communism – possession of the ojczyzna [fatherland] – means different things to older members of the first generation on the one hand and to younger members of the first generation and members of the second and third generation. It has a predominantly political and ideological significance to the former, while to the latter group, it is part of their claim to be truly Polish. If accepted, it implies that

there is a sense in which the Poles in the UK are actually more Polish than the Poles from Poland. This has been important to all Poles in the UK.

Given this analysis, it hardly seems surprising that more recent migrants from Poland have been coded within this moral framework: with the exodus following the 1980 Solidarity rising being potentially capable of being located within the virtuous category of political exiles, although qualified by their 'unfortunate' contact with communism, while the migrants of the last 15 years or so are unambiguously economic migrants, and, consequently, ambivalent members of any collective UK Polish imagined community. White (2011: 185), for example, on the basis of her research with recent Polish migrants, writes that: 'A high degree of connectedness to the Polish nation in abstract … coexists with a considerable capacity to criticize fellow Poles.'

Smith and Jackson's (1999) account of the Ukrainian population of Bradford reveals something of the same dynamics of the internal fracturing of any potential 'Ukrainian community' by the different narratives of a supposed common history that are in circulation within the population, which includes strategic silences as well as assertions of core beliefs. For the Ukrainian population, the demise of the Soviet regime opened up new realities that had implications for the renegotiation or defence of established narratives. Thus, as Smith and Jackson (1999: 384) observe:

> For many Ukrainians, therefore, the arrival of independence has unsettled a stable (though imaginary) sense of 'Ukrainianness', forged in exile with little reference to the changes actually taking place 'on the ground' in the Ukraine. For others, independence has merely confirmed their understanding of the complexities of national belonging.

Release of the 'homeland' from the oppression that forced the initial exodus for the political migrants constitutes a potentially radical destabilisation of the constructed identity that has been their mobilising rationale for generations. For different generations of this exilic population, the ways in which they encounter this transformation will be different, and the costs of adjustment may also differ widely. For those who have become 'more Polish than the Poles', the possibility of return opens up the possibility of experiencing the reality of the misfit between their imagined preserved identity and the currently lived reality, which could be distressing. However, the pollution of communism that they have avoided may then be invoked to provide a continuing legitimacy to their claim to be the true holders of the Polish heritage. At the same time, for the younger generation of this exile population, the removal of a hindrance to return, or at least to visit, opens up the possibility for them to escape from beneath the potent and sacred narrative of the older generation and establish their own reading of their relationship to contemporary Polish society, and to their sense of their Polishness.

This complex process of negotiating the narratives of identity and place against the background of different migratory histories, and different generations within migrant communities, provides a discursive terrain within which individuals seek to make sense of their biographies in relation to both the local context and the changing circumstances of the 'homeland'. The insights provided by Garapich and by Smith and Jackson underline the continuing relevance of historical events, and the meanings laid down around them, for contemporary intra-group identities. The distinctions made earlier by Garapich between virtuous communities of political exiles and the egotism of the economic migrant can be sensed within the analysis presented later from our data on the Bradford Polish population. Additionally, the comments of Garapich (2007) regarding the older settled Polish communities' response to the new economic migrant wave as being alien and contaminated by communism ('sovietised') may perhaps be seen in some of the data, as the older cohort respond to what they see as the lower values and behavioural characteristics associated with some elements of this recent Polish influx.

New settlers and the established Polish community in Bradford: the trajectories of intra-group dynamics

Polish Bradford: the people and the infrastructure

In Bradford, as elsewhere, the initial settling Polish population began to construct a community infrastructure around those existing structures that were deeply embedded in their identity as exiled Poles. One was the Catholic Church; the other was the ex-servicemen's organisations. Thus, in Bradford from the late 1940s, a number of institutions began to develop around the Polish Parish. These included the Polish Saturday School, the Polish Parish Council, the Polish Parish Club and the Polish Scouts. From 1984, a Polish Community Centre was in existence. In parallel to this, the Polish Ex-Servicemen's Association and the Polish Ex-Servicemen's Club provided important social hubs for the emerging community. Manningham was one of the neighbourhoods where this community settled in some numbers and the Parish infrastructure became complemented by shops meeting the needs of the Polish community. For this first generation, there was also the national *Dziennik Polski* newspaper published in Britain, and a Parish bulletin. The late 1970s–early 1990s was the 'golden age' of the Polish community, with prospering Parish institutions and a large number of active organisations, including a dance group, Polish Scouts and a Polish Catholic Youth Association. This was a period of community building, where consolidating the Polish infrastructure went in parallel with an increasing interpenetration of the Polish and majority cultures through the successful assimilation of the second generation into mainstream British life.

The irony for this population was that just as they had started to consolidate their economic and social position within Bradford, so, too, were the second generation developing their own syncretic relationship to their parents' vision of Polish identity and their own experience of being British born and British educated. A contributory factor in this transition was the significant loss of Polish language skills within this community. For those who had had a Polish father but non-Polish mother, the likelihood was that they would be English-speaking monolinguals, or bilinguals speaking English and their mothers' language (regarding language loss in bilingual families, see Moring, 2007). For those who had both parents from the Polish community, questions remained regarding their ability to withstand the dominant power of English in their life, and to retain competence in spoken and written Polish; not all succeeded. Another feature of the transition within this Bradfordian Polish community has been their economic success, and the consequent spread of their population outwards from the areas of Manningham and the city where their initial community infrastructure developed. The absence of sustained discrimination against Poles in the labour market, and the success of their children in the education system, aided their class mobility and spatial dispersion. (The permeability of the boundary between the Polish community and the majority Bradfordian population was much easier for members of the Polish community than it was for their fellow migrants, the Pakistanis, who had settled in the same city and in Manningham.) As a consequence of these changes, the cohesive nature of the Polish community in Bradford began to unravel. The older generation began to die off and Polish Parish life began to diminish, so that by 2003, there were only 36 students in the Polish Saturday School, and the Polish Ex-Servicemen's Club has now been closed down for several years.

For the Polish migrants entering Bradford over the last 10 years or so, the environment that they entered had a much more supportive infrastructure than had existed for the post-war immigrants. There was a depleted, but nonetheless extant, Polish population that had a potential to facilitate their entry and settlement, and unlike the earlier migrants, there was rapidly a very fulsome media environment to support their links with the homeland, and to ease their entry into the new town and country. As our research has demonstrated, there is a very extensive Polish language media infrastructure serving the Polish population of Bradford. The media environment is very rich, in particular, thanks to the Internet and digital and satellite media. There are a number of newspapers and magazines targeted at the new migrants, including *Cooltura, Polish Express, Lajf, Panorama* and *Polish Times* (available in at least four newsagents in Bradford and in several Polish shops), and they all have online editions, and so are available to anybody with Internet access. At the same time, in relation to print media published in Poland, all Polish newspapers and magazines are available online. Additionally, several Polish shops and some newsagents have a variety of both UK- and Poland-published magazines. In standard satellite and cable TV packages, there is usually at least one channel, Polish TV International Service (TV Polonia), available, but there are also Polish companies in the UK that install Polish satellite TV. However, Polish TV may not be easily available for those who rent property for a short period of time, since installing a satellite TV would not be practical. However, those who settle there for longer can easily have Polish TV, while some programmes can be watched online (eg from the Polish TV International Service website). There are a number of radio programmes, both national and private, that can be listened to online. Additionally, there are a number of portals with news and reprints of articles from the Polish and foreign press that can be accessed (wp. pl, onet.eu, interia.pl). Finally, there are portals targeted specifically at Poles in the UK and Bradford. Thus, they provide information for newcomers about various aspects of life in the UK, a sort of survival toolkit: news from Poland and Britain and about Poles in Britain; forums (again, usually regarding various aspects of life in the UK, from going to a doctor to Polish cuisine); and information about Polish institutions in the UK or specifically in Bradford. Probably the most informative one for Bradfordians was bradford24.pl. Thus, for those who want to use Polish-language media, there is ample opportunity as there is an extensive variety of media types and genres.

Given the range of competence in English of the recent Polish migrants, this media infrastructure provides a basis for sustaining those who cannot engage with their new environment through the English language, while also providing ready access to news about life back in Poland for all who want it. For the former group, this fulsome Polish-language infrastructure may facilitate a form of protective closure that enables them to find a viable *modus operandi* without having to commit themselves to a rapid acquisition of at least minimal competence in English. This is especially true for young parents staying at home with children, or low-skilled workers who work with fellow Poles and whose type of occupation does not require English-language proficiency. In other respects, the institutional infrastructure of the new migrant population is rather poor, even though constantly developing. There are several Polish shops, a newly opened Polish pub and a Polish Pierogarnia restaurant. While some of the shops are rather small, there is one Polish supermarket, where Polish food, a selection of Polish magazines and an advertisements board can be found. There are no associations of Polish migrants in Bradford. The Polish Parish structure, however, though less vibrant than at its peak, does continue to provide a potential source of support for these new migrants. However, as we shall see later, the utilisation of this resource varies quite dramatically between segments of this new migrant population.

The diversity of Polish perceptions of the Bradford 'Polish' community

What emerges from the interviews in this Bradford sample is a complex nexus of perceptions. On the one hand, the absolute numbers of the Polish community have increased, which is seen as positive. Yet, ironically enough, the settled community is ambivalent about the Polishness of these new Poles: they do not all meet the proudly nurtured community identity or the exilic cohesive sentiments of the settled Polish community. Thus, neither absolute demographic increase nor the recognition of this increase can be simply equated with a stronger sense of an expanded and vital Polish community. There is no single Polish identity since the identity-formation process has certainly been shaped by the differing patterns of migration. What is more, we cannot analyse the presence of Poles in Bradford exclusively in terms of the relations between the two cohorts: the settled community and the recent arrivals. The intra-groups dynamics within both cohorts are also significant here.

There are two dominant narratives to the story of adaptation of post-war Polish migrants: one of success and upward mobility; the other of loss and humiliation. Some of the representatives of this cohort mastered English and entered mainstream British life very quickly, often anglicised their names, and successfully blended in. Many opened their businesses catering to both Polish fellow migrants and the wider public and were generally rather prosperous. As one of the interviewees noted, the first TV sets, as well as other luxurious novelties in the neighbourhood, appeared in Polish houses. Yet, others, to a large extent due to their line of work, never managed to learn proper English, had few native English in their social networks and were locked into jobs below their qualifications. During 1968–70, many Polish exiles were examined in psychiatric institutions in Bradford, the investigation showed that after 20 years, some had never fully recovered from their wartime traumatic experiences (Hitch and Rack, 1980). Hitch and Rack claim that these problems were aggravated by the experiences of not-so-successful adaptation to the new country. Housewives, with limited contacts with the outside world, found themselves in exceptionally difficult situations, especially after their husbands died.

The differences in the perceptions of the adaptation process were not unrelated to the attitudes of the forced migrants themselves. Some of them decided that Britain was their new country, and that return to Poland would never be possible, so they should try and make the best of their new situation; hence, for example, the emergence of many flourishing private businesses run by Poles. Others could never get reconciled to the idea that Poland was lost to the new regime and they continued to nurture the myth of return, never being able to grow roots in the new place; a phenomenon that was paralleled in the Pakistanis' settlement (Anwar, 1979). We do not know the mutual perceptions of those who succeeded and those who did not. Yet, in the narrations of the second generation, these two approaches blend, producing an amalgam story of pride and suffering. What is also significant, irrespective of personal successes or failures, was that Polish settlers put a great emphasis on the success of their children, the key to which was good education. So, the second generation is largely well-educated, enjoying relatively high social status.

It is also worth mentioning a particular dividing line between the first and second generation of post-war Polish migrants. It was difficult for the first generation to share control and responsibility for community activities with their adult children, who, in their perception, were still too young and irresponsible, as well as being not 'Polish enough', to be really trusted. An example of this dynamic was the closing down of the SPK (Polish Veterans Association Club), where it has been argued that the leaders of the Polish community could not find adequate successors among the second generation, yet were also not able to run the club themselves, and, as a consequence, it was closed. Of course, the conflict between first-generation migrants and their children born and bred in the new country is nothing new, and is well described in the academic literature with regard to different ethnic groups (eg Tung, 2000; Berry et al, 2006).

Negotiating 'Polishness'

As is to be expected, there are a range of negotiations of 'Polishness' to be found among the settled Polish community that also has implications for the perception of the new migrants, as the following quotes illustrate. According to some, language competence is seen as important, yet not absolutely essential. One can be Polish without speaking perfect Polish:

> 'I don't speak very good Polish and I don't class myself any less Polish than the next person. I don't think it's about the language and things like that. It's more cultural. It's more the way we were brought up. It was the way of living rather than anything else.' (First cohort, original settler community, male)

This way of living included traditional Polish holidays, as well as recognising common values and norms – not necessarily living by them, but at least being able to name them. Such a list would include respect of elders, loyalty, bravery, the Catholic faith, much more traditional gender roles than within the host society and maintaining 'the old ways' (customs and traditions, including, eg, traditional Polish cuisine). Thus, some respondents claimed both identities, Polish and British, even though they did not possess all the qualities deemed significant for being Polish or British. Yet, others were much less tolerant of imperfection and demonstrated a much more essentialised and dichotomous approach. They claimed to occupy an in-between state, which was not that comfortable for them:

> 'To tell the truth, I am neither one nor the other. I do not understand the mentality of Poles, but I also do not understand the mentality of the English…. I would like to be among people like myself. My brothers are different. They married English women. They think differently, they act differently. They have become anglicised.' (First cohort, male)

Still others also emphasised the extent to which identity is relational and contextual:

> 'I haven't thought of myself as Polish, although I am very aware that I am not normal British. If I travel abroad, and somebody asks me, I might say I am British, not English, maybe Scottish. I was always aware when growing up that we were different, but you could swing from being proud of being different and being not one of the gang. I am British of Polish extraction.' (First cohort, female)

In general, we could differentiate two groups within this cohort. The first one is much easier to pin down, its members share a traditional diasporic and rather more essentialised identity based on the language of their parents, Polish customs and traditions, and Catholicism, as well as narratives of exile, virtue and suffering. The second generation within this group construct their Polishness around the memories of the experiences of their parents. Here, the distinction into 'political' and 'economic' migration is particularly important, and the emphasis is put on the significance of involuntary migration. For the majority of this group, the Polish Parish remains the centre of gravity, the symbol of the vitality of the Polish community in Bradford. In most cases, these are children of both Polish parents or of Polish mothers who were strong enough to pass on their heritage.

However, there is also the other group, uniting all those who have got some sense of affinity to Polishness, but the degree and means of exercising this identity varies considerably. In contrast to the more essentialist and traditional identity, this is a much more 'postmodern', cosmopolitan approach. For this group, the memories of the heroic past are one of many elements of their identity, not a measure of being Polish. Hence, the distinction between 'economic' and 'political' is considerably less important for them. Very often, these are children of Polish fathers and non-Polish mothers. Since, at the time, bringing up children was a task of mothers and not fathers, fathers were not able to pass on a strong traditional identity and thorough knowledge of Polish. Also, this group contains all those who, for different reasons, did not want to associate themselves with the Polish Parish institutions and social networks. Consequently, the responses of this cohort to the newly arrived Polish migrants are also widely diverse, although having some common themes. However, it is also worth mentioning the under-vocalised conflict between the two groups. If members of the first one consider the second as defectors who decided to blend into mainstream society and forsake their Polishness, for the members of the second, the Polishness of the first group is too parochial and unattractive.

As will become apparent in the analysis offered in the following pages, there is also an important distinction made within the recent population of new Polish migrants. As Ryan et al (2008) reported in a study of recent Polish migrants in London, language competence and education were strong factors shaping the pattern of social networks developed within their sample. Thus, for example, they reported that:

> While many participants spoke no English upon arrival and were dependent on the practical support of co-ethnics, it is important to differentiate between those who manage over time to improve their English and those who remain within a limited circle of co-ethnics. (Ryan et al, 2008: 878)

Also, among the established Bradfordian Poles, there is a strong perception that all recent migrants fall into two distinct categories: those who are seen as aspirational, self-reliant and engaged in making a success of their life in Britain; and those who are seen as poorly equipped to deal with the realities of the labour market and life in Britain, who have, therefore, become heavily dependent upon the British state and their fellow Poles. This distinction is strongly correlated with language competences. Indeed, the centrality of language competences in shaping individual Polish migrants' settlement in Britain is a point also noted by White (2011). Perceived success in this group is strongly related to the willingness and capacity to master English and thus gain independence and self-reliance. Indeed, while immigrants may be better off in the short run if they have the option of using social networks to find employment, a number of important long-term considerations come into play. The reliance on networks is associated with, and, in some cases, may directly cause, poor economic and socio-cultural integration into the host country (Sumption, 2009: 8). It is also significant that this is a distinction made by both the post-war cohort and the new Polish migrant cohort, and may be regarded as a novel extension of pre-existing Polish narratives of virtue that has relevance for both the self-esteem of the settled Polish community and for the independent and aspirational members of the new cohort.

Strategies of the new wave of Polish migrants

Ryan et al (2008) emphasised the difference in adaptation strategies between professionals and non-professionals:

> The networking strategies of the professionals included in the study were often markedly different from those of other migrants. They tended to develop both professional and personal relations with a wider group of people, including British people, and their cultural capital allowed them to build bridging networks both vertically and horizontally. (Ryan et al, 2008: 683)

While the same tendency could be observed among the Bradford sample, most interviewees claimed they were not specially looking for contacts with other Poles even though they did not necessarily deliberately avoid fellow Polish migrants: "it does not suit me to have only Polish friends. It is not important for me where someone comes from, but I would not like them to be exclusively Polish" (second cohort, female). Some put it more bluntly: "I don't live with Poles, don't work with Poles – I don't stay in the Polish ghetto" (second cohort female). It is also worth noting that important exemptions to the rule could be observed.

On the one hand, among those interviewed, there were Poles with higher education diplomas and professional careers in Poland who could not find the time and opportunity to attain an adequate level of competence in English, and who thus felt isolated and not interested in contacts with a wider group of people. Consequently, some of this group were convinced that the local population treated them with reserve, which reinforced their reasons for not being interested in developing contacts with the English. Predictably, they were highly dependent upon the Polish infrastructure and Polish networks. However, among those less educated and without professional careers or good English-language skills at the time of arrival, there were also people who managed to find contacts and build relations beyond their immediate group of co-nationals, which also helped them to improve their language competences, as well as consolidate their self-esteem and build independence. Thus, the Bradford sample shows that successful adaptation does not entirely depend upon the formal skills and qualifications gained prior to arrival, that is, professional experience, language skills and higher education. Attitude and motivation also play a significant role. Here, it is also worth mentioning some gender differences with regard to the patterns of adaptation of Polish migrants.

Women in our sample have a much more positive perception of their experience in the UK, and they see more opportunities than threats. They accept that migration may also mean initial status loss but work hard to improve their situation, and within several years, achieve positions that they are happy with. Women often claim that they doubt if they would have achieved as much in Poland. However, the orientation of men in this study strongly depends upon their initial experience: if they do not succeed from the start, they seem to find it much more difficult to handle status loss, blame it on discrimination and often lose motivation to further improve their situation.

Interestingly, for this sample, the majority of the new migrants who came to Bradford did not realise that there is a considerable settled Polish population there. Only a few came because members of their distant families belonged to the settled community. The Polish Parish network has predominantly attracted those less educated, with poor English skills, who sometimes rely on state benefits. The Polish Parish was a natural place for them to seek help and an important alternative to the services of the 'migration industry', being cost-free and more reliable. (Stories about Polish migrants being taken advantage of by other Poles providing services, including finding employment and accommodation and transferring money to Poland, are widely circulated.) Members of the Polish Parish have often been asked to assist with filling in benefits forms or seeking accommodation and work. As a result of contact with this specific group of Polish migrants, the 'traditional' Polish community has formed a rather negative opinion about the recent migrants, developing a somewhat stereotypical view that they lack a good work ethic and are too reliant on benefits to which they had not yet earned the right.

This perceived 'claiming culture' of the new migrants contrasts sharply with the self-perception of the settled community, which prides itself on its independence and self-reliance. Additionally, the new migrants are perceived as being impolite and heavy-drinking, making a sharp contrast with the code of behaviour of the settled Polish population. (In addition, this is a perceived characteristic of the new East European migrants that features in their inter-group perception by the established Pakistani community in Manningham.) Thanks to the objective changes of the situation of the Polish settled group (eg social upward mobility), as well as some social creativity strategies (eg positive comparison with the Pakistani communities), the settled community has developed a sense of relatively high prestige for the in-group (for an account of inter-group strategies, see Turner, 1999). They have also sustained a core of 'Polish values' that informs their in-group social identity. However, the memory of the past struggle for acceptance and prestige makes this subjective high status of the Polish community much more fragile than it might initially appear. Moreover, in the opinion of the settled community, the recent migrants neither contribute to the development of the Polish community proportionally to the support they get from it nor show their appreciation or gratitude. In fact, lack of involvement in the life of the Polish Parish is the most pronounced criticism of the recent migrants on the part of the settled community. They feel disappointed: their hopes associated with the arrival of migrants from Poland have never materialised. Given the earlier analysis offered by Garapich (2008a, 2008b) regarding the long-fostered distinction between the morally virtuous 'political' migrant and the dubious 'economic' migrant, it is possible to see this current response to the recent wave of migration as at least in part representing a vigorous reassertion of that core narrative of the older members of the established Polish community in Bradford.

From the perspective of the established Polish community, the perceived dubious qualities of some of these new arrivals are seen as putting into jeopardy the positive regard that these settled Poles feel they have earned with the majority population. Consequently, their status is seen as being threatened by the increase in the Polish population. At the same time, the new influx of Poles has provided a resurgent cultural market for 'Polish' food and services, and has thus added to the infrastructural resources of the total Polish community as new enterprises addressing these needs have sprung up again in Bradford following a period of decline. At the same time, the religiosity or, at least, the traditional allegiance to the religious institution of many of the migrants has helped replenish the numbers of the Polish Catholic Parish and revitalise the Polish Parish infrastructure. The following quote illustrates this ambiguity very well:

> 'Sometimes, I feel a little bit uncomfortable, to tell you the truth. Cause you see, we're sitting on our little root, and this is how things are, everybody is English and there are few Polish people. And suddenly they are all over the place, some of them not very nice, you hear a lot of swear words, which we didn't really have in the post-war – I mean, I'm not saying none, but you didn't hear them all the time. Well, somebody said to my partner – you are not Polish. And he asked why do you say that? Because you never say that word,

that begins with 'k' ['kurwa', a swear word]. Some people say it every word. There is some sort of funny feeling. I still feel Polish but this is feeling like, we have came first, we kind of have been accepted, this is how we are. And suddenly, a different sort of people are coming. They are younger, perhaps more sure of themselves, louder. And we are a bit frightened that we will be counted with those newcomers as Polish, despite having been accepted before.

On the other hand, the church was nearly empty. And I was thinking that eventually the church will be closed. Elderly people died off, their children spread off. Now we have some new blood, new people. That's a good thing. So, I'm ambivalent about it. But I still feel Polish, yes.' (First cohort, female)

Perceptions of the recent migrants

In looking at the perceptions of Polish community inter-group dynamics from the perspective of the recent migrants, the majority of the interviewees distance themselves from the established Polish community institutions. (It should be remembered in the analysis of this sample that the majority were bilingual and had a higher educational level than might have been found in the whole of the new Polish migrant population.) The majority feel well integrated into British society, and are self-reliant and well oriented with regard to British institutions. They have a rather positive self-perception, and they pride themselves on their achievements in the UK. For this sample, the Polish Parish institutions do not satisfy their cultural needs. These migrants are more interested in learning about the host society, its culture and institutions. When they miss Poland, they can easily contact their family and friends or just go back. The situation of this group is very different from that of the post-war settled community, whose ties with their motherland were cut and who had to recreate Polishness in the new country. What is more, many Polish migrants do not want to get entangled into the tightly knit and supportive, but also controlling, extant community. Finally, they also believe that they are not welcomed by the settled Polish community, who perceive the new migrants as a threat. The reticence of this cohort to engage with the extant Polish community is echoed in the reports of other comparable studies of recent Polish migrant accommodation to life in Britain. For example, Ryan et al (2008: 679) report that, 'In the case of recent Polish migrants, our research and that of others (e.g. Eade et al 2006) revealed a tendency to regard the wider "ethnic community" with wariness and even in some cases suspicion.' In fact, a lack of solidarity within the Polish community is a recurring theme in all of the interviews: the older settled population feeling the reality of the fragmentation and dispersal of their 'community' and the ambivalent implications of the new wave of migration, while the new migrants, in different ways, feel disassociated from the earlier community.

Echoing Ryan et al's (2008) findings, those study participants who were well-integrated professionals with good English skills, and who had had success in the labour market, tended to distance themselves from those 'other' Poles. The 'other' Poles is a very fluid category that includes what they call the 'pathological element' (thieves, thugs, drunks and criminals who have escaped Polish prosecution), but also those less educated, with poor English skills, and who are stuck in manual jobs and in areas of high concentration of Polish migrants ('Polish ghettos'). It seems that an imagined shared identity of 'aspirant migrant' is shared by these individualist respondents. They have a strong sense of a clear value base and an associated aspirational trajectory tied to economic and social mobility. What for the original exiles of the 1940s came to be regarded as the stigma of the 'economic migrant', are for this segment of the recent Polish migration markers of individual worth. It is a social identity that has little need of concrete ethnic-based sociability, focused as it is on individual and nuclear family aspirations. It is also an identity rooted in achievement that is likely to continue the centrifugal pressure of dispersal as they follow their own class-based ambitions in relation to housing tenure.

Another strategy that helps recent migrants to create a higher subjective status of their in-group – known already from the first cohort's experience – is using the Britons of Pakistani heritage as an out-group for positive comparison. In the opinion of our study participants, the 'host' population is more welcoming to Poles because they have a good work ethic, are closer in cultural and religious terms, obey local rules, and do not put forward too many demands, in contrast to Bradford Pakistanis. It is worth noting that this exercise in comparative identity management in many ways echoes the same criteria employed in distinguishing, and favourably distancing themselves from 'the bad and lazy Poles'. (The judicious use of selected out-groups as a mechanism for sustaining strong in-group self-regard is a phenomenon extensively reviewed in social-psychological literature; see, eg, Capozza and Brown, 2000; Dixon and Levine, 2012).

Yet another noteworthy trajectory of the inter- and intra-group dynamics of the Polish communities in Bradford arises from the fact that there are a number of Bradfordians of Polish descent who have remained detached from the Polish Parish network, and thus, for years, did not have the opportunity, space and tools to nurture their Polish identity. They drifted away from the Polish Parish, many scared away by social control exercised by a tightly knit, socially conservative group. The majority would fall into the group defined earlier as having a 'postmodern' approach to Polishness. Given the religious basis of the community, with some being non-believers and some being affiliated with other, often more liberal, churches, they were 'lost' to the Polish community, and, consequently, they themselves lost the hub, the uniting element of the identity. It is worth pointing out that maintaining Polish identity was more difficult in this case than for recent migrants, who have a very direct connection with Poland, as well as a wide area of Polish media and Polish-speaking friends and the possibility to rely on informal networks. In the case of the post-war second generation, those whose Polish language skills were underdeveloped: even in the surroundings of fellow second-generation Poles, they would stick to English.

Yet, some of them have been inspired by the arrival of Polish migrants to brush up their Polish and reconnect with their Polish identity. As one of the interviewees explained:

> 'I was looking for something, I was wanting to be part of some group.... And then about 2004, when all these Poles started to arrive, I thought, "Well, I've got some Polish roots, I've got speaking, reading and writing skills. Maybe I could put them to some advantage and also see if I could fit into that group."' (First cohort, male)

Thus, for example, a course at Bradford College, run by a recent Polish migrant, has become an excellent opportunity not only for improving long-lost Polish language skills among the established Polish community, but also for building social contacts with recent Polish migrants in a much more equitable environment. The Polish course has become a springboard for the formation of a social network, including both recent migrants and settled community Poles. The new Polish bar and the 'Pierogarnia' restaurant frequented by the members of this network have become hubs of Polishness, bonding the settled community members and recent arrivals, and are an alternative to the Polish Parish. Some members of this group went to Poland for the first time as part of trips organised by students of the Polish course, strongly encouraged and assisted by their new Polish friends. Polish migrants, for the settled community of Poles involved in this interaction, are not people seeking help, but partners in an intercultural exchange. The perception of the new migrants by this group is much more positive than by the 'traditional' Polish community consolidated around the Polish Parish institutions. Even if these settled community members come into contact with those 'problematic' migrants, they do not treat them as the epitome of the recent Polish migrants.

Thus, the arrival of new economic migrants gave an opportunity to this cohort to regain or reinvent their Polishness, which had not been possible before, other than through the established Polish institutions and thus by accepting and taking up a traditional, old-fashioned and exclusive understanding of Polishness – precisely something that they were not interested in.

Conclusion

The interviews with these two cohorts of Polish migrants in Bradford reveal a great deal about the transitory nature of community dynamics, and about the internal complexity of identities. The narratives provided in this analysis are comparable with other ethnographic accounts of migrant settlement and community formation. The 'founding' settlers of post-war migration established not only the basis of their physical community within Bradford, but also, just as importantly, the defining narratives that gave them their identity and core values. With the loss of linguistic competence in the homeland language in successive generations, and with a class-based capacity for movement out from the original areas of settlement, the Polish population of Bradford had lost a good deal of its cohesion over the five decades from the 1950s, and its institutional foci around the Polish Parish and the Ex-Servicemen's Club had lost their dynamism. In a way that would be entirely familiar to scholars of diasporic communities, this 'Polish' population of British citizens had developed a multilayered and diverse construction of their understanding of their Polishness. One consequence of this was a degree of tension between those still firmly attached to the Polish parish infrastructure and those who had come to distance themselves from it.

The recent wave of Polish immigrants found themselves arriving in a city in which the social infrastructure of the Polish community had undergone a significant decline. However, the decline had not been so disastrous that it was not able to provide succour to the new migrants, should they seek it. The Polish Catholic Church was able to provide a familiar religious base for those who found themselves seeking the comfort of their familiar faith in negotiating their entry into a new and challenging environment. This was a need more apparent among the lesser-educated migrants, and those with little English. Additionally, it was from this element of the new migrants that the demand for support from the Polish Parish system came, as they sought help in dealing with the British civil administration and in looking for work. The direct evidence from the sample of more successful migrants interviewed here is that they have found entry into and settlement in Britain to be relatively unproblematic, although there is evidence of significant gender differences in the personal adjustments needed in negotiating the labour market and building a future in Britain. A significant number of this cohort appear to have little motivation to establish any links with the extant Polish community. Yet, the example of the intensive interaction between some recent aspirant migrants and the members of the settled community detached from the Polish institutions is also noteworthy. It is not that significant in quantitative terms, but very much so in qualitative terms. As a result of this interaction, there are Bradfordians who managed to relearn their mother tongue (or the tongue of their fathers, to be more specific, as, in most cases, they are children of Polish fathers and non-Polish mothers) and reconnect with their Polish identities precisely thanks to their contact with the considerable inflow of Polish economic migrants.

The extensive growth in the Polish-language media environment, which is predominantly not located in Britain, but is transnational, is the only truly significant structural change that has resulted from this large influx of Poles into Bradford in recent years. The spatial dispersal of the post-war Polish population in Bradford is matched by a diversity of subjective positionings of individuals within the 'floating signifier' that is contained in the notion of Polishness employed by this sample: there may be a population of 'British Bradfordians of Polish heritage', but there is no shared identity that can be attributed to the whole of this group of people. A very significant change in the demography of the Bradford-based Polish population has not, as yet, resulted in a meaningful re-energising of a collective Polish identity, nor a greatly changed Polish social infrastructure in Manningham and Bradford. Yet, the process is dynamic and multidimensional.

In the context of this book, this account of the experience of the Polish population of Bradford provides an invaluable comparative understanding of the intersection of identities and opportunities in Bradford. At a time when nationally, and perhaps internationally, Bradford has become stereotypically associated with the 'problem' of Muslim communities in multi-ethnic Britain, this chapter indicates significant areas of similarity in underlying determining processes, while, at the same time, making clearer the role of those distinctive features of a particular community's biography that shape their experience and actions in the present.

CHAPTER FIVE

Manningham: lived diversity

This chapter provides an introduction to the wide range of data that was acquired through the many interviews that were carried out with current and past residents of Manningham. The fixed framework for the daily encounters reflected here is the topography of the area discussed in Chapter Two. However, even the physical properties of the area have a fluid dimension, as individuals bring their own, and familial, histories to bear in interpreting *their* reading of Manningham, and their own neighbourhood within it. The interaction of space, place and identities is vividly present throughout the experiences reflected in the account that follows. As with all ethnographic and qualitative data, the account presented here is an interpretation of a wide range of experiences tapped through the interviews, and, as such, provides a window onto life within Manningham rather than an exhaustive account of all the very different lives lived there.

Perceptions of Manningham

To an outsider, one of the most striking features of this, and previous, research (Alam, 2006; Alam and Husband, 2006; Phillips, 2006) may be the extent to which residents appear to have a deep, personal sense of attachment to and investment in what is, on paper, often deemed a 'deprived' area. Although there were one or two residents who 'hated' Manningham, and Bradford, with at least one considering the neighbourhood a "shit hole", most of those interviewed expressed pride and comfort when stating their views about the place. The reality is that Manningham has, in fact, a low crime rate. The crime statistics for Manningham, and its adjacent ward of Toller, place them as having the second-lowest crime rate in January 2014, compared with the eight neighbourhoods within a five-mile radius (UKCrimeStatistics, 2014). However, as is typically the case, fear of crime does not accurately track substantive crime statistics and a small study carried out in Manningham/Toller in 2010 revealed that some members of both the white and Pakistani population expressed concern about their safety in the area, and perceived some areas as specifically problematic (West Yorkshire Policing and Community Research Partnership, 2011).

In our data, in many cases, a highly positive perception of Manningham was complemented with a textured caveat that brought into play the idea of *reputation*, as well as the capacity for a historical narrative of a place, mostly written from the outside, to have a long-term and deep impact. One interviewee (M10), who works as a sports and leisure attendant, recalled this event about one of his customers:

> 'A lady from Baildon came to do swimming, old-age pensioner. She had some friends coming over to her house and saying, "Ethel where are you going?" She'd say, "Oh, I'm going for a swim." And they'd say, "All right, tell you what: can we come along?" And she goes, "Yeah can't stop you." It's only until next day when they said, "By the way, where is it?" As soon as she mentioned Manningham, they kind of came up with, "Oh, I have to get my hair done." She goes, "How do I tell them don't worry about it: I mean it's safe in there, I've been going years and never had a problem, they're very friendly and all that." Because of the reputation that they'd heard and all that, the other ladies, they kind of backed out. Ethel told us, "I asked them why they didn't come." They told her the cars get broken into, you get attacked and all that. Ethel goes, "Look, I park my car there all the time, it's safe round there, and it didn't get broken into there. I parked outside my house in Baildon and somebody came and broke the window and took the stereo and all that." It just tells you no area's safe but, at the same time, the reputation, you know, people take that on board.' (M10, late 40s, Pakistani male, Manningham)

Another interviewee, with a professional involvement that resulted in their meeting with visitors to Bradford and Manningham, deeply resented the negative views that such visitors typically held of Manningham. She reported that:

> 'They come with very fixed views as to what Manningham is about, and they expect to come to an area that's extremely disadvantaged, that's full of diversity, that's really run-down. They don't realise the wealth of history in this area; the amazing buildings, the architecture. A number of people say to us "Is it safe to walk?"' (Q1)

Outsider perceptions of Manningham as an unsafe place are something that many residents were mindful of and understood, perhaps even appreciated. For outsiders who, by and large, have an inchoate mix of ideas and rumours, Manningham does often appear to represent something dangerous, or at least alien. Again, in the course of the interviews, and echoing the previous reportage of M10, perception, often based on rumour and reputation, is a key aspect that helps define and, in some cases, maintain the meaning of place:

> 'I gave [driving] lessons to somebody in Queensbury ... we came up Carlisle Road, and he says to me, "Oh my god we need to get out!" He was genuinely really concerned that he was in this sort of area.' (M3, late 30s, Pakistani male, Heaton)

This view of the perception of Manningham was also reflected in the comments of a white female in her 60s who has lived in Manningham since the 1970s, who reported that:

> 'People have always sort of gone, "Manningham!" I mean, originally, they didn't because it was very posh. But certainly since I've been around, it's had a bad reputation, and I suppose, in a way, it almost prided itself on it. You know: "We are Manningham." And the white middle class that came to live in Manningham, "We're living in Manningham." And so there's still a bit of that around. I think people still think that it's full of drugs, but Manningham Park is attracting people bringing their children from Ilkley. You know, it's like saying one thing and doing another: like coming to restaurants or whatever.' (A15)

These quotations provide insight into one aspect of the existence of negative 'outsider' perceptions of Manningham, namely, that for a goodly proportion of those in Manningham, such opinions are merely irrefutable proof of the ignorance of the outsider. Consequently, for many 'insiders', their pleasure and satisfaction with *their* life in Manningham is framed by a pleasing self-conscious rejection of the outsiders' views. It is worth making clear the relevance of the italicising of the word 'their' in the previous sentence, for it needs to be remembered that while many of our respondents were happy with their life in Manningham, they were also aware that there were others whose life was harsher and more constrained than theirs.

More robustly, this following quote embodies some sense of mistrust and anger at how the packaging and retailing of the self-segregation thesis has come to be so potent and widely used as a defining aspect of Manningham, and Bradford:

> 'This thing about segregation and that we are segregated; we don't want to integrate and all that. I've always believed that that is the biggest lie and the biggest fallacy going … growing up, we've always tried to mix, we've always tried to sort of be involved with white schools or white children, but there's always been that reluctance, you know. I mean, you do get good white people who will mix but, in the main, they want to stick with their own as well: they don't want to mix with us. Heaton … was always regarded as a very well-to-do area when we were growing up. Heaton was a suburban leafy area, and I used to look at the gardens, look at the size of the houses: really nice. But when [Asian] people with good jobs – teaching jobs, professional jobs – started to move in, the white middle class here thought "Right let's get out of here, we're not mixing with this riff raff," although they were the best of our community, and so there's always been that attempt to keep themselves, you know, away and not to mix and maybe not to accept our middle class.' (M1, late 40s, Pakistani male, Heaton)

M1's experience and perception is not untypical and, indeed, also reflects a desire by many of the Asian residents to defend their reputation through voicing their critiques, often complemented with valuable anecdotal evidence, of what is a problematic and politically loaded discourse that while placing them, as Manningham residents, at the heart of the matter itself, often excludes their voices. Broadly speaking, this theme recurs in various ways, often the detail accompanied with qualifications explaining interpretations and perceptions of 'segregation'. For many of the Asian community interviewed, segregation[5] is viewed as an outcome, a symptom, of wider problems linked with, for example, education, employment, racism, values or other structural and symbolic forces. Again, for a majority of those interviewed, there is more to be gained through a genuine appreciation of and engagement with

---

[5] The idea of *self*-segregation remained contested for nearly all those interviewed, with some rejecting the term altogether, while others unpicked and deconstructed its meaning, and link with their reality, in the course of the interviews and discussions.

diversity. In order to achieve this, however, it is necessary to encourage the development of spaces where ethnicity and heritage is recognised and valued:

'When you grow up in a sort of monoculture, you then become disrespectful, you become insulated and you become disrespectful of others, whereas when you grow up in a multicultural way, when you have got different experiences, you learn to respect folk.' (M7, mid–30s, Asian female, Manningham)

One voice reflected on the changed demography as having an impact on changing current social competences:

'It's like when we were at school [approximately 30 years ago], we got to know about other cultures and that because they were all around us. So, it wasn't unusual, you might say – it was normal, natural … but kids today – and I'm not having a go – they don't know how to mix with, say, white kids, for example. Manningham used to be really comfortable with itself like that: down White Abbey Road and Green Lane and that area, there were a lot of different cultures, but for some reason, it's become very Asian; very Pakistani, I should say.' (M9, early 40s, Pakistani-heritage male, Manningham)

This theme of the changing demography of Manningham was strongly echoed in the account of a young white professional female in her 30s who had deliberately moved into Manningham because of its multicultural population. Speaking of her entry into Manningham in the late 1990s, she described it thus:

'At the time, it felt quite vibrant. It felt diverse in terms of the kind of waves of migration. You know, on our street, there were Sikh families, Muslim families, there was an old lady who came from the Netherlands, and all the waves of European and Italian migration round there. It had obviously, at the time, a sizeable African-Caribbean heritage community and also an arty-bohemian community.' (A2)

This same person goes on to reflect upon the gradual loss of diversity, with white and other friends moving out from an area where some had felt their presence increasingly challenged by a growing assertive Muslim neighbourhood identity. Despite this, some of the white residents of Manningham whom we interviewed had seen changes in its character and demography but remained very positively committed to living in the area. A professional woman in her 60s spoke of Manningham in the 1970s as being "kind of the heart of the immigrant community" (A15).

Similarly, an older white, devout Christian male relished living in Manningham and was very positive about his long experience of living there:

> 'I wouldn't personally be in any other place, you know. I don't envy anyone at all, because the experience of being here has been entirely wholesome. And, I mean, you talk to people living in the houses around here; and I remember one lady I went to see because her husband had died and she said "The first people that came to me were my Asian neighbours with baskets of fruit for me. They couldn't say much, but they wanted to express it in ways that they knew."' (T3)

This loss of diversity in areas that have, over time, become dominated by single minority ethnic or faith groups is a situation that is lamented across ethnicities, as it results in a loss of social, cultural and intellectual capital. For example, especially some older participants perceived an incapacity for young Pakistani men to 'mix' with other groups, an incapacity that was borne of circumstance rather than desire or motivation.

Negotiating alien territory beyond Manningham

When Pakistani residents were asked about their perceptions and experiences of zones and neighbourhoods that they felt were dangerous or unsafe, the locales that were mentioned included Ravenscliffe, Holme Wood and Buttershaw: council estates built after the Second World War, for the most part (temporally and spatially), housing white working-class residents. While the physical fabric of some areas, for example, Holme Wood, has been redeveloped and greatly improved over the last two decades or so, the reputation of such neighbourhoods remains, like that of Manningham, laced with negativity, fear and danger. As reported in previous research, there is a strong perception of which areas in the city are to be avoided; often, these perceptions are, indeed, racialised, as well as having a strong class dimension (see Phillips et al, 2002: 10).

That said, even some of those areas are undergoing changes in terms of their populations' ethnic profile. Despite the power of reputation, migration into those areas is certainly becoming noticeable, and this, in turn, is viewed positively:

> 'Our communities are now moving onto these areas: these particular areas were no-go areas, you know, probably a few years ago. Not any more. People are living there, Asian families living there … one of the lads I work with, he sent me a change of address and he's moved to Broadstone Way, and Broadstone Way is the heart of Holme Wood and I thought "Wow, he's an Asian lad and he's moved from Keighley to Holme Wood."' (M13, late 20s Pakistani male)

One thread woven into the fabric of many interviews was that Pakistani residents often had very little or no direct experience of the areas they ended up avoiding, and even the minority who did experience what to them were 'danger zones' were split into two camps: one set had no problems with these areas as they encountered them in a professional or work-related capacity; the other category, which included mostly older males, had only experienced these areas decades ago, when they attended school, for example. The element that unified those who had not experienced these white 'danger zones' was simply this: they did not *need* to visit those areas in the first place, so any present or future experience of them was unlikely and unnecessary. For many, a stock response seemed to be "I don't need to go there, so I can't say much about it other than what I've heard" (M2, 22 years old, Pakistani female). That said, for some, even if there was an opportunity or need to venture through areas that were rumoured to be especially unsafe for non-white people, strategies to play down any risk were often employed: being accompanied by others, as well as taking detours and, of course, complete avoidance of the areas altogether. For one resident, however, in the absence of apparent alternatives, more extreme action was necessary:

> 'They asked me to work up around Eccleshill and I did it for a day but I couldn't stand it because the other people working there, they were – well, they were racist. They didn't attack me or anything but some of the stuff they kept coming out with … these were young people, as well. So anyway, I did a day and said to my boss "Either you place me

somewhere else or I'm leaving."' (M8, late teens, Pakistani female, Manningham)

Regrettably, one consequence of strategies such as these is that the negative beliefs and associated affective feelings of fear and suspicion are rehearsed and reinforced through the very success of these strategies in 'protecting' those who have employed them from the anticipated threats. It should be noted that this utilisation of avoidance strategies to pre-empt experiencing the dangers of 'alien', threatening territory was not unique to the Pakistani respondents. Very similar views of white working-class estates were held by white respondents, who on class-based sensibility, regarded specific white working-class areas as highly undesirable, and potentially threatening, no-go areas.

For another resident of Manningham, it was, however, necessary to negotiate a form of acceptance within the white area in which he was asked to work. Here, the significance of 'role' was a key factor in gaining trust and reciprocal civility, while diminishing a sense of overt conflict and of being viewed as an unwelcome outsider. As he explains:

> 'I've worked at a lot of places where I wouldn't actually go, like I worked up at Queensbury.... I was a bit hesitant at first to actually go up there.... For the first hour and a half I thought "Wonder if somebody says anything", because they'd not had an Asian guy work up there.... After a bit: "All right how are you? We've not seen you before." So, that little fear had gone by then you know, so it was good.' (M14, early 20s, Pakistani male)

This experience was echoed by a young, hijab-wearing, Muslim woman, who had worked in an area of Bradford stereotypically perceived as being a white working-class enclave. She said of her experience that:

> 'When you start to speak to people and people get to start to speak to us, they realise that yes, I look a certain way, but the way I handle who I am, you know, for me, I'm British through and through, and that's where I was born and bred. And so nobody wants to change me – other than the way I look. And it was an interesting sort of time, working in places like X, because I think people's eyes have opened as to who we are, you know: we're not very different.' (A4ii)

As with this young woman, among the Pakistani interviewees, there were very few who had a need, either due to work, family or other social and leisure commitments, to visit areas outside of Manningham and its immediate periphery. While there was some discussion, and often comparison, of other cities in Britain, it seemed that many of the residents were, in some ways, quite content to live within a relatively small and local world. This does not mean, of course, that there was a resistance to travel or to widen horizons: many of the Pakistanis interviewed had not only been abroad to Pakistan, but travelled around Europe, the Middle East and the Far East. Rather than being defined as insular, it could be argued that residents of neighbourhoods like Manningham are actually behaving in a relatively rational and efficient manner; a rhetorical question echoed again from earlier research was often asked: 'why go elsewhere when everything is on your own doorstep?' (see Alam, 2006).

Comfort zone, neighbourhood and norms

The notion of 'comfort zone' more generally was also found to be of great significance in earlier research (Alam, 2006; Alam and Husband, 2006), and is repeated heavily throughout this research, which is built on data generated through a much broader sample in terms of age, ethnicity and gender. Arguably, this kind of disposition or attitude is more linked with a sense of localism and local identity, a trait also apparent in research that took place across West Yorkshire (Alam, 2011) that was built on a diverse sample, reflecting differences in gender and generation, as well as faith and ethnicity. In other work, there are to be found seams of data that reflect similar ideas. Lewis's (1985) description of growing up in London (see also Back, 2007) is partly defined by the salience, power and investment in the notion of *territory*. For Lewis, even everyday journeys and movements were negotiated through an embedded awareness of 'no-go and go areas', often acutely defined by race and the likelihood of racist abuse. Knowing which parts were safe and which were not was arguably a means of survival, but, at the same time, such knowledge and awareness was almost a taken-for-granted part of growing up in a world where race mattered in stark and subtle ways (Lewis, 1985: 219, cited in Back, 2007: 62). As Back (2007: 51) notes: 'she held in her head a coded map of the area in order to both make sense of it and to move through its hospitable and unwelcoming places'. The intersection of 'race' and place is echoed throughout our data, as the nationally racialised discourses of race and *legitimate* presence are given concrete expression in the unique lives of our respondents, sometimes producing unanticipated modes of expression:

> 'There aren't massive places that I feel unsafe. Maybe that's my own stupidity, but there are places where you feel safer you know ... don't feel safe when there's police around; I feel very safe when there's lots of criminals around!' (M5, late 40s, African-Caribbean-heritage male, Manningham)

The previous work of Alam (2006) has shown the close bonds of young Muslim men to specific neighbourhoods, and this is found elsewhere in our current data. For pragmatic as well as affective reasons, individuals develop their own urban terrain. One older white female resident living in housing association accommodation in Manningham provided an example of such a routine. She said that:

> 'I go all over the place; but I go to the top of the road and got a bus. I go to the top of the road on a nice day and walk round the park and get a bit of exercise if it's a nice day. Occasionally up Oak Lane to where there's some shops if I need something. There's a supermarket up there, which is Asian, which, as you say, "Have I shopped in the Asian shops?" I do if I go up there, but I don't go regularly. [The area] I really go is the little square bit where I live.' (T1)

Similarly, a single white male living in multi-occupied housing association accommodation appreciates the benefits of the local shops, while making use of the proximity of the city centre: "No, no. I do shop locally. It's very handy you know; the area itself is handy because everything's on tap" (T2).

However, significantly, in a way that echoes the non-stereotypical reality of this inner-city area, he also notes other valued features of the area where he lives in the centre of Manningham that make him distinctly disinclined to move out:

> 'I mean, I do like this flat. As my rented accommodation in this area, to be honest, I don't think I could do anything better because in a way, I mean, the housing association – we've got a lovely garden they've spent a fortune on: and, yes, it's a lovely house, plus we've got a lot of big established trees, so we've got a lot of wildlife: owls, woodpeckers. Quite a lot of wildlife round here, yes, it's all right, you know. I

mean, it's not perfect, you know, but, yes, on the whole, yes, yes – it's all right.' (T2)

Another single white male occupant of social housing greatly appreciated the size of rooms that his Victorian residence provided, and the history that came with it:

'Well, they're quite grand houses; and that's something I like about Manningham, and Bradford in general: the architecture. There's some pretty grand architecture. At one time, this was an affluent, wealthy area: these were houses for the mercantile class who were wealthy merchants and, I believe, quite a lot of Jewish people back then, you know, a hundred years ago it was quite a Jewish area.' (T5)

As a birdwatcher, he also greatly appreciated the bird life that shared his neighbourhood. In an account that echoed the challenge to the stereotypical depiction of the inner-city streetscape that we explored in Chapter Two, he proudly rehearsed the bird life of his section of Manningham:

'I like the grand buildings round here: the trees, the fact that we have a lot of mature trees round here and all the wildlife that supports…. We've got gold finch, chaffinch, green finch, long tailed tits as well as the normal blue tits. Blue tits and great tits, yes, but we get long tailed tits. I've even seen a migratory flock of waxwing in Manningham; I've seen a flock of migratory redwing in the park…. And in this garden, I've seen a sparrow hawk; we've got a very thriving population of Tawny owls; we have greater spotted woodpeckers; nuthatch.' (T5)

Thus, the elegant Victorian streetscapes discussed in Chapter Two continue to provide an environment that nurtures, and is appreciated by, a very different population to that of its original occupants. It is important to also note here the fact that the housing association accommodation that non-residents may look down on as 'multi-occupied social housing' provides not only highly valued accommodation, but also a social context in which mutual support may make the *coexistence* mutually enriching. This interviewee, for example, painted a very strong picture of the friendship and mutual support he enjoyed in this locale, which enabled him to say: "Oh definitely. Definitely, yes I feel like this is home. I mean, I loved growing up in [another area of Bradford] and I do like that area; but to be honest, I do feel more at home here" (T2).

Another respondent who lived in social housing (retired, white, male) also spoke of the civility of living in collective housing:

'Well, I meet most of my neighbours on a regular basis. There are chairs out there; I go there and sit down, someone will join me. It might be any one of my neighbours to say hello and have a chat for five or 10 minutes. It's nice. It's a nice atmosphere, you know.' (T7)

However, this gentleman also provided an example of the routine ability of respondents to make distinctions between good neighbours and 'the less desirable sort'. In his case, this included East Europeans who had recently moved into accommodation nearby, school children in transit to and from school, and his own examples of 'welfare scroungers': "In fact, some of these people have been in these properties for years and years, and some of them are really anti-social, they really are. They don't know anything else but just moping around" (T7).

This sense of people living on the basis of daily terrain that is quite narrowly prescribed, though extended by bus and car, provides a necessary reminder that the neighbourhood locale *within* Manningham is the de facto experiential basis of being resident there. At the same time, individuals' sense of both their own locale and of wider Manningham is framed by the descriptive narratives that circulate about the area. People position themselves in relation to both the direct experience of their neighbourhood and its explicit and implicit comparison with other neighbourhoods and other areas of Bradford.

There is an association, but not a linear casual link, between a subjective sense of one's own turf, one's comfort zone, and one's sense of identity within a specific neighbourhood. One interviewee who had worked as a community worker in Manningham reflected the earlier findings of Alam (2006) regarding the strong sense of neighbourhood felt by young Muslim Bradfordian men, reporting that: "I think Manningham's a really interesting space in terms of organising and identity. Yes, there's real narratives that people have with themselves in Manningham, I think, so Oak Laners really feel they are Oak Laners" (A2).

Her account of the young men, from their early teens to mid-20s, revealed a strong sense of local affiliation with this particular area of Manningham, and an associated claim of territorial ownership that reached into supporting a normative repertoire of acceptable behaviour for residents in the area. Furthermore, this repertoire is replicated across the city and within its neighbourhoods, each being home to young men, of whatever ethnic heritage, who are grounded within their locale to such an extent that it becomes an embedded aspect of personal and group identity, which, in turn, can become manifest in both banal and spectacular ways: merely an affirmation of self when describing one's identity, or a proud, loud and seemingly aggressive claiming of territory infused with an assertive masculinity that, it has to be said, is only one, albeit highly visible, expression of a broader hegemonic, patriarchal context.

A brief methodological aside

In fact, early in our fieldwork, Oak Lane provided an incident that was revelatory of both the sense of Oak Laners' ownership of *their* turf and the different perspectives 'outsiders' might bring to a situation. Charles Husband (English, male, white, in 60s) and Jörg Huttermann (German, male, in 40s) were walking down Oak Lane. Husband had lived in Manningham for 10 years and was introducing his colleague to the area. As we came down Oak Lane, I (Husband) noticed four young Asian men in their 20s walking up the same pavement towards us. Some part of me registered the fact that if I was on my own, I would have moved across to let the four claim the pavement. However, because we were in conversation, in the end, we only moved over to such an extent that one or two of the young men had to move out into the road. As they passed us the young man nearest to Jörg clipped him across the top of his head with a light glancing blow, and let out a whoop. His friends laughed and we all continued to walk onwards in the direction we were heading.

What was our reaction to this event? I felt responsible for not having given Jörg explicit guidance that we should more actively move over, but, at the same time, I thought that the event was essentially humorous. No one had been harmed and it seemed an unlikely, but timely, introduction of my German friend to the street politics of Manningham. I saw the behaviour of the young men as a piece of territorial behaviour. My friend and colleague, Jörg, felt that he had been assaulted. We were both right. In a technical sense, but not in a way that would attract police interest, Jörg had been the recipient of an unprovoked blow to the head. I felt that the blow had been carefully calculated to cause an assault to Jörg's dignity, rather than his person. However, importantly, I felt that this behaviour was not totally unexpected in the context of the street politics of Manningham, while he felt that such behaviour would have been out of the question in the streetscape of a comparable Muslim/Turkish area of Marxloh, where he was carrying out comparable research.

At the same time, it is worth wondering whether or not the same events within the encounter would have occurred had we been non-white. Similarly, had we been white but also young, wearing visible signs of street credibility and, to all intents and purposes, something closer to projecting an insider identity, perhaps there may not have been a physical rejoinder at all. However, in such a situation, the interaction may have been even more physical. While different permutations may have led to different processes within and during the interaction, it is clear that identity and its markers play a key role in even the most taken for granted of social encounters.

Nevertheless, this incident provides a useful foundational caveat to all the analysis that follows in this chapter, for it revealed that in the process of carrying out fieldwork in Manningham, I was not only observing behaviour, but simultaneously relating it to an extant, but malleable, framework of understanding about the differing norms that operate over the same area. As someone familiar with Manningham, and with some understanding of inter-ethnic relations in Britain, I brought a set of sensibilities to this encounter that were not shared with Jörg. In a similar way, as a male spending a lot of time walking through Manningham, I did not have the experiential repertoire of a female, who might be expected to bring a different set of sensibilities to walking these streets alone, which was, in fact, the reason why we employed a young female colleague to carry out that fieldwork for us. However, her experiences, and those of the young women she talked to, and of the other women in the sample, do demand that we be explicit in our analysis about the normative framework we wish to bring to bear in discussing this experience. As will become apparent in this chapter, very different normative frameworks are in existence within Manningham, as different interests seek to express the legitimacy of their presence, and power, in gendered terms. Consequently, in this chapter, the predominant mode of writing will be descriptive, with a modest amount of contextual analysis. A considered discussion of what we report here will be left to the concluding chapter.

Colour, race and ethnicity: identities and labels

Before proceeding any further, it is both necessary and helpful to self-consciously take note of the presence and role of modes of social categorisation that operate across Bradford and Manningham. As we noted in Chapter Two, the history of migration into Britain is marked by the persistent allocation of racial labels and racist ideologies upon the migration and settlement of different waves of new communities forming within urban Britain. In the present era in which this research is located, the phenomenon of migration, settlement and, now, coexistence is profoundly racialised. Whether it is the white population that is the majority population of Bradford, or the people of Pakistani heritage who are the majority population of Manningham, the language and sentiments of 'race' are readily available to provide the basis of both self-categorisation and stereotypical categorisation of others. This has consequences that we will explore further in the concluding chapter, but for our purposes here, it is important to see the capacity of this conceptual framework for shifting perceived interactions on the street from those seen as being between two individuals to those experienced as being between two groups: not me and you, but Us and Them (the latter variant being very much the salient framework for the encounter between Jörg and his assailant on Oak Lane). The discourse of race produces a permanently available basis for the polarisation of social relations. So, too, in more recent times, has the emergence of the powerful discourse of Islamophobia placed the possession of a commitment to the Muslim faith as a sufficient basis for again being placed into the polarising categorisation of Muslim versus non-Muslim. In the context of everyday interaction in Manningham, therefore, there is the ever-present capacity for interaction to be coded into quite rigid modes of categorisation that bring with them powerfully embedded stereotypes and feelings that can radically change the perception of interactions (see Jost and Hamilton, 2005; Yzerbyt and Corneille, 2005).

In Bradford, as is the case in most other multi-ethnic towns and cities across the UK, a close connection between place and race remains, with associations of one feeding into definitions of the other. Racism can become one controlling narrative of areas that have identities derived from the amalgamations of territory and 'race': there are white areas and there are non-white areas, and each of these has their own broader meanings and currencies across and within communities. Like Lewis (quoted earlier), a majority of those interviewed held racially encoded maps in their heads, often coloured with experience and reputation. Some aspects of these maps are fixed, while others change with sudden events or slow and gradual evolutions. Personal experience combined with rumour, hearsay and reportage form an ever-changing map. It should be said, then, that the universes and world views encountered in this research were far from simple black/white–good/bad dichotomies. For the respondents in this study, what defined safe and unsafe zones was the presence, perceived or otherwise, and likelihood of racism, not ethnicity per se:

> '[Holme Wood] had its good parts and it had its bad parts. I saw some poverty there that I've never seen before and since, you know: white kids coming out with excrement attached to their body.... There was only one guy that outwardly shouted at his front door, but you always got people calling you silly names but they didn't have the power to do it; just names and this that and the other. The discrimination was ingrained, then, within all aspects of society, the institutional racism that we now know it to be, and it's there still, it's perhaps not as obvious but it's there still ... the Polish ... they can pick up a perfect English accent and move on.' (M5, late 40s African–Caribbean-heritage male, Manningham)

The issue of being able to 'exit' (Tajfel and Turner, 1979; Tajfel, 1981) a stigmatised group has been central to the demographic dynamics of Bradford, for, as we have seen in relation to the Polish community, the permeability of the boundary between the Polish and majority English population was not rendered rigid by colour differences. There has been extensive intermarriage with the majority English population, and physiognomy and skin colour provide no basis for identifying people of Polish heritage as they pass by on the street. For the residents of Manningham of Pakistani heritage, their colour has provided a non-negotiable signifier of difference. As one Manningham resident noted:

> 'You can go back to the Irish, my ancestors were Irish and they lived in the poor inner city and all the rest of it; and the prejudice towards them was similar, but a generation down, once the accent had gone, the Irishness that remained really was the Church. But they fitted in: in looks and behaviour. Whereas once you get to the Asian and black immigration, they never fit in appearance-wise.' (A15)

Colour has provided not only a means of Bradfordian Pakistanis being the inescapable targets of white racism, but also a means of mutual identification that has aided the capacity to police the behaviour of in-group members within the Pakistani community, for one of the obvious findings to emerge from the interviews is the construction of neighbourhood and wider ward-based norms of behaviour that are regarded as legitimately applicable to anyone living in that (their) area.

In the intersection of 'race', faith and ethnicity, there is in a place like Manningham a rich environment of complex multiple codes being simultaneously put into play. Clothing that for one white observer may signify that a person is Pakistani (an ethnic and cultural coding), may for another signify that this person is a 'Paki' (a racial and racist coding), or that they are Muslim (which can be ethnic, racial or a fear-engendering Islamophobic coding). It should also be noted that while each of these codes can sit alongside each other, their meanings also have variance. For some, ethnic and cultural coding can also sustain stereotypical beliefs: Pakistani may well be an ethnic and cultural code, but it can also connote a lack of integration, difference, inferiority and so on. Nevertheless, the same appearance for a member of the Pakistani community may signify that this person is a 'sister' (female member of the community upon whom certain behavioural social norms may be placed). Furthermore, it is also possible that the style of dress and language spoken may indicate which specific ethnic subset of the Pakistani population this person belongs to. Thus, presence on the street invites a wide range of attributed characteristics being laid upon a person, accompanied by claims of presumed difference and similarity, and a belief in the legitimacy of expectations laid upon each party.

The boundary markers of identity in an area like Manningham reflect the salient identities in play. Accordingly, there are the banal ethnic markers of clothing, which may be essentially ethnic in terms of style and significance, as noted in Chapter Two. However, there are also other potential aspects of clothing that do not so much specify the precise clothing to be worn, but rather the connotations of the clothing style in question: for example, the degree of 'modesty' that the clothing offers the (female) wearer is significant in shaping reactions. Consequently, in an area with the demography of Manningham, there is a distinction between, for example, a preference for a certain style of *salwar kameez* that may signal specific values around fashion, and religiosity among members of the Pakistani community. The expectation that there should be modesty in clothing, itself borne of Islamic values, may be extended to all females living within the neighbourhood. Thus, for example, a female white respondent with a close affinity to Manningham reported how, on moving there, she became aware of a code of modesty that began to inform her dressing routine. She reported her perception that following 2001, "I think there were probably issues around religious markers becoming more apparent or a religiosity becoming stronger in a way: so, just small things that would make you kind of think 'Oh, that's interesting'" (A2).

It was not, however, merely a matter of benign observation of cultural change on her part, but also increasingly verbal sanctioning by male members of the Pakistani community that made her feel the growing impact of religious behavioural prescriptions increasingly impacting on her daily experience.

The imposition and response to dress codes is no simple thing. While some men may feel that they have the legitimate masculine neighbourhood credentials to explicitly pass comment on women's dress, many others may share their sense of distaste at a perceived impropriety, and possibly many more might enjoy the diversity of feminine clothing styles they encounter in a day, and make no comment at all. Equally, for Asian women, they, too, may have a range of views about the proper dress codes in their area but may make no verbal comment. Consequently, we have no adequate means of knowing whether there is, in fact, a consensual Asian subcultural dress code in operation in Manningham. However, we do have evidence that a visible minority of persons make it clear that they do seek to police dress codes, and their activity will have a disproportionate impact upon the persons they sanction. We tend not to go through our day and note the many occasions on which we experienced no exposure to social criticism or discomfort whatsoever, but we may well rehearse isolated moments of public abuse for a prolonged time. The very many acts of mutual recognition of similarity, as individuals go about their daily business, shopping, strolling or going about our work, are based upon an acknowledgement of the similar roles we fulfil in the social environment of our neighbourhood. Individuals passing each other in their cars on the street do not ask why cars are moving from A to B, nor do they routinely trouble themselves with the motives of those in transit. Cars, streets, mobility are all part of our routine streetscape. In 'rubbing along together' (Watson, 2006), residents play out a shared understanding of the reasonableness of most people's actions. They may not always find the actions of others in close proximity to their own norms of behaviour in this specific context, but they recognise that the roles being enacted are well established and usual. It is when the behavioural expression of these roles deviates beyond a *locally* negotiated range of acceptability that the interaction is experienced as offensive and meriting sanction. *Rubbing along*, in this context, does not mean that there is an absence of latent conflicts of interest, nor of negative judgements of others encountered on the streets. However, what is in place is a normative level of behavioural civility that sets limits on the expression of these interpersonal sentiments. The idea, highly visible in a range of urban theory (Simmel, 1950 [1903]; Lofland,1989), that at the core of urbanity lies a state of indifference that underlines the freedom at the heart of urban life, seems too simplistic in accounting for the interaction in Manningham. Apparent behavioural indifference may be reflections of the local normative constraints placed upon quite salient inter-group sentiments, and territorially grounded perceptions of legitimate authority may, as we see in our data, facilitate direct attempts to police others.

Additionally, in the dialogic nature of interpersonal perception, it is also possible for individuals to feel an outsider in a specific social setting. These can, for example, be acutely real in class terms in Britain, where participating in a friendly social event takes you to a locale in which *you know you don't belong*. In such circumstances, the highly sensitised personal scanning of the interaction may lead to the perception of signals of rejection or criticism from others present when none was intended. Thus, in everyday interaction in Manningham, expectations on the part of all the persons on the street may skew the perception of the nature of the encounters experienced.

Staying and going: the multiple dynamics of residence

Across the interviewees, Pakistani and non-Pakistani, male and female, there is a strong thread of stories that build up a picture of the dynamics that shape individual and family reasons for wanting to stay in Manningham, or for wishing to exit to other locales. Individual cases include all the expected complexity of life choices, but there remains an overarching repertoire of experiences and rationales that can be drawn out as identifiable themes.

While there is a sense of confidence that comes from familiarity with place, in the case of Manningham, as we saw earlier, it is richly complemented with concrete examples of the support and social and cultural infrastructures that enhance everyday living, with specific reference to modalities of culture and community.

When asked about the topic of 'integration', some residents explored their earlier memories of moving into 'white' areas that soon became 'brown' through the process of 'white flight'. Interestingly, this previous 'white flight' has now mutated into a 'middle-class flight', where class, as opposed to ethnicity, has become a potent marker of identity and appears to be a significant driver that explains migration out of working-class zones into those that can be defined as having a more middle-class demography and character. It is worth reminding ourselves, however, that discrimination and, in particular, poverty remain strong features of minority ethnic communities in Britain (Dorling, 2010).

Reasons given for movement out of Manningham into 'better' areas included the chance to gain better educational provision for children, the need for larger accommodation with gardens and an appreciation of the greater privacy that detached and semi-detached housing affords. While, as we have seen, there were other strong 'pull factors', perhaps most significantly, however, were the push factors that emerged, including a lack of ethnic diversity, as well as an acceptance of, and resignation to, the impact of the external perceptions of Manningham. So, while some residents expressed deep commitment to and connection with the area, at the same time, the area's reputation seemed a powerful push factor for some. Indeed, when the small number of former residents of Manningham were asked why they had moved out, their responses reflected ambivalence: the area felt safe to them, they knew its nooks and crannies *but* there was also a growing problem with educational provision, road safety and, especially, young men and drug dealing:

> 'It's [drugs] just been flooded in the streets and it's too many role models that are out there that are driving the flash cars and have got a spliff in their mouth, and the young think it's a good thing to do I suppose.' (M12, 33 years old, Pakistani male)

However, it is not just Manningham that suffers from this perception. Some interviewees were quick to assert that inner-city Britain on the whole suffers from various problems associated with youth and criminality. This acts as a necessary reminder that individual residents of Manningham do not construct their perceptions or situate their experiences in isolation from the wider debates about contemporary urban life. Contemporary political assaults upon the urban poor as welfare scroungers and as 'skivers' rather than 'strivers' has inevitable implications for an area with high levels of deprivation. Indeed, the association of those inner-city areas inhabited by large proportions of Muslims with terrorism and criminality inevitably form part of the available repertoire for and reputation of Manningham – for its residents as much as outsiders. Within Bradford, there are other areas that although having undergone some changes, are essentially perceived as remaining the same:

> 'Do you know something, I stayed at somebody's house in Girlington and it used to be really bad at one time. There used to be a lot of white people round there and they used

to get drunk and swear on a night and you could hear them swearing and we used to be scared, now it's totally opposite [in terms of ethnic composition]. Now, it's just all Asians, a lot of asylum seekers now, but a lot of Asians and there's all the pubs are gone. It's just local lads round there, guys, drugs, flashy cars.' (M4, mid-20s, Pakistani-heritage male, Manningham)

Although having been born and bred in Manningham all his life, a successful Pakistani man (M12) now lives in Heaton in a large house with its own garden, garage and all the trappings that his successful business affords. 'Pakistani' people with his class and professional profile were not a rarity among the residents interviewed: many were either aspiring or already achieving professional/middle-class individuals. Granted, there were also some who were on a personal economic trajectory that was less than positive, but the noticeable aspect across the sample is the extent to which Manningham elicits hope despite its reputation and lack of formal economic and social infrastructure. Manningham's identity as a zone of transition is also somewhat underlined in the following quote, as is the notion that locales can also have porous, ambiguous and open boundaries: "Well, to me, I am not out of Manningham, this is part of Manningham, because you see Manningham folk have moved outwards, a lot of my friends from Manningham are living roundabouts here, they're all from Manningham" (M2, late 30s, male, Heaton [an adjacent ward]).

Although not all of its schools are failing, residents across the board were negative about education in Bradford as a whole. Indeed, there is also some popularity in the view that school admissions policies are themselves counterproductive and have enabled the formation of areas and neighbourhoods that lack ethnic diversity. As another respondent put it:

'Asian parents ... want to get their kids into more mixed schools, where there's more white children and it's impossible. They say, "Oh no, sorry, you're in the catchment area for this school, so your kids can't go to that school", and yet white children who live in the same catchment area, they manage to get schools. So, they use it as a stick to keep us a limit to the school ... and the thing is, our parents want children to go and mix with white children but they're not allowed to.' (M1, late 40s, Pakistani male, Heaton)

Thus, for residents of Manningham, as much as anywhere else, one reason for movement is the desire to move to an area that provides a better social and educational environment for their children, despite the fact that they currently find much in Manningham that is congenial and valuable. Over the generations of Pakistani residence in Bradford, there has been a significant growth in the number of people who have enjoyed economic success. So, while Manningham continues to be an area of higher-than-average social deprivation, there is a significant distribution of families that are more than economically comfortable. A small proportion of these will be the white 'cosmopolitans' who specifically value the ethnic diversity of the area, but a much larger number are those members of the Pakistani community who individually, and as families, have come to enjoy a considerable degree of economic success. Consequently, residents in once working-class terraced housing may have disposable income that the outward appearance of their homes might not suggest. Some of the larger houses described in Chapter Three have, indeed, acquired outward and visible signs of the prosperity, and self-declared status, of their current occupants. Others, however, maintain there external modesty, which may be betrayed by the high-end luxury car that is parked outside. (Of which, more in Chapter Six.) The fact remains, however, that for an increasingly large number of Pakistani residents over the last few decades, the economic restraint on their capacity to move out of the area has been removed. Consequently, it can now be observed that some choose to remain in the area because of its biographic and cultural value to them, while others find themselves now more exposed to a consideration of the balance between forces inclining them to stay against those that might motivate them to leave. Here, as in other areas of their positioning in the life of Bradford, such people have their immediate views about life in Manningham shaped by the broader awareness of changing social realities in Bradford. As one respondent commented: "Our people, we're arriving. We have got professional people all over the city now. It's a shame we don't have more power, but that will come slowly with each generation" (M6, late 30s, Pakistani male, Girlington).

In one joint interview with a mother and daughter, both of whom lived in a large, detached Victorian property in the heart of Manningham, there was a reflection of the aspirations offered and given legitimacy by these changes within the Pakistani community, especially as expressed by the older interviewee. Indeed, for this person in particular, an original desire to move into a 'better' area was met with some resistance by those who can be perceived as informal gatekeepers to better areas:

> 'I looked at places like Ilkley, Harrogate, Leeds – in more conservative-type areas – because I wanted to move away from the Asian community and that was only because I thought maybe a majority of Asian people are not interested in perhaps to be educated and to be more outgoing activities, and this type of thing … I think I was influenced, and I was impressed, by my own white colleagues – doctors, social workers and so on … I didn't want to move into a completely white area where I would have no contact with people with Asian backgrounds; I wanted a semi-type of area. But the experience I had: on a couple of occasions I was refused to view houses in Harrogate and other places because they thought an Asian person is coming. That was a good experience for me … a learning experience.' (M11, late 40s, female, Manningham)

It seems, at least for this interviewee, that despite over 40 years' worth of progress in the sphere of race and ethnic relations, things have not changed so much. Echoing our concerns with racism earlier, this interviewee's experience sheds significant insight into how ethnicity is still visible, and coded into racism, even when it is only apparent at the end of a telephone, when a speaker's accent is recognisably non-(indigenous)British. In sum, this experience of rejection from apparently 'better' areas, perhaps by self-serving estate agents, echoes Hiro's (1973) earlier assertions about how the ethnic character and demography of areas are defined and maintained. As one other interviewee reflected:

> 'There was an estate agent that used to be predominant in Heaton … they had this saying about the 10 effect … and what this was was that when 10 Asian households move into an area, Asian or black moved into a white street or area, that would become the tipping point, and they called it "the 10 effect". Now, this was based on what they'd seen … as soon as it got to that number, the whites said "Right, let's go, we're out of here" … if you speak to a lot of these Asians, they would love to live next door to white people but the problem is they won't stay, they want to move to areas where there's more white people.' (M1, late 40s, Pakistani male, Heaton)

Although M11's interpretation may well be wrong (that her being barred from viewing properties in 'better' areas was actually due to the houses already being sold/under offer, etc), any misinterpretation becomes less convincing given her capacity to read between the lines: she is not only a professional, but she takes an active role as a citizen and community member. In other words, she has a keen ability to recognise racism and articulate its existence. Meanwhile, M1's belief in the existence of a 'tipping point' also adds depth to M11's experience, while also reintroducing the relevance of power and access. (Rationally speaking, and given the significance of race/ethnicity within the construction of what constitutes desirable/undesirable areas, it may seem rational for estate agents to ensure a tipping point is not reached as a means of maximising commission.)[6] At the same time, this negative experience enabled her to revisit the positive and beneficial aspects of Manningham, in part, the character of the housing and the extent to which 'our' people were now investing in the maintenance and renovation of their homes:

> 'Recently, the other house just behind this street ... it belongs to meat business people ... and they made it really, really beautiful. It seems like they're going to stay for good years because of the amount of money they spent on it. So, seems like people are becoming interested [in renovating their homes].' (M11, late 40s, female, Manningham)

Thus, it is reasonable to speculate that with segments of the population of Manningham becoming increasingly diverse in terms of class and wealth, some reclaiming of Manningham by a bourgeoning Pakistani-heritage middle class is taking place.

Over the last 10 years or so, however, with the maturation of subsequent generations, formerly working-class Pakistani families have started to move into larger housing, both within and outside of Manningham. For those who have moved into neighbouring Heaton

---

[6] Although the link is admittedly tenuous, see Levitt and Dubner (2005: 55–88). Here, the authors give a rational choice theory-based explanation as to why it serves the interest of US real estate agents to sell clients' houses at lower prices than their own; the argument presented also sheds some light on how maintaining levels of desirability within a locale serves the vested interest of real estate agents. Of course, this does not mean that estate agents are de facto operating in an essentially discriminatory way, but their practices can and do result in unintended social consequences that are often deemed free and independent of them.

especially, there appears to be a minimal amount of upheaval, partly because the neighbourhoods are next to each other and also because the 'ethnic' character of Heaton has changed to resemble Manningham's over the last three decades. In many cases, interviewees expressed some degree of ambiguity, and ambivalence, as to where Manningham ends and where another area begins. For others, Heaton – although often deemed to be a slightly 'better area' – is nevertheless perceived to be an extension of Manningham. When discussing boundaries around Manningham, one interviewee simply stated: "I think it's still part of Manningham, isn't it, really?" (M3, late 30s, Pakistani male, Heaton). Another, respondent reported that her professional family had lived in a predominantly white area of Bradford, but that following a serious racial attack upon one of the family members, her father "moved to Heaton, which is quite a middle-class mixed community, but he feels that he needs people around him from his own background and religion" (A8). The 'safe' familiarity of the fusion of class, ethnic and religious identities within a relatively newly established 'middle-class' adjunct to Manningham proved a very strong pull factor to a family that had felt the cost of racist rejection elsewhere in Bradford.

For many, Manningham's appeal lies, first, in familiarity and comfort with the place itself and, second, in a growing aesthetic and functional appreciation of the area's 19th-century housing stock. Indeed, as we saw earlier, the 'character' of some of Manningham's housing became a point of discussion for some interviewees. Reference to the height of the rooms, the density of the walls and the quality of the materials used was often made in comparison with more modern housing. As alluded to by M11 earlier, a resurgence of interest in Manningham as a place to live – and to live comfortably – is significant, despite the stigma and reputation that the name still carries.

Despite this, the majority of interviewees expressed, at times, an overwhelming sense of pride in the area. The interesting thing is that, at the very least, it is more than mediocre; that it is in whatever ways special, especially to the people who continue to occupy it, and even:

> 'I don't think we leave Manningham, we are Manningham. Our home would always be that, that's what we are. We are Manningham, and I'm Manningham. That's our birthright, our central thing, and when we go to Manningham, it's like we're coming home. I don't feel like I'm coming home when I come to Heaton. When I go to Manningham, that's the place where I belong. I really feel a sense of oneness with that place....This is just the place where I live. I don't

feel I belong here. I don't feel anything special about this.'
(M1, late 40s male, Heaton)

Residence, diversity and change

It is clear from our data that the streets of Manningham mean very different things to different residents and to those who are merely passing through. It is clear that for some residents, Manningham is a locale where the history of the collective settlement over time of 'people like them' has given Manningham a specific affective sense of belonging. Thus, for some of our respondents of Pakistani heritage, Manningham in its current form is experienced as a terrain that is imbued with a sense of collective ownership of the neighbourhood. It is a presence that is experienced in relation to a shared history and a significant current infrastructure of culturally appropriate shops and services. In this sense, it reflects Amin's (2012) concern with the role of *material attachments* within an environment in shaping the experience of connectedness. The appreciation of the familiarity of their locale is made real through a subliminal appreciation of the fact that this was not always the case, and that in other neighbourhoods in Bradford, this is still most certainly not the case. For such individuals, Manningham has the virtues of a valued 'created' home ground. Its particular ethnic profile – which includes demographic, infrastructural and cultural features – is a shared achievement, with its own histories and explicit territorial parameters. As such, it can be seen as a distinctive neighbourhood whose valued integrity may not be taken for granted, and that, consequently, may be subject to threat and unwelcome change. In this regard, we have evidence of members of the Pakistani population of Manningham having acute sensitivities to changes in its character. Specifically, for example, the relatively recent arrival of incomers from Eastern Europe has provoked, for some, a sense of violation of the dominant ethnic contours of life in the area. A successful Pakistani businessman who has lived in Manningham all his life expressed the view that:

'You just have to walk around, especially down Whetley Lane now…. That whole neighbourhood is becoming Eastern European. You just see them walking around. So, I think that they are having the same kind of experiences that our parents had when they first came in – not knowing the language, doing odd jobs for Asian businessmen now. There's a certain resentment going on: which at the moment, there's a lid on it.' (A16)

Despite his sense of appreciation of their difficulties as recent immigrants, and an appreciation of the similarity of their experience with that of his parental generation, he is still able to produce a pretty damning stereotype of the new Eastern European population:

> 'They look different, you can tell even though most of them look English the way they dress, you know, they're always huddled together, always together. They're crossing the road together and they have this sense of lack of purpose and they're standing around doing nothing.' (A16)

Another Pakistani male in his 40s who had established a successful business spoke eloquently of his affection for Manningham and then broke into a long litany of problems associated with the arrival of Eastern European migrants in his area. He spoke with feeling about how their children played out on the streets and were noisy, of how they sat out late at night drinking, of how they had loud parties, and of how all of this was making him think that he might have to leave Manningham. However, he then said: "That's how you lot used to talk about us" – a recognition of a common experience, and memory, of having been newly arrived migrants.

Additionally, a young female Pakistani community worker, reflecting upon the response to Eastern European migration, reported that:

> 'I think to a degree – especially, for some reason, with a lot of young people – they feel that they own this area now, and even though they've been told, or their parents were told for so long, 'You don't belong here, go back to where you came from' … they feel kind of like these Polish people have come into our community and this is our community, for some people.' (A12)

However, she is careful to qualify this view, arguing that:

> 'However, I think because we've built such a diverse community, it hasn't been so much of a problem, and its just a sense of intrigue and more of a media narrative that the Polish are taking our jobs, so then its our turn to turn on the Polish because we're used to people turning on us. But, generally, I think we are [all] quite comfortable here.' (A12)

A single white male resident of Manningham also reflected on the recent changed demography of his area, stating "round here, it's become slightly more ethnically diverse really because of the new influx of the East European population" (T2). However, he is a self-defined liberal and has a multi-ethnic friendship network. His sanguine response to this new development is framed by placing this recent change in the context of the history of Manningham:

> 'I mean, this area of Bradford always has had a large immigrant population and, you know, there's been like the Lithuanian clubs and Hungarian clubs and Russian. A lot of these little social clubs have disappeared, but, yes, there's always been for a long time, you know, some sort of immigration from somewhere coming into the area.' (T2)

He is himself an immigrant into the area and in accepting the established 'tradition' of Manningham as a place of social flux, he sees the new arrival of the Eastern European migrants as a current instance of an established phenomenon. Of course, not all established residents shared this perspective and some were happy to express clear resentment at what is perceived to be a large East European presence within their area, a view exemplified by a white, male pensioner, who said:

> 'Believe it or not, the houses you saw coming up on the right-hand side, they are, believe it or not, a lot of foreigners. I shouldn't say this – what's the proper word – foreign nationals live there. Poles, Ukraines, you name it – they all live there…. But some of the people in this country feel, not just residents, they feel they are getting away with everything these foreign nationals. Why should they? I've had to work all my life for what I've got.' (T7)

It is clear that change can be perceived as problematic for an ethnically grounded, and defended, status quo, or it can be seen as a de facto social reality within which there may be both change and continuity. One elderly, white male resident, who very much liked living in Manningham, provided an interesting case study that echoed the consideration of the streetscape and toponymy from Chapter Two. He observed that:

> 'Well, I've worked here for 42 years and I've seen the whole demographic development really. Because, if you looked at,

for instance, the streets round here and the shops – they've changed enormously, so that now they're all geared into the Asian culture, whereas at the time when we first came here, they were all the sort of shops that probably I grew up with. Barber shop, fish and chip shops; actually fish and chips is a great leveller. There's a fish shop down the street called Vitties, and it was kept by some folks. They sold out to some Asian proprietors, and they kept the name on, of course: Vitties. There's a shoe shop up the road called Ackroyd's, but it's an Asian one; there's a chemist called Shakespeare, and that has an Asian proprietor.' (T3)

For this resident, the change in the area is marked by a continuity in both signage and, importantly, usage. There are many examples of shops and other spaces having a similar trajectory of usage but it has to be borne in mind that the change is driven by changing demographics: culture and identity, in some regards, underpinned by economic/ commercial dynamics. An area's changing demography dictates the market and that, in turn, responds to the (new, but growing) demand of the (new, but growing) consumer base. It is no surprise, therefore, that in parts of Bradford and elsewhere throughout the UK, there are countless specialist 'ethnic' outlets/stores. In some cases, the nature of the new specialist wares does form a discontinuity. The larger and more noticeable disruption in usage, however, occurs when the purpose of one space is replaced with a new purpose. In Manningham and its surrounding areas, for example, there are many examples of this having occurred over the last 50 years, including end-terraced houses converted into shops, churches becoming furniture outlets and even bingo halls and pubs becoming places of religious worship and instruction. What is important here is that these are concrete examples of a changing landscape that, for the most part, certainly in the Bradford context, appear to have become accepted with relative ease.

The historical pattern of settlement, discussed earlier, for many Pakistani residents of Manningham, has provided not only a neighbourhood in which they can sense the nurturing, and protective, presence of co-religionists and people with shared history and culture, but also a neighbourhood in which close familial ties are replicated in the proximity of family members in the same street and neighbourhood. Thus, the double bonds of family and culture, which were once rehearsed as the valued characteristics of traditional white working-class communities, have been a distinctive feature of the Pakistani communities' experience of Manningham. Generational changes in the normative claims of the *biraderi* and individual variations in class mobility have provided a basis for introducing new dynamics into the cohesive pull of these established values and practices. As Simpson (2004, 2007) has shown, the internal class dynamics within the Pakistani community have created a flow of more affluent members of the Pakistani community from inner-city areas of Bradford like Manningham to more affluent and ethnically mixed areas. However, increased affluence has not proved to be an irresistible force driving individuals and families from their home in Manningham. The continuing attractions of neighbourhood and family proximity palpably remain strong reasons for continued residence in the area, irrespective of generational changes in affluence and status. As the chapter on the presence of the car will show, there are notable instances of 'high-end' cars parked outside traditional Manningham terraced houses. For members of the Pakistani population resident in Manningham, these features of the ward, and of their specific neighbourhood within it, makes it their chosen and valued place of residence.

Importantly, it is precisely this predominant Muslim/South Asian ambiance of Manningham that has made it so attractive to some members of the majority white population. Such individuals fit rather well the loose definition of *cosmopolitans* (Appiah, 2007): being people who actively wish to live in an area that is multi-ethnic and that provides them with the possibility to live within a social environment in which any notion of *their* cultural hegemony is routinely disrupted. They thrive on the daily negotiation of difference and explicitly value the possibility of moving through a culturally diverse environment.

One older white female resident who positively relished living in Manningham commented that "People who come and do studies and write books and things; they all think they've got it, and none of them have because it's so fluid. And I mean that's what so joyful about it; it's a fluid place" (A15). A older white male who positively loved living in Manningham proclaimed that "This is the most wonderful place we've lived in by far … it's been extremely positive moving here" (A17).

The social dynamics revealed in the last three sections of this chapter are highly consistent with an established trajectory of work on multi-ethnic inner-city neighbourhoods (Keith and Pile, 1993; Back, 1996; Eade, 1997; Westwood and Williams, 1997), in which the space–time transformations of transnational identities are grounded in the lived experience of specific locales. Despite the significance of transnational linkages and diasporic identities among the residents of Manningham, their presence in a city and neighbourhood has an anchoring reality in their lives. In the words of Durrschmidt (1997: 64): 'People's extended "fields of action" are still woven around significant places, where their daily routines are focused, providing a localised kind of situatedness.' Consistently with other contemporary literature, the significance of place and space for the residents of Manningham is not a given, but an ongoing negotiation of historicity, identity and the opportunity structure of their lives there.

Gendered space and the relationship of experience and framing discourse

For some individuals of a cosmopolitan disposition, the determined aspiration to live in a multi-ethnic area has not proved to be possible because specific facets of their identity – in particular, their gender – have proved to be an uncomfortable fit with some of the social dynamics of Manningham. The recorded accounts of a few young women speak directly and strongly of their experience of sexism on the streets of Manningham, and elsewhere in Bradford. Writing in the context of a recent political and media furore over the 'grooming' of young white women by 'predatory Pakistani men', this is a topic that requires careful analysis. Perhaps we should first provide some account of the nature of their experiences. One respondent, who usually lives overseas but spent three months doing fieldwork in Bradford for this project, recorded how she experienced the way in which her person was routinely sexualised in Bradford as shocking in comparison to her ability to walk through the streets of her current home town with no such intrusion upon her sense of identity. In this section, I will draw upon this work extensively, as it brings together not only her own experience, but also that of the other females she interviewed and encountered during her fieldwork. Of her own experience, she reports that:

> 'If we think of comfort as a relationship of power in a social setting, the fact that the majority of women I have spoken to admitted that they (myself included) often feel uncomfortable because of being commented and stared at by men – mostly Asian and black and sometimes white – is quite disturbing. Harassment was something I personally experienced almost on a daily basis.'

This is an account that was powerfully echoed in the experience of a white young professional woman in her 30s who had deliberately chosen to live in Manningham because of her cosmopolitan values and her active engagement in intercultural community political action in the area. She found the extent of sexual harassment by young Asian men to be so intolerable that despite her political commitment and deeply held values, she felt that she was forced to leave the area. A young Polish woman experienced the impact of this sexist male behaviour when she lived on Oak Lane. She records that:

> 'For two months, I was living on Oak Lane and it was like I was going for a pizza or something like that – so, you know, they're shouting. *Even if I was dressed in my trousers.* It was only two o'clock [14.00 hrs] when I went there, you know!' (T4, emphasis in original)

These are disturbing direct accounts of gender power on the streets and introduce a layer of interpersonal dynamics that run counter to the benign account of the physical streetscape presented previously. The young researcher's further discussion of this experience serves to remind us of the intersectionality of identities discussed earlier, as it is clear that it is not a female identity alone that shapes the nature of such sexist behaviour. This young researcher was female, in her late 20s, slim and blond, and as her account reveals, other females might have to negotiate different facets of the interaction of their gender, ethnicity and age:

> 'Most of the time, I was walking around by myself, with no other friends, whereas I would always see young Polish women walking in groups or with their partners. In any case, I could clearly feel that a white woman walking alone in the streets of Manningham attracted attention as something odd to see and when I would pop into a restaurant on Lumb Lane at around 2–3pm after my walks and there would be only men sitting inside, I clearly felt I was not supposed to be there. There was no adversity, but there were constant stares questioning my presence there. Being a woman, alone, white and East European-looking singled me out.' [Note: that is a self-definition of the researcher; this white male British writer would have comfortably perceived her as a young English woman.]
>
> 'I was a body that did not belong there, I did not fit in. Neither did I fit in the Asian jewellery and clothes shops in Manningham, which were somewhat in the domain of women: other female customers, especially older ones, stared at me with quite serious faces. Meanwhile, my Pakistani

friend admitted whenever she was planning to go to Asian clothes or jewellery shops, she would think carefully what to wear before going there and choose traditional Pakistani clothes; otherwise, she would feel uncomfortable and people would stare at her. So, whether it was shopping in Asian stores or visiting her friends in "Asian areas" (Girlington), she would always wear something traditional so that men harass her less.'

This brief account opens up the nature of gendered interaction dramatically. Clearly, it is not only gender, but also skin colour and perceived ethnicity/nationality that, in interaction, shape the range of responses attracted. A young '*Asian*' woman wearing 'traditional clothing' in Manningham might attract less sexualised comment than one who chose to wear the contemporary fashion of the majority population. This researcher, as a white woman, clearly attracted a lot of unwelcome sexist comment and behaviour from men, but also constituted an anomalous presence to 'Asian' women within *their* shops. Yet, another of our white female respondents, who was also a committed cosmopolitan with an explicit commitment to living in Manningham, reported that she never felt threatened walking the streets of Manningham.

This older white resident presented an account of why such behaviour may occur, couched in the language of a trans-cultural understanding of South Asian expectations of decency suggesting that, 'Yes, I think there is a sort of predator male thing to do with young females depending on how the young female is dressed. You know, if they see it as being sexually provocative' (A15). Her own pleasure and ease in living in the same area she explained thus: 'Nobody would look at me kind of thing; so I'm quite happy. And I think its one of the joys of being an older person that you're not treading on people's toes' (A15). However, she was a lady in her 60s for whom age clearly qualified the other shared characteristics as being female, white, vital and attractive.

The concept of being potentially perceived as being 'sexually provocative' indicates a sensitivity to the cultural mores of the majority Pakistani/Muslim community who live in Manningham, providing a framework for female propriety in the area. There was, in fact, a wide awareness of this phenomenon among our female respondents, and a wide willingness to seek to work within its requirements. However, some of the interviews also seem to indicate an intersection between the criterion of proper dress and the independent variable of being a known member of your neighbourhood. The young white woman who felt compelled to leave Manningham because of the experience of sexist behaviour towards her, and because of forms of random violence, also had a friendship network with members of her neighbourhood Pakistani community that afforded her significant degrees of particular inclusion. Interviews with young Muslim Pakistani female community workers showed a similar range of considerations in play in relation to their presence in Manningham. They situate the behaviour they experience in Manningham within the wider patriarchy of Bradford as a whole. Speaking of sexist behaviour on the streets, one said:

> 'I think that it's in Bradford. I don't think it's specific to Manningham because if you walk around Bradford and whatever area in Bradford, whether it's an Asian young man or a white young man, it's the same thing. I don't know whether it's just Bradford or other cities are exactly the same, but it's throughout Bradford. I think if you live within that community, you don't have that issue; but, again, when you are an outsider and you're something slightly different within that community, that's when that sort of whistling and, you know, shouting at a girl.' (A12)

In the following statement, she makes clear the distinction between wearing appropriate dress and between being in your local area in terms of their independent impact upon the degree of harassment:

> 'Within the Asian Muslim communities, when we walk through an area, it's not as bad as when somebody who doesn't wear a headscarf would; but it's not that we don't [experience harassment], we have, but it's less likely to happen because we wear headscarves. I think within the community we live in, it doesn't really happen; but if I went into another Asian community, or I went into another white community, then it's more likely to happen because they don't know me; so, therefore, it's OK to make comments because it's not going to go back to somebody I know, because I don't know who they are. But I think it's not just specific to Manningham.' (A12)

These interviews reveal that overlaid upon the preponderantly Pakistani streetscape of Manningham, which we explored earlier, there is a behavioural code that is heavily informed by the Pakistani/Muslim values of the dominant community, which are themselves linked to wider, and often more subtle, patriarchal structures and values. This, in itself, links back to the question of territory and identity and the legitimacy of the claims that one member of the area can make upon another. It is because Manningham has evolved as a predominantly Muslim terrain, within a city where the settlement of this community was characterised by marginalisation and struggle, that the ownership of this area is seen in terms of possessive territorial claims by its majority ethnic, Pakistani, population. The literature that we explored in Chapter Two relating to housing preference showed the significance of concerns with security and ethnic infrastructure. Everything we have seen about the motivations of Pakistani people to remain in Manningham supports this view that there is an affective association with this area as one that they have historically shaped, and that they currently see as being distinctively 'a comfort zone' compared to other areas of Bradford. Therefore, the reality of the strong claims to ownership of the area in terms of regulating its streetscape rests upon a strong shared conviction of the legitimacy of this behaviour. Fenster (2005b) provides examples from Israel and London where similar intersections of ethnicity, gender and a territorialised sense of local norms inform the patriarchal encroachment upon the lives of women as they go about their business on the streets of the neighbourhood. The fact that the regulation of women's lives in public life by patriarchal power, typically mediated through specific ethnic/class cultural mores, is widely evident in the research literature (MacMillan et al, 2000), may make the findings here relatively unsurprising, but their significance for people's lives remains to be recognised and discussed in the concluding chapter.

Young men in context

Across the interview data, the respondents frequently offer explanatory accounts for the circumstances that they experience in Manningham; this is equally true of their experience of young men in their neighbourhood. M12, for example, gives context and a not-unreasonable analysis as to why and how social relations across the generations have developed as they have:

> 'I think the kids nowadays know a lot more what's going on around them than we did, because we had that routine when we were set to go to school, after that go to the mosque and if it's summer long sort of days, we'd go for a game of cricket, football, even tennis sometimes. And nowadays, the kids have got, we never watched as much television in comparison

to what kids do nowadays, the decent ones, the ones that stay at home and stay indoors, they'll be watching telly or playing computers, the ones that have got mates outside, the ones that hang around streets, they're obviously getting up to no good anyway. Even the teachings on television I completely disagree with so many things, there's so many messages in there in watching television that it affects.' (M12, 33 years old, Pakistani male)

Another respondent, speaking of sexual harassment of women in Manningham, stated that:

'I would say that it's probably exaggerated to a certain degree, but equally not dismissing the fact that I'm sure harassment does take place, but I would say that would probably happen across most of the areas across the district....

'I would say that inevitably you will get fractions or you will get groups of lads hanging around on street corners with nothing better to do.' (A8)

However, as a professional Asian woman, she also linked this to "the times that we are living in": with "high levels of unemployment, low education attainment, lack of basic respect and lack of parenting, I guess, and the lack of respect within the home that then translates onto the streets" (A8). However, she clearly saw this as symptomatic of contemporary urban life, rather than being a unique feature of young Muslim Asian men in Manningham.

Similarly, a number of older interviewees, both male and female, discussed what they perceived to be an appropriation of a 'gangster' or 'thug' identity by young Pakistani men especially. Not infrequently portrayed as aggressive, or as criminally minded, this is yet another variation in a long line of 'folk devils', where ethnicity, class and generation combine to form a potent threat. A resident who has lived in Manningham for his whole life complained of crime as a general fact of life, as well as the risks posed to his young family. A theme that recurred throughout the interviews was reference to the salience and impact of drugs. In M7's case:

'Well, the issue I have is that the area we have at this moment in time, we have issues with drugs, we have issues with graffiti, crime ... the problem is that a lot of the children that go to the school now, they are either involved in gangland war, crime, graffiti, drugs you know … I may well have to move out of the Asian community now to go to primarily or 50% at least white, for example, like Shipley or Bingley or towards Haworth Road, Sandy Lane, Cottingley, so that, yes, you've still got the links with the Asian community and I'll always have the links with my mum and my brothers, my nephews and nieces, but however they're not getting their ears filled in all the time by these negative images.' (M7, 40 years old, Pakistani male, Manningham)

More broadly in Britain, there has been a strong series of associations between crime and violence with ethnicity and gender. Young black and Asian working-class men in particular continue to be demonised as a group guilty of anti-social behaviour due to their involvement in gangs, street crime and car crime, as well as knife and gun crime. These powerful associations between young people and violence, real or perceived, remain items of 'news' reportage, whether it is the occasional instance of 'black on black' violence or the dangers posed to society by the wearing of hoodies. With a long history in urban folk lore, violence has once again become racialised, now in the stereotypical form of a commonly feared folk devil: the young, Pakistani Muslim Male. This is one powerful variant of several that represent – and, in some ways, epitomise – all that is wrong with especially working-class inner-city Britain and the failings of multiculturalism (see, eg, Alexander, 2004; Husband and Alam, 2011).

Although many of the interviews referred to the broader problem of 'failing youth', or to young people lacking opportunities in education and employment, there was nevertheless a capacity to recognise the folk devil within the real world: young men, albeit in a minority, possess the capacity to be perceived as carriers of social threat and, in some cases, violence. However, for most, this grounded vision differed quite markedly from the world as it is represented through reportage, fiction and other sources of information. There is a sense of proportionality in very many of the comments that are made by residents, who distinguish between the concrete instances of problematic individuals and the wider stereotype of a cohort of antisocial young Muslim men.

In all youth cultures, there has been the generation of a current style that young people may employ to distinguish themselves as a unique cohort in relation to others defined by, for example, age, gender, class or sexual preference. So, too, in Mannigham, in association with a claiming of territory that we noted earlier, there can be found examples of an assertive *machismo* that owes a lot to pop and media cultural influences.

Not all young Pakistani men are threatening, and very often those who appear to be, only *appear to be*. That is, machismo, adopting the 'gangster' walk and talk, are largely elements of performance. The forms and shapes of these performances are a reflection, in part, of media influence (eg the prominence of hip hop/thug life culture was also reflected upon in many interviews), as well as reflecting, in some ways, a romanticised connection with the 'ghettos' of Los Angeles, New York and other hip hop heartlands. Given the salience of hip hop culture throughout the world, regardless of class, ethnicity and other markers of identity, the adaptation and adoption of an 'alien' *subculture* ought not to be seen as too remarkable (see Hesmondhalgh and Melville, 2002; Drissel, 2011). Indeed, it may only be because Manningham's Pakistani young men are packaged as problematic that the hip hop/gangster-inspired everyday social performances that may be encountered are an issue at all.

Conclusion

This chapter has revealed something of the many ways in which Manningham both has an existence as a place of everyday interaction – as people move through a physical environment that both constrains and facilitates the mundane business of being in the social world – and provides the locale, with its particular historicity, for the necessary engagement with the process of sustaining meaning in that world. The perpetual interface between the individual pursuit of the daily tasks of making a living, going to school or to a place of entertainment, or going shopping, and experiencing this in relation to group-based identities that provide a framework of meaning and expectations for the interactions that consequently arise is apparent everywhere. Manningham, within Bradford, has a salient repertoire of historically layered conceptions of its character that are actively reaffirmed, or self-consciously negated, by its inhabitants as they bring their understanding of the relevance and virtues of living there to bear on their daily experience of interaction. Across the interviews, we have seen evidence of the importance of a positive affective bond with the area in shaping individuals' experience of living there. The nature of these bonds can differ quite dramatically. For an older cosmopolitan, Manningham is the terrain on which their political and aesthetic commitments can be validated in practice. For members of the Asian population of Manningham, a familial, and personal, biographic connection to the area is framed by a particular understanding of the historical *making* of this area as an area of Pakistani settlement. Additionally, Manningham is understood in a dialogic relationship with the areas of Bradford in which individuals feel that they would not – could not – live, and areas to which they might prefer to move.

In the daily flux of movement between the routine destinations of everyday life in the area, multiple interactions take place. The very great majority of these take place within the over-rehearsed activities of a personal daily routine. Included in this routine are the ossified patterns of shopping in particular shops, going to and from specific schools, or going to and from work. Shared neighbourhood norms frame these interactions and provide a framework for facilitating a capacity to 'rub along together'. The many occasions on which this fusion of patterns of behaviour and normative framework synchronise provide the basis for confirming the viability of coexistence within this multi-ethnic area. On those occasions when interaction is perceived as jarring, unpleasant or directly abusive, the impact of such an event stands out in strong comparison to the routine de facto banality of coexistence. While these interactions may be between individuals, we have been clear in wishing to assert the significance of the availability of strong social categories – ethnic and religious labels, age and gender categories, class and status attributions – which, when mobilised, can shift the perception of events from having relevance as an expression of individual personality and style to a perception of the opposition of group interests that have a history of contestation within the area. This is a reality that has very considerable significance in shaping the possibility of shared *civility* within an area like Manningham. The implications of these findings will be developed more fully in Chapter Seven.

CHAPTER SIX

The car, the streetscape and inter-ethnic dynamics

Introduction

> **Respondent:** 'Me and my mate, we've both got the same car. Almost exactly the same – same year, same spec and same colour, but mine's better than his.'
>
> **Interviewer:** 'Yeah? If they're both the same, then how's yours better?'
>
> **Respondent:** 'Cos it's mine.'

Through drawing on a range of qualitative research, this chapter explores the often complex and occasionally curious relationships we have with cars, and links this to the experience of living within and moving through ethnically demarcated urban spaces. Part of this involves the extent to which cars connote meaning not only about the individual behind the wheel, but also about the 'group' that appears to drive the kind of car in question. As such, the car can help us to see and understand the dynamics of in-group–out-group relations and culture more broadly. In the context of this book, the car has proved to be an irresistible theme within the developing story of this research inasmuch as it emerges as a pervasive presence in the multi-ethnic dynamics of Bradford and Manningham. Part of the story rests in the rich texture of meanings that car ownership has for some of Bradford's Pakistanis. It is a physical presence that has the capacity to trigger acute moments of inter-ethnic sensibility that may be characterised by envy, suspicion, resentment and anger, each with the associated attribution of legitimating beliefs about the character and intentions of the car driver/owner.

The car as object and symbol

The car, described by Sheller and Urry (2000:738) as the 'quintessential manufactured object', carries a lot of symbolic meaning. This mass-produced object, through specific companies and particular models, can provide a concrete expression of national pride and identity, with subsequent expressions of national tropes and stereotypes: engineering skill (German – Audi, BMW, Mercedes Benz); design flair (Italian – Alfa Romeo, Lancia); democratic accessibility (French – Renault, Peugeot); or valued consumer goods (British – Jaguar, Range Rover). Car ownership has been desired for its pragmatic utility and its material expression of affluence and status, and it has been integral to the emergence of distinct lifestyle performative practices, such as cruising urban streets or the Sunday afternoon family rural excursion. In contemporary Britain, the car has been instrumental in a radical transformation of urban landscapes, with throughways bisecting communities, acres of land being given over to supermarkets and their car parks, and the routine congestion of local roads during peak transit times. The car is a frequent and highly salient element in the lived environment of many citizens – it has visibility and banal societal impact – 'But the way that the car has introduced new forms of social action in late modernity, thereby contributing to its distinctive nature, has not yet been the focus of serious sociological attention' (Dant, 2004: 61).

There are a few authors who might take offence at Dant's categorical assertion, but it remains the case that the car's significance in contemporary society is worthy of greater systematic attention. With this in mind, we seek to explore the car as a distinctive element within the complexities of inter-ethnic contact in Bradford. We note the literature on the synergistic relationship between driver and vehicle, not because this is an agenda we wish to particularly develop, but because it is essential in providing a basis for understanding the power of the car as an instrument of personal agency and collective identity. The phenomenon we seek to explore is not an ephemeral expression of advertising copy and over-learned urban myths about the car. It is significant precisely because of the *assemblage* of car and driver, because of the powerful ego involvement that may be associated with car ownership and usage:

> Automobility indeed constitutes a civil society of hybridized 'car–drivers', dwelling privately-within-their-cars, and excluding those without cars or without the 'licence' to drive from the car-dominated public realm. Such a civil society of automobility transforms public spaces into public roads, in which to a significant extent the hybrids of pedestrians, cyclists and even public transport users are marginalized. Only those moving (however slowly) in

private vehicles can be public within a system in which public roads have been seized by the 'auto-mobile' private citizens cocooned within their 'iron-cages'. (Sheller and Urry, 2003: 115)

As Edensor (2004) argues, all driving takes place within a specific cultural context, within which the element of national identity is important. In sketching the distinct *motoscapes* in Britain and India, he provides a contextualised account of the very different driving cultures that develop within these particular contexts. This leads him to argue that:

> driving is a culturally bound procedure organized around which manoeuvres, forms of etiquette and gestures of annoyance, for instance, are 'proper' in particular contexts. Once learned, not only are such practical norms unreflexively embodied but fellow-drivers monitor the driving performance of others through a disciplinary gaze which expresses rebuke if these communal conventions about driving performance are contravened. (Edensor, 2004: 112)

Thus, it is essential to frame the experience of driving in Bradford within a specific national, local and ethnically demarcated context. This is a context with a very evident external regulation of driving through a considerable body of relevant legal prohibition and an extensive armoury of signage and road furniture that seeks to regulate the behaviour of road users. Additionally, through nationally validated driving tests, there is an expectation of a minimum level of driving competence and familiarity with the normative expectations of the *Highway code*. Linked with this, there is, of course, a national-cultural aspect related to compliance with traffic legislation. British tourists overseas, for example, are often bemused by well-behaved pedestrians waiting for traffic lights to change in the absence of any traffic whatsoever, whereas in Britain, personal agency is typically seen as being appropriate in overriding a pure obedience to the law. Similarly, strict adherence to speed limits is not necessarily typical of British drivers. There is, in other words, a wide cultural accommodation that has come to overlay the formal rules of British traffic behaviour. These normative shared expectations of driving behaviour frame the interpretation of the behaviours of other drivers. While these expectations may be operative in the Bradford context, additionally, the power of race/ethnicity, as well as gender and age, remain pervasive and visible. Thus, there is also the possibility of subcultural mores further shaping the behaviour of particular cohorts of drivers. Sometimes, as with the mythic 'white-van man', collectivities are constructed around the perceived driving habits and lifestyles of specific vehicle users. Our study here explores both the possibility of an externally attributed identity such as 'young Asian men' and the possible existence of specific car-related identities within the population of young, and not so young, people in Bradford.

Culture and 'car culture'

Culture is fluid, its change oiled through evolutions in thought, technology and, of course, mobility itself. Migrations small and large, rapid and long-term, occasional and frequent all feed into where we are from and to where we are heading. Culture is as much about routes as it is roots (Creswell, 2006). We move in various ways and for various reasons, but in contemporary cities, much of this movement is aided through systems of transport that we take for granted and accept, though perhaps consider being in need of change. Today, cars are an integral aspect of our psychological, economic, physical, political and especially cultural discourse: we see our children interacting with car facsimiles in the world of play; in one way or another, we all pay towards maintaining the roads upon which cars live; we negotiate their presence in traffic as pedestrians or drivers; we may share a sense of angst or guilt about the damage they do to the environment; and we watch films in which characters depend upon their cars for making getaways, chasing criminals or even for the purpose of character development.[7] In one way or another, we interact with cars and their ongoing legacy on a daily basis.

As symbol, economic entity or merely a piece of machinery to be used pragmatically, the car has grown in relevance over the last 50 years and continues to make inroads across the globe. Partly, this has been

---

[7] A good example in which the latter becomes important is the 2009 film *Gran Torino*, directed by and starring Clint Eastwood. Although the film explores, in arguably simplistic and racialised/racialising terms, issues linked with ethnic diversity, the role of the car is significant as a marker of identity and ethnic difference. Eastwood's character, a white Anglo-Saxon Vietnam veteran named Walt, with his US-built Ford Gran Torino, serves as a foil against the newer, foreign Japanese cars, mostly driven by the neighbourhood's relatively new South East Asian Hmong community, itself comprised of first-generation immigrants and their second-generation children. For a fuller discussion of the film and its use of racial stereotypes, see Schein and Thoj (2010).

made possible by the relative decrease in the costs of car production and retail prices (Paterson, 2007: 95), while, at the same time, rises in income and individual cultural capital have helped to ensure that car ownership is 'enjoyed' by more people than ever. Furthermore, the global infrastructure devoted to the car, along with an array of 'forward/backward economic linkages'[8] with the car (Paterson, 2007: 96), continues to expand. Everything from drilling for crude oil (a backward linkage) to the production of drive-time radio (a series of forward linkages) is connected closely with the car. Furthermore, today, the state – through national governments – has little choice but to promote the economic, and thus cultural, social and political, presence of the car. Indeed, the car and its manufacture is the exemplar of capitalist production (Paterson, 2007: 92). Across the UK, the centrality of the car can be seen in the day-to-day management of cities and towns and their economies: law enforcement, traffic control and the health and safety of the populace are all aspects of management that, in large part, attend to the consequences of cars and motorised vehicles.

Alongside its passengers, the car carries a range of other connotations linked with class, gender, generation and, powerfully and complexly, ethnicity. At one level, the car is merely an object that facilitates transport, but it does have a myriad of layered meanings above and beyond the scope of transportation. Indeed, over the decades, the car has become even more acutely tied into the realm of popular culture and consumption (Miller, 2012) and is therefore a potent symbol that both flattens and homogenises identity on the one hand, and laces identity with very sophisticated levels of nuance and individuation, on the other. While the same model of car may roll off the production line in its thousands, car customisation, tuning and enhancement produces objects inscribed with distinctive, personal aesthetics and contemporary forms of working-class artisanship.[9]

Within some of our previous ethnographically grounded work with young Bradfordian Pakistani Muslim men (Alam, 2006; Alam

---

[8] This term refers to related infrastructure that enables, or is a consequence of, the car: the acquisition and production of items manufactured from steel, plastic and other materials all service the car in a backwards linkage, while filling stations, motor mechanics and spare parts dealers service the car in a forward linkage.

[9] See Warren and Gibson (2011) on their discussion of 'vernacular' and 'blue-collar creativity', and Bengry-Howell and Griffin (2007) on the individualised discourse of consumption evident among working-class male car modifiers.

and Husband, 2006), a regular feature and topic of discussion was the significance of and meanings associated with car ownership. For some, a 'nice' car was important, not only as a symbol of personal economic success, but also as a means of expressing identity: car manufacturer, model and the presence of after-market modifications resulted in either a high- or low-value commodity as defined by an 'imagined' community of drivers, with its attendant tastes and preferences. At the same time, several of those who prided themselves on modifying their vehicles, and, in some cases, owning unadulterated prestige or sports vehicles, were fully aware that doing so attracted particular attention from members of the local community or the police. Often, such car owners were conscious of the risk of being labelled as, or perceived to be, corrupt or criminal (drugs-related crime being cited most often), an idea that remains prevalent today:

> 'In Bradford, it [the Range Rover model] does have that gangster image, so a few people have said to me: "Why you driving a gangster car for? You should have a respectable car." I mean, what is a respectable car? The gangsters have them all! Everything what you drive in Bradford, above a certain price tag, it's a gangster car.' (SJ, early 30s, Pakistani Bradfordian male)

This quote strongly illustrates how the car seems to represent and reflect, and can become an extension of, the driver's identity without the driver doing anything other than occupying the vehicle. Once this association becomes embedded within a public sphere of whatever depth and reach, the capacity to link all drivers of the same type with all cars of the same type becomes realised and feeds back into the cycle of representation, association and knowledge making.

Cars and their representations are ubiquitous: as toys, as objects and subjects of art, and in advertising as well as mass media more generally. Cars continue to be evocative of freedom, autonomy and independence (Gilroy, 2001; Thacker, 2006; Paterson, 2007) and increasingly somehow speak about group and individual identity, whether this is associated with class, ethnicity or gender.[10] The connections between the car and identity are made meaningful through normative channels of socialisation, as well as more complex and often mediated routes that establish norms and values. Tragos (2009: 542), for example, argues that US shows such as *Monster Garage*, in which the presence of the car is central, represent 'a nostalgic desire for traditional masculine identities'. In Britain, of course, there are also TV shows, as well as rows of magazines and pages of newspapers, devoted to the car in all its forms, which echo a similar reclamation of masculinity. The BBC's motoring programme for over three decades, *Top Gear*, is presently introduced by three men, including the proudly traditional and uber-masculine Jeremy Clarkson, who, along with his co-presenters, continue to ensure that the domain of mediated car culture remains largely white and male-dominated. His status as one of the most highly paid BBC presenters of a programme that celebrates speed, style and excess[11] is an unobtrusive statement about the place that the car holds in the British male psyche.

Car manufacturers, advertisers and retailers have developed a highly refined system of language and symbolism to 'package' specific cars for specific consumer clusters defined by purchasing power and lifestyle aspirations. A sports car and a multi-purpose vehicle may cost the same, for example, but they will have very different symbolic value. Within the many expressions of 'car culture' (Miller, 2001a), the capacity for creating coherent subcultures are legion. For example:

---

[10] Class: a Citroen Saxo with performance and aesthetic enhancements, including Burberry motif paintwork, connotes a particular class taste when compared with an unadulterated Bentley Continental. Ethnicity: certainly in the 1970s and 1980s, BMWs were somewhat stereotypically associated with black males (for more discussion on 'ethnic taste', an area we do explore in due course, see later). Gender: one of the most obvious means of identifying gender is through colour scheme and, to some extent, texture: pink, fluffy things on the parcel shelf can strongly suggest a an owner/driver who projects feminine and female characteristics. Indeed, there are even some particular cars that are stereotypically defined, often by males, as those more suited to females ('girlies'/'chicks') usually because of their lacking performance and looks (eg the new VW Beetle, Ford Ka, Mini Cooper, Audi TT). The importance of stereotypes in all these schemes, of course, runs deep, to the point of inducing bias and discrimination along the markers of identity, and corresponding behaviours/traits, that each vehicle type represents/connotes.

[11] While issues linked with fuel economy and general fuel sustainability are occasionally discussed, such topics are often relegated to fleeting, light-hearted and sometimes disparaging commentary.

> Around each specialist or classic type of car a whole world
> develops with its own form of specialist knowledge and
> publications, practices and argot, which seek to explore
> and define the details of car anatomy, 'look', styling, image
> and ride. A world which offers the pleasures of common
> knowledge and distinctive classifications, which work with
> shared embodied habitus and membership, through car talk
> as much as car driving. (Featherstone, 2004: 14)

As Featherstone notes, the activity of such car subcultures is realised
through talk as much as through driving itself. It is through such talk that
the salience of specific elements of a car is defined and given legitimacy,
and behavioural expectations and characteristics are elaborated and
policed. 'Off-road' driving requires at least a persuasive attempt to tell
tales of rugged terrain negotiated, whilst the family estate provides an
invitation to elaborate upon the unlikely shape and amount of loads
it has accommodated. To the extent that car ownership operates as
a basis for group identity, that group must have a dynamic that goes
beyond the mere possession of a shared category of 'owner of an X or Y
vehicle' (on the dangers of 'groupness', see Brubaker, 2004). Ownership
of a Ford or of a BMW does not necessarily make you a member of
a distinctive group, but if you have a *specific type* of BMW, and if you
have customised it in a *specific way* or have a very specific (and relatively
rare) variant/model, then you may well be claiming a *distinctive identity*.
Thus, in the context of Bradford, it is necessary to demonstrate the
existence of specific, collectively shared understandings of car ownership
in relation to, and cross-referenced with, ethnic/age/gender/class-based
identities. The car's capacity to be an expressive *vehicle* for collective
identities may be a matter of widespread 'common knowledge', but,
in this argument, it also requires ethnographic support.

In the context of this book, this chapter explores the power of the
car as a symbolic presence at the very heart of the everyday experience
of multi-ethnic coexistence. We will primarily explore the potential
significance of car ownership among members of the Pakistani/
Muslim population in Bradford, and, in a complementary manner, the
impact that minority ethnic car ownership can have on inter-group
relations. While the book focuses upon Manningham, in this chapter,
we will perforce develop our general argument about the presence of
the car in Bradford as a whole in order to outline the multiple layers
of significance that can be inscribed upon car ownership. Indeed, it
is not merely car ownership that gives such *personalisation* of the car
a potential for collective group affiliation and inter-group posturing,

but the multiple ways in which a car can become affectively developed as an extension of individual identities, and how the semiotic space within which such meanings can be developed as a shared semiotic code (for an introduction to some of the elements of the dynamic of social identity and inter-group dynamics, see Capozza and Brown, 2000).

The research background: a brief review of relevant literature

Given that cars are firmly embedded within everyday life, it seems odd that more in-depth social research around car usage, culture and significance more broadly has not been undertaken. While there is extensive writing around the origins, development and chequered life of the car, the nature of the literature has ranged greatly, including: the ups and downs of the UK's car manufacturing sector (Adeney, 1988; Wood, 1988; Whisler, 1999); the systematic approaches within Japanese car production (Kamata, 1982); the impact of globalisation, along with the opportunities and challenges it presents to manufacturers (Humphrey et al, 2000); the potential development of non-fossil-fuel-driven vehicles (Westbrook, 2001); and the growth and nature of car and car-related crime (Light et al, 1993; Browne, 2001; Corbett, 2003; Kellet and Gross, 2006). There are also cultural theorists who explore how the car and its associates resonate and tie in with contemporary popular culture. For example, Thacker's (2006) work on the car/oil/war subtext within *The Big Lebowski* is fascinating and offers insights into the nexus-like relationships between the car, the state and consumption. The broader range of present social science literature is largely theoretically driven and, generally speaking, tends to lack the voice of car and road users (whether pedestrians, motorists or car enthusiasts).[12] This chapter, however, aims to address this gap.

Of the writers who have nevertheless written extensively on and around the car while remaining attentive to how automobility is experienced, John Urry (2000, 2004, 2006, 2007; see also Sheller and Urry, 2000, 2003; Dennis and Urry, 2009) and Daniel Miller (2001b, 2012) have fed into the development of an interdisciplinary/'post-disciplinary' (sociology, anthropology, geography, cultural studies, social policy) approach in which the study of cars is framed, in part, by culture, globalisation, sustainability and consumption. Sheller and Urry's (2003) work exploring how a 'sociology of mobilities' can help explain the

---

[12] While there are some texts that do include the voice of the user, these are usually mainstream and may not require the strength of sociological insight in achieving their aims.

forces that are redefining the boundaries of public and private life is both interesting and relevant. Contemporary mobilities include the concrete and physical (the car, public transport and any actual movement of our bodies), but also refer to those aspects of transport that are increasingly becoming abstract and virtual (eg in the form of digital communications technology). It is with some attention to this broad, but still growing, area, and through its fluid methodologies, that we situate our discussion. It is worth asserting that a large aspect of this chapter draws on a flexible and active notion of consumption helpfully alluded to by Miller, whose position is outlined thus: 'Rather than seeing consumers as the merely passive end point of economic activity, I argue that they actively transform the world. They too see both the negative and positive consequences of consumption and have their own critiques' (Miller, 2012: 39–40).

Miller's in-depth appraisal of consumption includes reference to a range of contemporary popular artefacts. From meanings associated with soft drinks to the economic and cultural scope of the car upholstery sector in Trinidad, his analysis makes links with the ways in which objects have connotations with ethnicity and class. Indeed, a structural element of his narrative is the historicism of ethnic heritage and how it continues to play out in present-day Trinidad. The different meanings afforded to the different types of drink ('red' or 'black') can be traced to the real and metaphorical routes that the original migrant (slave/labour-oriented) communities had taken to reach Trinidad. The taste in soft drinks held by Indo-Trinidadians, whose presence in Trinidad is connected with the colonial system of indentured labour, is different to Afro-Trinidadian taste, whose heritage is linked with slavery. While there is a suggestion that this variance in taste is somehow connected to the very nature of the routes themselves, what is also relevant, however, are the ways and extent to which these markers feed further into the construction and perpetuation of what group (ethnic) identity entails:

> There is today the red sweet drink and the black sweet drink. The red drink is the quintessential sweet drink in as much as it is considered by consumers to be the drink highest in sugar content. The Indian population is generally assumed to be particularly fond of sugar and sweet products. This in turn is supposed to relate to their entry into Trinidad largely as indentured labourers in the sugar cane fields. They are also thought to have a high rate of diabetes, which folk wisdom claims to be a result of their over-indulgence of these preferences. (Miller, 2012: 44)

In much the same way, one element of our broader concern here is to assert and illustrate how cars also have the capacity to become rich with meanings and connotations linked with both class and ethnicity, which, while underscored by variances in taste, can be seen within the 'motoscape' of a multicultural city such as Bradford. At a very fundamental level, this can be interpreted to be a repetition of the oft-cited claim that cars can carry and project high or low status. The car, as a consumer object, therefore 'embodies a cultural logic that is relatively autonomous from and often contradictory to other dimensions of automobility' (Gartman, 2004: 169). Furthermore, cars offer much richer and more vibrant forms of data that connect with issues linked with the realms of economy, employment and identity, as well as aspiration, leisure, conflict and art (Warren and Gibson, 2011), and with a range of human emotions that the car facilitates and conveys (Sheller, 2004).

Cars in their social context

Amy Best's (2006) work provides insights into the ways in which class, gender, ethnicity and generation inform and develop attitudes towards the car. While her work is based in the US (San Jose, California), it holds rich ethnographic data that, perhaps unusually, can be related to distant geographical research sites. One of the reasons why she decided to locate her ideas around cars was because they 'provided a way into the worlds occupied by young people' (Best, 2006: 3). Similarly, Warren and Gibson's (2011) examination of car customisation situates the salience of class, and especially the nexus of connections between 'blue-collar' occupations with creativity, in an Australian (Wollongong) context.

For us, there is a similar concern with younger people and the car as an equally appropriate means that can be used to tap into their experiences. Like many material artefacts, cars have the capacity to confer status, but they can also conversely mask or distort aspects of an individual's, or group's, identity and position. For example, this and earlier research we conducted indicates that some spend what seems to be a disproportionately large amount of their income/wealth on cars. While highly customised standard cars may further reinforce negative associations of working-class culture and taste, a high-status prestige car steered by unexpected hands can be a source of confusion, or result in biased thinking. For detractors, high-status-conferring cars strongly indicate success through illegal or criminal activity if the driver does not happen to fit the expected profile, while the same car can draw attention from admirers for whom the car may connote success and hard work. As one of Alam's respondents observed:

> Before it used to be just any ordinary car, but now, more than whites, the most prestigious cars would be Asians'. I wonder if that's causing friction. I think *gorays* [white people] look at Asians and think, 'How did they get that car?' When I see Asians I presume there are some who do work hard and deserve what they've got. Some have worked hard for it and some have done it the other way. (Alam, 2006: 181)

In short, the symbolic power of the car is such that it can be readily deployed as a means of aiding race and class thinking, which leads to what are now deemed as reasonable and acceptable tropes: the black or Asian male behind the wheel of an expensive car *must* be dealing drugs or engaging in some other illegal activity. Conversely, as Paul Gilroy (2001) points out, when high-prestige ('white') cars are appropriated by African–Americans, they appear to become a means of challenging and resisting prevailing racial, and racist, hierarchies while, at the same time, maintaining them (see also Böhm et al, 2006b: 8). For others, however, it is the young white male driving the souped-up hot hatch that is problematised as an integral aspect of unruly 'chav' behaviour: the car (the make and model, its aesthetics, and its [amplified exhaust and music] aurality) serves to reinforce the pathology of the behaviour and its meaning. What are often overlooked are the positive aspects of car ownership and the sometimes close-to-emotional relationships some develop with their vehicles simply because they are an extension, or reflection, of their identity and creativity. The notion of ownership, therefore, extends beyond the usual understandings we have around the term. Apart from having legal entitlement to the car, ownership elicits emotional responses (Sheller, 2004) and, arguably for many, personal well-being. While Sheller's work explores the ways in which emotional currents can be underscored by personal, national and cultural memories and understandings of cars, she also touches upon how individuals feel about cars: again, freedom and control are key aspects of car ownership. For car enthusiasts, in particular, those of working-class backgrounds, additional investments in their cars signify deeper layers of ownership and attachment. Here, there is a new kind of hybridisation in which the self is fused with the object in a highly creative way. The redesign and reinvention of a car occurs through labour, capital and articulations of taste and identity that, of course, come to reflect and project something of the owner (see Bengry-Howell and Griffin, 2007). Changing the 'look' and 'feel' of a car is as much about investing in oneself as it is about investing in an otherwise mass-produced object. In the many interviews carried out for the research underpinning this chapter, the deep sense of personal investment that the owners reveal for their cars is striking. In such instances, the car is no mere casual appendage to their self-presentation; it is a much more powerful synergy of identity, aspiration and social expression.

It is worth noting at this juncture that our sample ranged across those variables that constitute social class. Some interviewees are professional and clearly occupy middle-class positions: their homes, educational background and income are all aspects that seem to be further reinforced by their taste in, and practice with, their cars. For those inhabiting a professional, or entrepreneurial, position – those who can be described relatively confidently as 'on paper' being 'middle-class' – cars are usually not heavily or noticeably customised. Instead, such drivers favour the acquisition of relatively new, upmarket models of different categories: executive-level saloons, sports coupes and four-wheel drives. For the majority of this layer of the sample, modifications are either very subtle, hidden (for example Electronic Control Unit [ECU] reprogramming, often called 'remapping') or simply unnecessary as the car itself is already a high-performance or niche model. However, something close to the opposite of this feature of *habitus* seems to operate for those who occupy what we can term as working-class positions. There is diversity in terms of employment type, as well as neighbourhood and, importantly, type of house. Indeed, some of those defined earlier as 'middle-class' may well have working-class neighbours (see Chapter Two). Class distinctions around employment, income and education can become manifest in the disposition towards, and practice with, the car. Especially for the younger, working-class subcultural element in the sample, cars are much more likely to be older models, and if customised or modified, explicitly distinct from the original object when initially manufactured. Despite this distinction in practice, however, what also comes through each class cohort is a recognition of each other: the working-class driver may even aspire to, or certainly be appreciative of, the middle-class driver's taste; similarly, the middle-class driver, though not always appreciative of it, is acutely aware of the appeal within the working-class car repertoire and culture. We make no suggestion that there are clear, non-porous boundaries between the two or, indeed, that these categorisations of class are non-problematic in exploring these issues. For example, in some of the interviews with middle-class drivers, stories of first cars often held data that echoed the present stories of the working-class drivers. At the same time, this class distinction does not necessarily result in class segregation. For example, while the interactions between (working-class) motor mechanics and (middle-class) customers indicate a degree of instrumental knowledge sharing, there is often a complementary, and more embedded, discourse around the car as a shared object. Alongside this, both elements of the sample share a heritage that goes beyond the history and impact of post-Second World War migration into the UK. Across the sample, there is a working knowledge/memory of the first-generation experience and position as not only working class, but also, in the context of race relations and racism, second class.

For some working-class younger people, considerable time and large amounts of wealth are funnelled into the production of their own cars. While owners know that these investments are unlikely to ever be returned in financial terms, the rewards are personal and real: achievement and creation being principal drivers of satisfaction. When this happens, cars become something similar to objects of art. They are objects imbued with artistic insight, artisanship and identity. While contemporary street artists such as Banksy and Roadsworth use the road and the streetscape more generally as their canvas, often layering their work with political or countercultural messages, working-class car culture is perhaps more mundane and democratic: the artistic statements often subject to questions of personal 'taste' instead, arguably ego-driven and not in any discernible way linked with a political counter-hegemony. However, and despite the fact that the products of a mainstream capitalist hegemony are being appropriated, these cars are corrupted through processes of individuation that does suggest a subcultural form of hegemonic resistance is taking place. Similarly, for Paul Gilroy, black car culture and practice is located within a historical and political context:

> this tentative consideration of cars within the wider framework of America's racial politics is not a means to present US blacks as special dupes of consumerism. Instead, it raises the provocative possibility that their distinctive history of propertylessness and material deprivation has inclined them to a disproportionate investment in particular forms of property that are publicly visible and the status that corresponds to them. (Gilroy, 2001: 84)

Meanwhile, for Warren and Gibson (2011: 2705), the car becomes a locus point for the realisation of a 'vernacular creativity' that has spawned its own organic infrastructure of 'skills, networks, circuits, and spaces of production'. The discussions around young people's behaviour with and around cars further reinforce and often revive and add dimension to youth moral panics more generally. These debates, aided by newspaper reports, academic writing or politicians' rhetoric, are often loaded with class bias and discriminations because the behaviour is judged to be anti-social, irresponsible, lacking respect and often illegal (Warren and Gibson, 2011: 2705–6). What this narrative also does is discount any creativity, let alone acknowledge or appreciate artistic or cultural endeavour. Echoing arguments by the likes of Hoggart (1957) and Williams (1958), it seems that definitions of art and creativity are still tied to a relatively narrow, elite and middle-class sensibility and taste. Like working-class culture, this kind of 'Vernacular creativity typically relies on oral forms of knowledge production and stems from personal passions, reliant on generosity and sharing, as well as the quest to perform idiosyncratic elements of personal identity' (Warren and Gibson, 2011: 2707).

One of our aims here, therefore, like Hoggart and Williams, is to revalidate or at the very least bring to the fore aspects of working-class cultures and, in so doing, challenge forms of mass, dominant culture, whether they are by design or manifestation elite or popular aspects of hegemonic control. While Fiske maintains that within capitalist societies, the occurrence of 'authentic' folk culture is unlikely due to the homogenising impact of mass culture, (class) cultural excorporations and De Certeau's (1984) 'appropriations' are taking place all the time:

> The creativity of popular culture lies not in the production of commodities, so much as in the productive use of industrial commodities. The art of the people is the art of 'making do.' The culture of everyday life lies in the creative, discriminating use of the resources that capitalism provides. (Fiske, 1989: 27–8)

Cultural objects do not necessarily have fixed meanings, despite the fact that producers of everything from sportswear to cars need to instil coherent and usually consistent meanings, attributes and associations that conflate quickly and sharply with brand identity (see, eg, Goldman and Papson, 1998; Choi and Rifon, 2007; McDonald and Scott, 2007; Springer, 2009). What is relevant here, however, are the ways in which the car can come to hold a new identity that is completely different to that which its brand stands for when it rolls off the production line. Some of these meanings are organic and grow over time through mainstream usage only to be further enhanced by the circularity of reputation. Others, however, change with severe, brutal and very rapid interventions.

Cars are perhaps one of the best examples of objects that hold the potential to become enhanced in order to suit environments, whether fashioned by broader mainstream cultures or, more especially, by smaller subcultures. Like the car itself, meaning and value is modified through investment in terms of time, money and cultural knowledge. For any car enthusiast, and certainly for many in our sample, up-to-date knowledge about modifications, repairs and maintenance is important. This knowledge may be focused on one or more areas such as in-car entertainment (ICE), performance modifications and upgrades to a car's interior, bodywork and wheels. However, this knowledge may also be relatively superficial and only include awareness of cost, increases in brake horsepower or insights into the anticipated aesthetic improvements. For some, however, a more in-depth, technical knowledge, along with aesthetic sensibility, is part of the process and, indeed, also comes to speak of personal identity. To some extent, there is as much of a fusing of the intellectual with the leisure as there is with the self and the car; the car–driver hybrid (Urry, 2004) can be a much more rounded entity through which identity is not only carried, but expressed, reinforced and even developed.

The car, in some cases, can very explicitly enable further labelling. In the interviews, for example, and echoing Miller's earlier discussion of Trinidadian taste in soft drinks, there was a sense that participants could identify what were deemed to be typically 'white cars' and typically 'Asian cars'. Admittedly, some of the discussions with participants around this aspect were elicited through asking whether certain cars are/were more 'Asian' or more 'white' than others. Partly, this eliciting was based on an extant knowledge of car-buying patterns in Bradford over the last 30 years, a knowledge base built on observation, as well as countless discussions and interactions with those in the motor (retail and repair) trade, along with those having a general interest in cars. Through combining more systematically generated interview data, observations and diary entries with existing background knowledge, a brief overview of Bradford's relatively recent car-ethnicity narrative is now offered.

The co-evolution of the car and Bradford's Pakistani community

In the 1970s, the majority of Pakistani Bradfordian car drivers were male and working-class (many of whom still worked in the textile industry as 'unskilled' machine operatives, particularly in spinning and weaving).

A significantly large, and thus noticeable, proportion of these first-generation immigrant-settlers tended to buy Japanese-manufactured cars, principally those produced by Datsun (later to become Nissan) and Toyota. Of these, most commonplace were small- to medium-sized saloons.[13]

For second-generation Pakistanis of the 1980s, particularly and arguably almost exclusively males, acquiring a Provisional Driving License and then taking driving lessons, passing the driving test and either being a 'named driver' on an existing car policy or purchasing a car seemed to be a natural thing to do and was a move often supported by parents. At this time, access to a car was not especially about elevating/projecting status, but it did enhance the family's cultural and economic capital as it enabled the kinds of freedoms discussed elsewhere (Paterson, 2007; Thacker, 2006; Gilroy, 2001). A car, for example, would not just be useful in completing usual family undertakings around the city (shopping, doctors' appointments or visiting relatives locally), but also reduce the family's dependence on others who did have cars, especially around the times of births, deaths and marriages among the geographically distant family and *biraderi* more generally (on the significance of extended family, family culture and *biraderi*, see, eg, Werbner, 1990; Shaw, 1988, 2000).

It is no surprise that with a British-born second generation, educated and socialised within both Pakistani and British culture, came a fusion of taste in the cars they would prefer. However, while there was some broadening in brand preference, there was also a broadening in car type. So, while first-generation Pakistanis were more interested in functionality than style, the inverse occurred with the second generation. Indeed, a continuing preference held by older Pakistanis is for cars with four or five doors. At one level, this is a common-sense preference as a four/five-door car has a greater range of practical uses in terms of carrying passengers and bulky items. This preference is not particular to ethnicity, but, rather, more tied in to taste as defined perhaps by generation, and also comes with having responsibility for family and its commitments. Younger, second-generation drivers, however, often preferred three-door coupes and hatchbacks because aesthetic value started to become more compelling than function. During the 1980s especially, the inner-city motoscape became populated with a growing car population

---

[13] Among Datsuns were 120Y (Sunny), 100A (Cherry), 140J, 160B, 180B (the numbers within the model name signified engine size: 120Y had a 1200cc engine, etc) variants, while the most popular Toyotas were the Corolla, Carina and Corona.

that, while not dominated especially by 'hot hatches', was certainly becoming more diverse.[14]

Within this general picture, there are two important caveats to bear in mind, however. First, cars were often bought second hand, with some passing from friend to friend or relative to relative, and with newly arriving (second-hand) cars being purchased by Pakistani drivers with competence in the craft of car purchasing and knowledge of what to look for in a good used car: a car-cultural capital. It should also be borne in mind, therefore, that the vast majority of these second-hand cars were originally bought (new) by white drivers. Additionally, while there was a strong preference for Japanese cars, this was by no means exclusive. Even during the 1970s, for example, certain European-produced cars were also favoured: Ford's Cortina, Escort and Capri models; Vauxhall's Victor, Viva, Chevette and Cavalier; cars produced by Hillman (Avenger, Hunter, Imp); and British Leyland's Princess and (Morris) Marina. Among wealthier Bradfordian Pakistanis and Indians (particularly those with Sikh heritage), Mercedes Benz appeared to be relatively favoured, with BMW and Audi yet to have established solid credentials within the mainstream semi-prestige UK car market. What is also worth noting is that by the second generation, there appeared to be an echoing of Gilroy's (2001: 84) 'disproportionate investment' in the car as an object imbued with strong public visibility and, especially 40 years ago, an object that connoted status.

Cars in context: descriptive accounts of the cultural incorporation of specific marques

Sixteen valves and a twin-cam engine. The making of a Japanese GTI: an illustrative case study

While it is not our intention to explore the subculture of car customisation in depth, a brief outline of the arguably conflicting facets of one mainstream car manufacturer's identity, certainly among one of its more unusual (second-hand) markets, may prove useful as a means of illustrating how existing cultural objects are appropriated

---

[14] Japanese coupes and hatchbacks (Toyota's Corolla, Celica, Supra; Nissan's Sunny and, to a lesser extent, its Z/ZX coupe variants; Honda's CRX, Civic, Prelude); European high-performance/'hot hatch' models (Ford's Sierra Cosworth, Escort XR3i, Capri 2.8i; Vauxhall's Cavalier SRi 130, Astra GTE, (GSE/Lotus) Carlton; Rover's SD1 3.5 Vanden Plas; Volkswagen's Golf and Scirocco); and, gaining a reputation for build quality, BMWs (in particular, the 3 Series).

and reinvented to stand for values and meanings contrary to those that the original mass manufacturer first intended.

Toyota is one example of how a brand stands to represent some very simple and clear ideas: among other qualities, and despite high-profile safety issues between 2009 and 2011, Toyota continues to mean reliability, along with efficiency and economy. In relatively recent years especially, however, Toyota has been one of several Japanese manufacturers whose cars have developed a very different set of connotations that are rendered meaningful in more localised contexts, where age, ethnicity and class appear to become more salient markers of identity that enable a new form of brand appreciation and loyalty to take place. One of Toyota's most successful and perhaps 'ordinary' models, the Corolla, has become something alluring and emblematic for a distinctive population, which includes younger Bradfordian Pakistanis especially. Indeed, for car enthusiasts in general, one generation and variant of the model in particular is appreciated through a very different cultural and aesthetic lens.

In 1983, Toyota, like many other manufacturers, followed Volkswagen's[15] lead and began producing its own version of a 'hot hatch'. Perhaps an unlikely candidate for the 'GTI' treatment was Toyota's small saloon/hatchback model, the Corolla. The 1983 base model came in a number of body-style variants, including two, three, four and five doors, but all had small (1.2–1.6 litre) petrol engines. The GT itself (and the later GTI variant) had two versions: a rear-wheel-drive three-door fastback coupe (known as the 'AE86'[16]) and a front-wheel-drive three-door hatchback derivative (known as the 'AE82'). Both models used the same 1.6 litre, twin overhead camshaft, fuel-injected, 16-valve engine and Toyota manufactured both with a range of cosmetic and structural modifications, including uprated suspension,

---

[15] In 1979, Volkswagen produced the first version of what has been one of the most groundbreaking cars ever, the Golf GTI: a small hatchback car that soon established itself as the benchmark within the class. At the time, it matched the performance (including top speed, acceleration and handling) of 'authentic' sports cars but was also practical and relatively affordable in terms of purchasing and running costs.

[16] To insiders, mechanics and Toyota enthusiasts, AE86 is a manufacturer code that represents four aspects that enable a form of specific vehicle identification: the 'A' referring to the engine code (the 4A); the 'E' being shorthand for Corolla; the '8' denoting the code for the series (E80); and the '6' standing for the variant within the range. The AE82, therefore, shares many of the same features (engine, model, series) except for the variant. The appropriation and use of this manufacturer code/symbol further reinforces and legitimises, of course, in-group (subcultural) identity and boundary maintenance as it readily yields common meaning to the group's members.

colour-coded bodywork, rear spoiler, alloy wheels, sports interior and so on. As well as Toyota, other Japanese manufacturers 'souped up' versions of their standard hatchbacks, Nissan with a Sunny GTE and Honda with their Civic GTI, for example. All of these cars were adorned with aesthetic and performance-enhancing modifications, many of which subsequently filtered into mainstream production even for standard/baseline models.

While it is difficult to pin down any overarching reason for its revival, if its allure ever declined at all, there are some clues. First of all, even among mainstream car experts (principally journalists), the AE86 has been given a certain amount of respect as something of a 'driver's' car. It has relatively few driving aids, it is robustly built, relatively quick and allows the driver to take part in the experience of driving in a close, attached and sensitive manner. Furthermore, it has a reputation for being a fun, lively and exciting car when driven to the limit. The car's nature and 'behaviour' is, in part, due to its rear-wheel-drive orientation. By 1983, the majority of mainstream car producers (with the exceptions of BMW, Jaguar and Mercedes Benz) had, in large part, switched from the earlier rear-wheel- to front-wheel-drive orientation. The front-wheel-drive system became popular partly because it yielded much greater levels of leg room in the cabin (especially the rear) and also because front-wheel-drive vehicles had a further advantage, particularly in Northern and Western European markets. Rear-wheel-driven cars – with relatively light rear ends sitting over the rear driving axles – often struggled to gain and maintain traction/grip in countries that had periods of snowfall and frost. Front-wheel-drive cars, however, because of the weight of the engine and transmission across and around the front drive shafts, were relatively comfortable in snowy or icy conditions: the weight and downward force yielding higher levels of grip and traction. Even in wet conditions, rear-wheel-drive cars were more likely to enter rear-end skids than their front-wheel-drive counterparts. Front-wheel-drive cars, originally at least, had practical benefits that the mainstream driver would appreciate.

Over the last decade or so, what was once deemed a major disadvantage of the rear-wheel-drive car – its relative propensity to skid compared to the front-wheel-drive car – has been subverted to become an aspect of appeal within our car-based subculture and beyond. Controlled skidding – often known as 'drifting'[17] – has become a performative art form that has already made its way into mainstream culture. This has been done through a strong presence and range of references in cinema (the *Fast and Furious* series of motion pictures has one film sub-entitled *The Tokyo Drift*) and television ('drifting' has been showcased in *Top Gear* and the language of the drifting subculture has also made its way into wider motoring media). Added to this, a large body of computerised gaming features the car, enabling players to race, customise and drift their digital, four-wheeled creations. For those particularly interested in the drifting scene, an expansive repertoire and knowledge base around which cars are more suited to drifting than others has evolved. Nissan's Skyline, 200SX, 240SX, Silvia, 300ZX and GT-R models, Mazda's RX7 and Toyota's various Supra models, along with some Mitsubishis, all have a strong 'drift' identity – some are even referred to as 'Drift-Mobiles/Machines' – as do a range of 'M'-specification BMWs and AMG Mercedes Benz.

It is within this milieu that the AE86 not only sits, but continues to feed back into the mainstream. Toyota itself has capitalised on the broader cultural value of the AE86, especially with its launch, in 2012, of a new coupe model, the GT86. What is more relevant is that this new model was marketed with explicit reference to the AE86. To push the point further, Toyota has very consciously woven the AE86's identity into the new car's through not only incorporating part of the model code (AE86 becomes GT86), but also tying in the new car's credentials and packaging with the older car: heritage, engineering, design and pedigree, and even 'feeling', all come together to form a set of meanings that link the old, and established, with the new.

Today, as we might expect, very few fifth-generation GTI Corollas remain. Of course, rarity does give any surviving cars a premium, collectible value. However, what is more interesting is the extent to which these cars, in particular, the rear-wheel-drive AE86 coupe/fastback variant, have become popular especially among younger Bradfordian/Pakistani drivers and enthusiasts – a smaller but noticeable aspect of the car (sub)culture that is present in Bradford. One of the elite respondents – a mechanic specialising in Japanese performance

---

[17] A complementary term, 'power sliding', applies to front-wheel-drive cars. The actual technique (the Scandinavian or Finnish 'Flick') was developed during the 1960s by Scandinavian rally car drivers in their negotiation of usually icy corners and bends; through a combination of throttle, steering and sometimes braking control, the car slides, or drifts, around bends and corners.

cars, himself the proud owner of a high-end performance Subaru –
illustrated the value of the model thus:

> 'I know lads who've been all the way to Scotland looking
> for one of them [AE82/AE86 Corollas]. And not runners,
> neither. To look at them, they look like they're scrap but
> they'll pay strong money for them; at one time, you could
> pay a couple of grand for a non-runner. A lot of these young
> lads, they buy them and spend a fortune doing them up....
> It's cos they like the look of them, cos they're unusual and
> they've still got a bit of something to them. So they ferry
> them down the M1, stick them in a garage and then throw
> money at them: strip it and rebuild the whole thing from
> scratch sometimes.' (AS, 45 years old, Pakistani-heritage
> male)

This echoes Warren and Gibson's (2011) broader thesis around
'blue-collar creativity', positing car customisation as a form of living,
working-class art that is lubricated and nuanced with forms of
communication including song, image, film, social activities and oral
traditions. Added to this, the evolving aesthetic manages to influence
wider (mass-market-influenced) notions of taste and style. With this
appropriation sits reinvention: the growth in custom paintwork, custom
stencils/wraps, spoilers and wheels are purpose-built enterprises for the
subculture. So, like all subcultures, some taking from and giving back
to the mainstream is present. Cars designed by Ford today have the
adornments and features that enthusiasts were trying out two decades
ago fitted as standard; twin exhausts, ornate interiors and multi-format
ICE are all elements that can be traced to fit within a feedback loop
involving the subculture and the mainstream.

The car's performance, capacity and driving 'nature', essentially
built on a combination of physics and engineering, adds a further
dimension of appeal that sits within discourses of speed, danger and
skill. However, for some younger drivers who are aware of this appeal,
the car's *capacity* to outperform other cars is more important than the
practice and performance of drifting itself:

> 'I've never raced my car like that. You know, I've put my
> foot down here and there when I can but I don't like to
> screw the shit out of it for nothing. If I wanted to, I could
> do doughnuts and drift round car parks but why bother?
> You know how much the tyres alone are on this thing? I

can't afford to blast my car around in case something goes wrong with it: an engine rebuild, that'd run into thousands for me.' (AA, 30 years old, Pakistani-heritage male)

When this respondent was therefore asked why he felt there was a 'need' to own, maintain and enhance a car that was rarely, if ever, driven for what appeared to be a substantial element of its purpose, he stated:

'Because I'm into it. I know what my car can do and, for me, that's enough. And other people, they know – well they have an idea – about what my car can do as well. They can see it, they can hear it when I pull up next to them. One look and they know not to mess because my car, it looks fast.' (AA, 30 years old, Pakistani-heritage male)

One of our other respondents echoed these sentiments when he suggested that there was a pointlessness, at one level, to having so much power that is rarely used. However, there was also, again, the surfacing of meaning, not only to the owner/driver, but to others who hold the shared cultural capital:

'It might be the fact that you know what it can do and other people – people who know about them as well – they know what it can do. And because people know, that's enough. I think there's some of that going on.' (IP, 23 years old, car retailer)

As well as any aesthetic appeal intrinsic to modified cars, whether based on a broader 'retro'[18] sensibility or not, there is, of course, the driving experience itself. Although Sheller (2004) does touch on how we feel when we drive and the feelings that arise through owning or even having access to a car, and Katz's (1999) discourse centred around anger and its consequences while driving is similarly helpful, there is relatively little writing around the performative elements of car driving, of which there are two distinct elements that hold relevance in this discussion: the driver's performance within the car and the

---

[18] By this, we mean the perennial nostalgia for all things retro; in the world of cars, the original Mini variants have remained consistently fashionable, chic and generally appealing. There have also been examples of contemporary cars that have a 'retro' feel – the Nissan Figaro perhaps being one of the best examples of a new car that was purposefully designed to look old/retro.

performance of driving as perceived by those outside of the car and looking in, or at. In this latter regard, the aesthetics and aurality of car culture is significant and also, once again, ties in with the subculture of customised vehicles in general, as well as with 'grey imports' and older cars that are now revived as Japanese 'classics'.

The presence of cars, as well as motorcycles and quad bikes, in the soundscape of Bradford and Manningham constitutes a distinctive element of the automotive inter-ethnic experience. Whether it is the percussive assault of the boom box at full blast or the tuned rumble or cacophonous roar of the customised exhaust system, there is a planned aural signature to some urban driving that is intended to claim an audience. While there is an intrinsic pleasure in customising your own car, there is a closely related frisson in ensuring that your car is seen and appreciated. Making sure that it is heard is one established means of ensuring that your car, and, by extension, your presence, is noticed on the street.

Unlike Warren and Gibson's (2011: 2711–15) respondents, who had a central role in the production and development of their own customised cars, the same cannot be said for the majority of our sample members who own modified cars. Many will source cars that may already have been through a process of individuation wherein the previous owners have envisioned and then created cars according to their own tastes and preferences. However, notwithstanding this sense of 'completeness' at the point of purchase, some degree of creativity often continues, occasionally with further modifications and maintenance:

> 'You never stop sort of doing stuff to it. Like mine, it had some nice wheels on when I bought it. Not standard, but nice split rims: 19 inch with low-profile tyres. Nothing wrong with them but I fancied some nicer ones, ones that would make it stand out even more. So, I bought some … put them on and it looks pretty mean now. I got a few other things I need to do to it but I've already spent a lot so it'll have to wait.' (AA, 30 years old, Pakistani-heritage male)

The same respondent also talked about the constant maintenance his car 'needed' – from checking fluid levels to regular servicing, from minor bodywork repairs and modifications to regular polishing – this 'need' to be involved with the car's well-being might appear to border on the obsessive. However, for this individual and others who share similar dispositions towards and practices with their car, the object is a source of pride and, thus, a repository of investment. The amount of time and money invested in its condition, and its evolution, however, will never be returned economically; yet, the emotional investment being returned every time the car is looked upon, sat in or driven is deeply rewarding. Conversely, if the car befalls a tragedy (an accident, an act of vandalism, a major repair), the emotional investment partially sublimes to become sorrow, loss and anger. However, even the labour and economic costs are rewarded through something that extends our usual understanding of ownership and consumption. As noted earlier, it is the owner, driver and enthusiast who somehow feels inscribed upon and within the fabric of the car; at the very least, and using even the loosest capacities of creative/artistic endeavour (Cropley, 2004), the car – how it looks, sounds and *is* – comes to be a 'living' art form, embodying something personal about the artist and artisan.

This subculture, it has to be noted, is one that is class-relevant and class-dependent. As with all subcultures, it exists at the margins of mainstream driving culture, even if that mainstream itself is, in some ways, marginal. In this case, the broader marginality refers to the social and political position of one minority ethnic group, which, of course, is far from homogeneous to begin with. So, while this particular car scene in Bradford involves usually[19] younger, Pakistani-heritage males, the appeal is by no means shared among all young, Pakistani-heritage Bradfordian males and, at the same time, it is not necessarily exclusive to only the young (indeed, some had come back to this practice after many years of driving 'standard' cars). That said, within Bradford's Pakistani-heritage population, there is a rising middle class for whom this car subculture is unattractive as it represents ethnic differentiation and suggests a lack of integration and, arguably, a form of resistance to and defiance against white, middle-class mainstream society. This working-class subculture may well be a means of giving voice to its members, but for its middle-class peers, this voice says the wrong thing. Yet again, therefore, questions of taste along with class *habitus* and practice are relevant (Bourdieu, 1984 [1979]).

---

[19] There are, of course, males and females from diverse ethnic and class backgrounds who are also part of the Japanese car scene, but for the purposes of this discussion, the generalisations regarding 'ethnic tastes' are a necessary and fundamental aspect of the argument, itself grounded within and reinforced by our empirical data.

Ownership and identity: examples of Pakistani investment in their cars

In this section, we explore some empirical examples that illustrate divergent tastes, as well as practices and dispositions, towards the car. This section is heavily dependent on data generated through semi-structured interviews and observations, some of which are presented in the form of diary/journal entries, field notes and reflections upon encounters with not only human respondents, but also aspects of the city's motoscape.

Black VW Golf MK5 2.0 GT TDI

This car has been owned for two years by a 28-year-old British-born Pakistani male (AB). AB likes Golfs. Apart from two Subaru Imprezzas (both top-end WRX models, one a saloon and the other an estate/station wagon), an Audi A4 and a 5 series BMW, he has owned about four VW Golf GTis, so far: a Mark 1, a Mark 2, a Mark 4 and now a Mark 5, which he has owned for over two years. Every car he has ever owned has been either modified or restored. He is not a trained mechanic but can service his own cars and has friends and contacts in the motor industry who give advice, assist and, in some cases, work on the cheap over weekends if more complicated work is required. When buying a car, he usually plans to make sure it is 'the right one' – mileage, condition and overall 'look' of the car. While this can mean weeks, but usually months, of scouring websites such as autotrader.co.uk and pistonheads.com, once sourced, the car usually then becomes subject to some modifications but he does not consider himself to be extreme. He usually sources modification materials and items from online sellers (often second-hand through, eg, ebay) but also uses local retailers. On his latest car, for example, he has completed the following work/changes: 19-inch alloy wheels, uprated/lowered suspension, custom exhaust, sway bars, K & N[20] air filter, Alpine audio equipment, uprated/tinted rear light clusters and, most recently, the car's ECU has been remapped to increase power while improving efficiency (something he is not entirely convinced is possible but has nevertheless decided to experiment with). The cost of these modifications runs into the thousands but this he justifies by saying:

---

[20] The US company K & N Engineering, named after its owners Ken Johnson and Norm McDonald, began operations in the late 1960s developing intake components for motorcycles. See www.knfilters.com/knhistory.htm.

'I don't spend much on anything else much anyway. It's just sort of spare cash, if you know what I mean. I work pretty hard and I don't drink, don't smoke or anything like that. I do shop around for bits when I need them. Like the alloys, I got them from X Accessories on X Road. I know the guy who owns it and he sorted me out. So, with the tyres that came with the alloys, they worked out to be a good, cheapish sort of deal.'

In its present condition, his car is probably worth a little more than the market price for a standard, unadulterated model, certainly nowhere near the actual sum the car has absorbed through aesthetic and performance modifications. On this note, AB was relatively relaxed – the money spent was never going to be recouped, but, rather, was and continues to be money spent in the pursuit of leisure and even creativity. While he makes no claim about an artistic endeavour, certainly not in the traditional understandings of the idea, the car comes to be a device within which his reinterpretation of function and style is layered. During one conversation with AB, it struck me that distinctions invoking class and culture were at play. Middle-class people may spend part of their income on creative and leisure endeavours (stereotypically speaking, this might be painting, wine tasting, theatre, etc), projects around the home or even on art appreciation. With AB and people with a similar class-cultural location, and this is not to suggest that this is a widely held class-located practice, the car becomes a pivotal point that continues to stimulate interest and elicit personal reward for no easily discernible or practical point. In other words, AB gives his car attention because doing so is fulfilling in a number of ways that are closely tied up with his internal (self-) and projected external identity.

AS and SM. Two mechanics with a garage in Manningham (January 2012–present)

AS, the owner, has been in the car repair/service sector since leaving school. SM, a decade or so younger, is experienced enough to take on anything that comes through the garage doors. They have no specific clientele: relatively plain vehicles, taxis/minicabs and cars that, to varying degrees, have been or are being modified. The garage owner has a reputation for being a reliable and highly knowledgeable mechanic with a wide range of experience across different manufacturers; his particular expertise is with Japanese and German cars – especially those that have a sports/performance orientation. Indeed, both mechanics are keen car enthusiasts themselves, owning high-performance Japanese sports saloons and occasionally testing their prowess during 'track day' events. While they do undertake performance modifications and enhancements to customers' cars, the bulk of their work is maintenance- and repair-oriented.

Over several visits to AS's garage, I observed and engaged with a diverse range of car owners. In most cases, their cars become the channel through which our conversations are carried: 'What's wrong with it?', 'What are you getting done?', 'How long have you had it?' are all used as triggers that help me delve into the life of the driver and his car. Nearly all are male, mostly of Pakistani heritage, but there are a few women who come to either drop off or collect their cars.

Many of the (especially older) men are not particularly interested in their cars in the way I am; they have been let down and this trip to the garage will burn a hole in their pocket. They do not resent their cars, but they do not love them, or have affection for them in the way some do. There are a few taxi drivers who, for obvious reasons, see their cars as objects that principally facilitate income, and they therefore seem less enthusiastic than those customers for whom a car seems to mean so much more. Some drivers especially like to talk about their rides in the here and now, whether they are only in for a service, some MOT work or a new gearbox; the more drastic the work, the more detailed the storytelling about what brought them to this point:

> 'Lent it to my younger brother a couple of times. I could tell there was something wrong with it when I got it back: you know, just didn't drive right. Found out he'd been hammering a bit; screwing the shit out of it. Knackered the gearbox, killed the brakes. Costing me a fortune, now.'

> 'Failed MOT – nothing major: brake pads, a couple of hoses. Last year, it went straight through, though.'

Some are young, some are older, closer to my age, and I connect easily with all those who are 'into' their cars. They tell me how long they have had it, what has been done and what it is like. Personalities given to objects – adjectives, metaphors, similes and alliterations – abound. I struggle to hold in memory the more interesting ones: "Like shit off a shovel"; "Fast as fuck"; "Handles like it's on rails"; "Sticks to the road like glue". Then come the comparisons, the decisions and the mistakes: "I had a Scooby before and that was quicker than this"; "It's better/

worse than my last one"; "It'll eat an M3 for breakfast"; "Might not be as fast as X, but it's got a better ride/better handling/looks".

AS tells me stories, small and precise, explaining the presence of the cars on his ramps:

> 'Engine gone. It's what happens if you don't look after it and drive like a fucking maniac.'

> 'Been back to me three times with the same problem – I don't know what he keeps doing to it.'

> 'The guy who owns this car, he treats it better than his wife.'

AS, while not revered, holds a certain power we all respect, and possibly even admire. We take him something broken and through a form of diagnosis and then surgery, he makes it better. He has one of those electronic code readers that he pulls out from time to time, plugs it in – usually somewhere around or under the dash – then scrolls through the various menus and options until the machine tells him the fault code. Anyone can do that but only people like him – people who know the language of the machine – know how to read and interpret; only some have that knowledge and that makes them special. Not quite gifted, but something close. Three decades, near enough, AS has had his head under a bonnet, and now, thousands of cars later, he is as close to a car whisperer as you can get.

SJ, a late 30s professional male who drives a fairly new (at the time of writing, less than one year old) and reasonably high/sports specification Range Rover (January 2013)

SJ is a partner in his family-run wholesale business that, while based in Bradford, has a broad, semi-national customer base. With the exception of a private registration plate/number, SJ's car is factory specification and has had no post-purchase custom work undertaken. SJ professes not to have any significant interest in this or any car. Indeed, prior to the interview, he stated that he had to look at the vehicle handbook in order to become familiar with some of the fundamentals (eg precise model and engine size). During the interview, however, it became clear that his insights about the car – while not those of a 'petrol-head' – were certainly borne of his own observations of and experiences with car culture.

While he acknowledges his car's 'presence' and what it might suggest to others – including having characteristics typical of a 'gangster car' – he values its practical benefits. Here, however, there is a need to explain what the car does for him and his business. For example, how others (clients and suppliers) perceive and interpret his car also feeds into their subsequent perceptions of him and his business. In his own words, the following extensive quotation explores this and other features of car ownership linked with image, perception and meaning:

> 'All of the cars that belong to the company reflect the company in a way. You've got two X5s, you've got my Range Rover, then you've got a Land Rover, and then you've got a BMW M5 and they're all pretty big cars. When I look at it, I actually get the feeling that the company is trying to send out a message through its vehicles. And the message is this: when you walk in, or when a rep walks in or when a customer walks in, they should get the feeling that this is a pretty big company, a successful company, the people who are running this company are doing well, and it should give the impression that this company is doing something right. What I've found is the cars are a kind of a symbol, a sign to the rest of the community out there – especially those stakeholders who interact with our company – that you're dealing with somebody who's doing well; have confidence in this company and this company is going places. So, for us, the cars are kind of a tool, a method to convey a certain message to a particular group of stakeholders, namely, most importantly, the suppliers. When a supplier comes, and on purpose the car park is next to the reception, he'll walk past this fleet of cars.'

As for the experience of actually driving a large car with a relatively high seating position and vantage point, here, too, SJ expressed a departure from his original uninvolved stance, which itself was also linked with the fact that he is 'semi-detached' from this car, which is, in effect, owned by the company. Notwithstanding this ambivalence, there are aspects of SJ's experience as a driver that reinforce some of the notional idiosyncrasies that we all may have in relation to cars in general: we may find them interesting as objects of engineering, design, speed and even art but we can also bemoan their appalling fuel economy or wider ecological impact. SJ's capacity to make sense of such contradictions is perhaps not unusual, but it does offer some insights into the trade-offs a much wider population may well make without too much distress. Again, while initially asserting that he had little or no interest in 'the type of car, the model, the engine size', SJ went on to reveal the following when asked about his feelings about his relatively recent car-driving/semi-owning history:

'The first one was a BMW 7 Series so that's the biggest you can get. It was absolutely brilliant, really liked it. It was smooth. It gave that impression of style and sophistication. And then I went to the Audi A8, which again is a very big car – probably the biggest in the Audi range – and it was brand spanking new and gave the same impression [as the BMW 7 Series] again. The latest car, which is the Range Rover, which is like a four-by-four type of a car, is the best car I've had so far. And the reason for that is that it does give all the right messages to the people. I know it has an image of a gangster car but when you're not a gangster and you're doing business and you're working hard, it gives you that feeling of driving a big car because you deserve it and because you've earned it. And power, it's a very powerful engine. It really does roar; it's the Sports Special, so it's got the voom factor in it. It gives you the power, the height, the looks, it gives you the wow factor and people notice you. I found that none of those cars did that, whether it was the 7 Series or the A8, it just wasn't big enough. This car's big enough to get noticed. It's a car you can't miss. It stands out.'

Of course, the fact that it stands out also means that SJ has to acknowledge the meanings that others may lay upon his possession of such a car:

'You can quite easily fall for that stereotype: it's the drug culture. The drug culture is minute and doesn't actually account for that much. This is the hard-earned money of these business people who are the cutting edge and they're bringing Bradford lots of variety, colour and style. Whatever we do in Bradford, we're gonna be stereotyped, we can never do anything right. You go out of Bradford, you meet people from the South and, you know, we're the people who are grooming, burning books, we're the people who are demanding this god damn halal food and we're the people who are throwing out Labour and voting in this loony crank from the Respect Party [here, the speaker was referring to the Member of Parliament for Bradford West, the Right Honourable George Galloway]. We've got this reputation out there of being quite out of the ordinary. That doesn't worry me. That's something we should be proud of. We're actually good at being different.'

SJ is one of several respondents who extolled the value of Bradford's car scene. Often, statements such as "Bradford has all the best cars" were followed by an expert endorsement or qualifier: "Even Jeremy Clarkson said if you want to see nice cars, go to Bradford." Although it has been difficult to find unequivocal evidence for this statement having ever been made[21] by the presenter, for those who claim and use it, it is neither unreasonable nor unrealistic.

ZA, a 22-year-old Pakistani Bradfordian female who works in retail clothing and drives a seven-year-old factory-standard Toyota Yaris

Although ZA bought her car with the money she had saved, it was her father who 'helped' her decide which car to purchase. She did not want this car, does not like it but has kept it for about three years (she bought it about a year after she passed her driving test). When asked why she did not like it, she said that it was because it was boring and dull: it had a small engine, it was a small car and it was just too 'tinny'.

> **Interviewer:** 'Has it ever let you down? Breakdowns or anything like that?'

> **ZA:** 'No. Nothing like that. No, wait – we had to change the battery on it once, soon after we bought it, but since then, nothing. To be honest, it's a really good car. It's good on petrol [fuel economy], reliable and it's all right, you know.'

> **Interviewer:** 'But you don't like it. Did you ever like it?'

---

[21] The statement, or myth, does occasionally appear online – see, for example, the following web forums for evidence not only of the claim, but also the discourse around Bradford, its cars and its drivers. See: http://pistonheads.co.uk/gassing/topic.as p?h=0&f=23&t=1232079&i=20&mid=0&nmt=Eyes+on+a+Diesel+GT and www. toyotagtturbo.com/forums/archive/index.php/t-32416.html

ZA: '[Laughs] No. I didn't want it but my dad sort of convinced me to buy it as like a first car: cheap insurance, easy to drive and all that, you know.'

She explained the process and reinforced the logic behind her father's thinking. The car, while certainly not as inexpensive as some others of the same age and category, was cheap to run, cheap to insure and, above all, would not give her any problems. Nothing, according to her father, could beat a Toyota. As a first car, it would be ideal but, if she wanted to, she could later switch to something she liked better – once she had built up some 'no-claims discount' and had become a more experienced driver.

For ZA, what constitutes a 'better' car is certainly not a Toyota or most other Japanese cars. When I probe further, it turns out ZA also dislikes Toyotas because they hold a certain stigma and because they lack some of the qualities she finds appealing in other brands/manufacturers:

ZA: 'Well, they're typical Asian cars, if you know what I mean. Corollas, Auris, Yaris and all that – they're just too Asian. Pakistani more than Asian.'

Interviewer: 'Any others that have that sort of Asian or Pakistani vibe?'

ZA: 'Like, the Japanese are like that but even, like, some others that aren't Japanese as well. You know, like BM's, VWs, Audis and all that – our lot, we drive everything now but there's some cars that only we will drive and those are some of the Japanese ones. Like, I never see a white person driving in an old Corolla. They might have, like, a new, a brand new Auris or Yaris or that Hybrid one or something like that, but you hardly ever see white people driving older Japanese cars.'

Interviewer: 'So, what do they drive instead, then?'

ZA: 'White people? Well, depends on sort of how rich they are, I suppose. For poorer people, it'll be like Fords and Vauxhalls. They're more common and so are Citroens and Peugeots and Renaults. If you're poorer and white, you'll drive one of them cars but poorer and Asian, you might be driving something Japanese.'

Interviewer: 'And if you're not poor? If you're rich?'

ZA: 'Doesn't matter if you're rich, you'll buy whatever you like, whatever takes your fancy. Doesn't matter what colour you are then. But I noticed that our lot are more into posher, nicer cars – bigger, expensive, showy cars. X5's, Q7s and Mercedes and even sports cars as well, our people buy a lot of, I think. You see them, don't you? Around here [Heaton] you do anyway.'

Interviewer: 'So, what sort of car are you getting next? What do you want to get?'

ZA: 'Something sportier and slicker than what I've got. A [Seat] Leon. I like them. [Volkswagen] Golf, obviously.'

Interviewer: 'Why obviously?'

ZA: 'Why? Because it's the best car for what it is. Everyone says good things about them: white people and Asians. It's a car that everyone can like because it's classy, I think. Not posh, but it's got a bit of style to it and, obviously, it's got a really good reputation and everything like that.'

Interviewer: 'Any particular one you prefer?'

ZA: 'Obviously, I'd like to have the best one, the R32 – the Mark 5 – but I could never afford that. It's got a big engine, very fast and it's expensive to insure. I wouldn't be able to get it insured, actually. So, I'll probably just get a diesel one, the 1.9TDI, which is also really good in every way, really.'

Interviewer: 'Do you know a lot about cars?'

ZA: 'No, not really. I mean, I read a bit about them, or talk to my friends and cousins about them, but I'm not what you'd say knowledgeable about them. I just know what I like!'

Regrettably, the number of female respondents we engaged with was small but those in our sample strongly indicated that they were as attached and interested as their male peers, and had their own concerns that were highly reflective of their connections with automobility. With

ZA in particular, for example, there are strong references to ethnic taste, as well as how class itself helps form and perpetuate taste distinctions: "Doesn't matter if you're rich, you'll buy whatever you like, whatever takes your fancy. Doesn't matter what colour you are then." ZA's interview also suggested that while ideas around 'ethnic taste' can be invariably skewed according to prevailing narratives and stereotypes, they remain concrete and arguably benign in some contexts. However, as SJ illustrated, conflating a car type with criminality exists on the spectrum of associations between the car–driver hybrid and behaviour.

One other female respondent (MK – a 22-year-old student from Bedford studying in Bradford) echoed much of ZA's views. For example, when asked what kind of car she would buy, she said her ideal car was a high-specification Audi hatchback (an S3 variant) but also mentioned a number of other exclusively German brands, including Mercedes, Seat, BMW and Volkswagen. Despite her preference for high-performance variants, she was also aware of their expense and that they can be perceived as 'boy racer cars'. When asked about the option of buying a Japanese car instead, her reaction was quick and forceful: "Never a Yaris or a Nissan Micra. They're like TP[22] cars. In Bradford, you can get away with it because there's a lot of Asians." When asked if she had no choice but a Micra or Yaris, she replied:

> 'I'd rather not drive! It's about your identity; you can't be driving a crap car like that. It's not about them being beneath you, but you have to have something more acceptable. If you can't afford it, then take a taxi or use public transport!'

Bradford's other car culture: sports, prestige and exotic cars

YA. Diary entry. Tuesday evening. 14 August 2012. Pakistani/Indian Restaurant in Bradford, 7

> I'm having a meal with friends. We're at a table by the window but I can see out, onto the main road and the three way mini roundabout. During the meal and conversation, I'm distracted by the number of high end cars that I see negotiating the roundabout. I count two Lamborghinis (a

---

[22] Pronounced 'tee-pee', this has been a long-established shorthand and informal phrase, principally used by British-born Pakistanis as a derogatory term against non-British-born Pakistanis but it has various applications that connect with signifiers of non-British Pakistani taste, including dress/fashion and, in this context, cars.

Murcielago and a Gallardo [I think]), one Ferrari (unsure of model, but looks modern/newish), a Bentley (a coupe of some sort – probably a Continental) as well as Porsches and Audis (one RS8). As well as these 'exotics', there are numerous prestige cars – too many to count – but I make a mental list to jot down later: BMWs (X6s, X5s, 7, 5 and 3 Series models are like dirt and I even notice an older [early 2000s model] convertible M3); Audi Q7s and S Line/RS variant A6s, A4s and A3s; some high spec VWs including Golfs and Sciroccos and also see a few large and well kitted out Mercedes Benz models; Range Rovers – again, high end Vogues and Sport variants – seem to be relatively common. Perhaps these cars are not that common, I wonder, but they are certainly noticeable and there are patches of time when there is at least one above average car passing through every minute or so.

The palpable visibility of so many 'high-end' cars is given a greater *frisson* by the very fact that they are encountered in a city, and in an inner-city area, that has a dominant imagery as being economically deprived and imbued with some miasmic Northern decline. So frequently being driven by persons of a non-white identity, these cars only serve to amplify their hyper-visual presence within the streetscape. In the city's inter-ethnic dynamics, this automotive assertion of affluence and self-regard cannot be assumed to be an unremarkable aspect of the daily inter-ethnic scanning of the streetscape.

IP, a 23-year-old car retailer

IP and his brother buy and sell cars. I visited them on a cold Sunday afternoon in January 2013 and I am surprised by two things: first, they sell their cars from home; and, second, they have some interesting, not to mention expensive, cars. Their front yard/garden accommodates about 15 cars in all, and most of these are fairly large: three Range Rovers, one BMW 5 Series Touring, one BMW X5 and a Bentley Flying Spur. Alongside these are a VW Golf GTI, an Audi S3, an Audi S4, a Seat Leon and a Mitsubishi Lancer, as well as a couple of others that seem average by comparison. He tells me about their approach to the bigger cars, in particular, the Range Rovers. They will buy a less-than-perfect example that may perhaps have some scratches and scuffs to removable body trim. Rather than simply repairing these cosmetic problems, they will send the car for a complete reinvention. Such a car becomes a candidate for a 'project': it will be stripped down and painted – inside and out – in a completely new and 'individual' colour (eg BMW Estoril Blue). The door cards, bumpers and other trim will be replaced with newer, fresher and upgraded kit. New, 22-inch alloy wheels will finish the job. The car, in his own words, will be 'pimped out'. As we talked, he priced up the shopping list for the recently completed dark blue Range Rover Sport: the enhancements came close to £8,000. While spending this sort of money and enhancing the look and appeal of the car will make it more marketable, it will also increase its sale price and, thus, profit. However, that is not the only reason why this kind of work is done:

> 'It started its life as a standard Range Rover Sport HSE. Basically, the car got stripped down to bare metal. Then he [IP's brother] painted it to his own colour. Land Rover never did them in this colour; this is like BMW M3 Estoril Blue. So, it's bespoke, then, isn't it? He's put the big body kit on, the big 22-inch wheels, give it a remap to make it smoother, lighter. To get it to this spec, you're looking at two grand for wheels, another three and a half grand for bodywork, and then there's body kit, headlights, LEDs – you're looking at eight–nine grand. Totally changes the car. He gets a buzz out of it, you know – going to the garage and seeing it changing.'

Woven into this interview was not so much the pursuit of profit, but rather the dovetailing of work, creativity and pleasure. IP's older brother is a keen car enthusiast and he not only manages to make a living through sourcing and selling cars, but more than occasionally finds the practice of 'changing' them into something different, 'individual' and 'bespoke' rewarding – in an artistic/creative sense. Once they are changed, he gains yet more pleasure in experiencing them while in motion. At some point, there is the third prong of pleasure in the making of a sale and profit. At the very beginning of the process, however, is a sense of visualisation and of having an image of how the car will look and feel when it is completed.

As documented in an earlier chapter and as strongly evidenced here, a proportion of Bradford's Pakistanis have at least started to show signs of upward economic mobility over the last decade. As a result of this, there are increased levels of disposable income. Indeed, as explored elsewhere, this disposable income is now free to be spent on the home (Husband and Alam, 2012), the body and on travel (Haj/Umra and holidays), which indicates that there is a discernible and varied growth in conspicuous consumption. In some ways, the increase in international holidaymaking (to places other than Pakistan) further suggests that a larger economic middle class is becoming established. Alongside this, there is a continuing expansion of business infrastructure that supports the consumer needs of this community: beauty salons, jewellers, wedding planning services and relatively upmarket eateries all cater for British, middle-class (aspiring or actual) Pakistanis.

A further result of these economic and cultural shifts is changes in attitude towards the car. Encapsulating the development of this community more broadly, including Anwar's (1979) *Myth of return*, one of our respondents stated:

> 'They were thinking of moving back, you know, at some point. The big thing was these big buildings, you know, mansions they're building in Pakistan, they're sitting there doing nothing now because people don't want to go back there. So, the parents have decided we can't invest in that kind of thing. The kid wants a car and just to make him happy he's gone into education like we said, and he's got married where we wanted to, so let's buy him a car.' (JP, 47 years old, Pakistani-heritage male)

It is within this context that a different aspect of Bradford's car culture can be situated. Alongside the Japanese imports, the revived and revitalised AE86s, and other models upon which young, working-class owners inscribe facets of their identity are the relatively unadulterated but equally impressive cars that fit into the sports, prestige and exotic categories. However, despite their relative newness, these cars, which even second-hand cost in excess of £20,000, are no less distinctive than their cheaper, downmarket cousins.

One of the most highly visible features of the *motoscape* in Bradford and Manningham is the very real visibility of '*top-end*' cars driven by members of the Pakistani community. The frequent presence of Bentleys, Lamborghinis, Ferraris and Porsches, as well as top-of-the-line Audis, Range Rovers and BMWS, on the roads of Bradford is itself striking. However, the intersection of these exclusive cars with the streetscapes in which they may be encountered gives their presence a very potent 'edge'. Driving through the 'working-class' backstreets of Manningham, there *is* something counterintuitive about seeing an Aston Martin Vanquish parked at the kerbside; or while walking up to a relatively basic Pakistani curry house with American friends, to have two Ferraris pass by in the matter of a few minutes presents a sharp challenge to stereotypical expectations. It is the nature of stereotypes to seek to resolve complex realities into simple, and simplistic, coherent patterns of fact and expectation. The diversity of car ownership within inner-city Bradford does not sit easily with such cognitive sketches of multicultural inner-city locales. The presence of stereotypes about inner-city areas like Manningham and other notions of the presence of a Pakistani-controlled drug trade provides an easy facilitation of assumptions about the probable basis for the viability of such car ownership. The de facto reality, however, is that Bradford does have an exceptionally high level of ownership of elite cars. Britain's now-established minority ethnic groups in general, and Bradford's Pakistani-heritage communities in particular, have undergone immense economic and cultural shifts, and some of these have become reflected in the changed attitudes towards income, in particular, in relation to how and upon what it is spent.

Nevertheless, the high visibility of high-end cars in the hands of non-white people continues to feed into perceptions that explain their presence. Indeed, the 'gangster' or 'doing something dodgy' thesis remains a fairly powerful, normative and widespread disposition. Sometimes, its expression does come from sadly unsurprising sources.

In 2010, one of the authors, along with several other Pakistani Bradfordians, attended a talk given by a senior civil servant with some responsibility for law and order across the region. The speaker made a particularly interesting comment about Bradford's reputation as a 'hub' for the drugs trade. The qualifier that accompanied this assertion was even more interesting in that it conflated the relatively high presence of expensive cars with illegal activity. Of course, a number of the audience, some of whom also happened to own high-end cars, rose to challenge this comment and the speaker quickly took a different stance, claiming that the comment was made in the spirit of provoking intellectual discussion. The fact remains, however, that there still exists a very real sense of correlation between the kind of car a person drives and the kind of person who drives it. In the 1970s and 1980s, for example, a stark racial stereotype had significant reach and resonance in many parts of Britain: BMW (*Bayerische Motoren Werke*, translated into English as Bavarian Motor Works) stood for 'Black Man's Wheels', its underlying, connotative meaning in effect justifying and explaining the apparent anomaly of a desirable vehicle being driven by an unworthy driver.

However, today, this racial coding is no longer entirely a process or means through which a minority ethnic group is labelled from outside of itself. Indeed, even among Bradfordian Pakistanis today, questions are asked when an especially young driver is seen behind the wheel of an expensive-looking car: 'How can such a young person even afford the insurance and running costs, let alone the purchase price?' As noted earlier, there can be a propensity for gaps to be filled when that which challenges established meaning and interpretation is encountered. The 'must be doing something dodgy' thesis is easily deployed when an expensive-looking car is driven by someone for whom the same car appears to be out of reach. This reasoning is simple enough: the only way such a car can be afforded by such a person has to be through illegal means, usually drugs. What is often overlooked is that despite a general socio-economic position that invariably has reference to forms and forces of deprivation, there is a growing middle class of entrepreneurs and professionals who buy and run cars that, given the strength and pervasiveness of racial coding, appear to be outside of their reach. In addition, there are individuals who still live with their parents and although only earning a modest income, it may be enough to pay for their car. Added to this, of course, we have to remind ourselves that, until relatively recently, we were all encouraged to live beyond our means through taking on more debt and buying more consumer goods simply because they were there and, to some extent, because doing so was good for the economy.

Ethnicity and car culture

In the previous examples, we have evidence of a 'Pakistani' car culture in which the car has taken on a role as an *empty signifier*, whereby through shared subcultural aesthetics and involvement, the car, as physical entity, has become a means of signifying a distinctive collective identity within an ethnically sensitised and possibly racialised (Rattansi, 2005) urban context. The evidence we have drawn together does not suggest that there is a dominant and singular set of car-mediated identities, but, rather, that there is a widespread acceptance of the car as a highly salient, material means of cultural expression. Within that context, then, there is an apparent range of niche sensibilities that are shared and actively rehearsed, and, just as importantly, there is the opportunity for car enhancement to provide a means of claiming a unique individualism. The richness of the data that has been revealed in carrying out this study has eloquently outlined the potency of the car's place within the cultural life of a minority community. It provides a locus for individual pride and creativity that merges into a subcultural collective sensibility, giving positive self-regard to some who might externally be seen as being relatively marginalised. Furthermore, the car provides a flexible and quietly intrusive way for more affluent members of the community to signal their success in intra- and inter-group encounters on the street.

As Best (2006) indicates, the modification of the standard specification of a particular car not only changes its external appearance, but also crucially changes its performative capacities. Increasing the brake horsepower and adding new exhaust systems can, for example, facilitate dramatic acceleration, accompanied by a cacophonous aural blast that ensures the immediate and non-negotiable visibility of the car and the driver. The car and the driver in that unique fusion of Urry's *car–driver* has already appeared in our examples as being potently expressed through driving *behaviour*. Thus, we must also give consideration to the expressive driving behaviours that can be found among Bradfordian Pakistani drivers, as it is these as much as the distinctive physical presence of the cars that feature in the inter-group experience of the streetscapes of Bradford.

Beyond the car: driving as cultural expression

Best (2006) situates part of her discussion within zones and places, in particular, discussing the significance of areas where enthusiasts take their cars and show off, cruise or race – usually, a main 'drag' or road that has an established identity and reputation associated with youth car culture. In Bradford, however, there is no single road, strip or even area more generally that has come to be the city's centre of car-cultural performance. However, along with some (supermarket/shopping centre) car parks (see, eg, harry4lyf , 2011), many of Bradford's inner-city roads do appear to become a venue or gallery in which especially young men will showcase their cars. In particular, and unsurprisingly, the road around the city's university and college seem to be used as advertising space, as do all other roads upon which there is a strong density of traffic (around businesses, eg, White Abbey Road, Leeds Road, Oak Lane), both vehicular and human. Thus, 'cruising' around with friends is an element of the Bradfordian/Pakistani car subculture, which, although engaged in by a minority of their cohort, may have a disproportionate social impact, a point we develop later. However, there are also some specific venues and events when this subculture is not only given wider legitimacy, but also cuts across the previously mentioned Bradfordian Pakistani class divide, with the allure and presence of the exotic car in the hands of the young heightened and sanctioned. On any given weekend, especially during the summer months, it is likely that this informally licensed/allowed car excess will be witnessed by road users and pedestrians within areas that have relatively large Pakistani-heritage populations. Weddings,[23] for example, give the green light to hire prestige and exotic cars. Formally, these cars form part of the motorcade from the groom's home to that of the bride's (if the cars are hired by the groom's side), from the bride's house to the wedding venue and so on. Informally, they are also used to cruise, show off and, for some, test driving prowess through drag races, burnouts, doughnuts and other feats of driving skill, as well as risk. The street becomes the performative space in which car drivers choose to display their cars as distinctive physical artefacts and as integrated expressions of their *car–driver* identity.

On the streetscape of inner-city Bradford, young men, four up, in a car, are routinely to be found in specific locales at specific times 'cruising'. From the perspective of an alien observer, this behaviour might be construed as some brutal form of social control order, whereby able-bodied young men are required to spend large bodies of time confined to an enclosed space from which they can only observe the world outside. Deprived of their full repertoire of interactional capacity, they are only able to shout comments at people they observe on the street and fix them with their gaze. Such engagements are necessarily temporarily constrained as the car passes along the street, leaving the pedestrian targets of their attention in their wake. Perhaps, precisely because of this, each encounter is experienced as being highly compressed, with all the emotive and cognitive impact given increased resonance because of its immanent loss. For this reason, too, the dialogue among the occupants of the car is powerfully charged as they rehearse the performance, as discourse, during and after each event.

Similarly, the theatrical machismo of rapid acceleration and braking over a distance as short as 20 metres has about it the benefits of immediate gratification. The intended audience do not have to explicitly signal their response to this performance, their presence on the street is sufficient to trigger the behaviour, with, for the driver, the vicarious satisfactions of a car-body act none-negotiably imposed upon them. In Bradford, the routine presence of such behaviour constitutes a familiar element of the automotively charged streetscape, and it attracts social comment.

---

[23] Other occasions for which high-end cars are hired are the Eid celebrations and, for some, to celebrate birthdays. Often, groups of friends, both drivers and non-drivers, 'chip in', usually to hire a Lamborghini, Porsche, Audi or whatever else their budget, and driving experience, will allow.

Being 'cut up': the personal becomes interpersonal

The most xenophobic citizen of Bradford may deliberately locate themselves in a white suburb where their neighbourhood demography will ensure that they have a minimal risk of encountering anyone of a different ethnicity, or class. However, if their weekly routine requires that they must drive through central Bradford, then they cannot avoid the possibility that they will have an encounter with that urban myth, *the young Asian male driver*. As we have seen, as part of the folk culture of Bradford, the young Pakistani male has a salience in many forms, not least as the rioter, book burner or drug dealer, but it is as the car driver that he takes on a form that everyone has a realistic chance of encountering, and reading/perceiving, in real life. Statistically, the 'Asian' (people of Pakistani, Indian, Bangladeshi heritage) population of Bradford is youthful, and, as we have seen, car ownership has a real popularity and cultural significance within their milieu. Young men and their cars are not a phenomenon unique to Bradford (Thomas et al, 1998; Wollen and Kerr, 2002; Swanton, 2010), but in Bradford, the *racialisation* (Rattansi, 2005) of the construction of the popular perception of the issue is profound.

Young Pakistani men have been rendered problematic in the local public sphere through their association with the drug scene, with crime, of specific areas coming to be seen as hostile to white people and through their association with 'grooming' young white girls. As recurrent, or occasional, foci of local media representation, these tropes have had a significant vitality and impact. However, it is the extent to which they are capable of being raised as the dominant imagery of a cohort of young people in the popular imagination that makes them so significant. In essence, in the context of Bradford, the category 'young Asian male' has become heavily permeated by negative connotations of threat and alien difference. In a purportedly academic account of Bradford's demography, for example, one writer takes the time out to propose that:

> These structural features of the migrant experience mean that young people in the District with different backgrounds may have experienced quite different forms of socialization, even if they are living in close proximity to each other. This is likely to have complex and potentially confusing effects on the identities of young people, and the ways in which these are expressed. On the one hand, young people of Pakistani Muslim background in effect have two kinds of

career option, in addition to facing whatever obstacles White racism throws in their path. They can make their way either in the White institutions or in their 'home' or community institutions, and this may place conflicting demands upon them. (Carling, 2008: 573)

This unyielding picture of polarised options is then followed by a footnote that indicates the inherent possibility for pathology in these circumstances. Carling continues:

Another possibility is that minority ethnic young people may fall between two stools, into the alienated space that exists in the gaps between these two sets of institutions, through criminal activity and gang membership, say for young men.... For young women this possibility is more likely to translate into psychological stress and mental health issues, through an internalization of anger and aggression, for example, which cannot be outwardly expressed. (Carling, 2008: 583)

Thus, when these same young men emerge onto the streets of Bradford in cars, they do not appear as tabulae rasae, as neutral and unobtrusive elements in the vehicular flux of urban life. They sit within a broader racialised narrative that is itself permeated with their racialised presence as key actors: underachiever, rioter, dealer, radical, groomer. First, they are visible because of their ethnicity, gender and age, and the prior expectations they elicit; in other words, they are primed for a process of selective perception when viewed from an external, majority perspective, and it is this, in a cyclical manner, that dominates the construction of their identity Second, they are visible as young Pakistani *drivers*: they have an extant reputation as a particular type of road user, and that reputation is similarly replete with imagery of assertiveness and its adjunct, aggression. The notion of being 'cut up' by a young Pakistani driver is part of popular street lore. It would seem that in both the Pakistani and majority populations, there is a widespread belief that this cohort of young people constitute a distinctly visible and disruptive presence on the roads. Indeed, anecdotes from individuals of their personal experience of being 'cut up' or in some other way being discommoded, challenged or threatened by the driving behaviour of such young men can be elicited with relative ease.

In the language of the social psychology of inter-group behaviour, such experiences might be regarded as generating a sense of 'realistic threat' (on Integrated Threat Theory, see Stephan and Stephan, 1996a;

Stephan et al, 1999), namely, a feeling that *our legitimate interests and security* is being put in jeopardy by these *others*. Equally, encounters with young Asian drivers can be seen as a *symbolic threat* in that *THEY* are perceived by majority ethnic drivers as an intrusive and unwelcome presence on *OUR* roads. Of course, within Integrated Threat Theory, these two processes interact. In this case, the behaviour and, in some cases, even the presence of these young men is perceived as all the more provocative and unacceptable precisely because they are Pakistani; their behaviour is thus pathologically tied with their ethnicity while their ethnicity explains their behaviour. That such incidents might constitute a minute part of a year spent driving in Bradford, or that the young men involved might be a minute fraction of the total ethnic/age/gender cohort that they are associated with, has little, if any, impact upon the resonance of the experience over time. Selective retention and recall, the close cousins of selective perception, ensure that these personal incidents are available for rehearsal when triggered in a social context.

Katz's (1999) evocative account of the road rage that frequently occurs as a response to experiences of being 'cut up' provides us with an insight into the ego involvement of the driver with their vehicle. The driver's engagement with their vehicle creates a synergy that renders a peculiarly ego-involving claim to competence, and *performance*, as a driver. Seeing driving as performative is, in fact, helpful to understanding the response to encounters with other drivers. At one level, driving a vehicle is essentially a pragmatically acquired skill that enables an individual to expedite their removal from one place to another. However, this is a definition that few drivers would accept as anywhere near complete. Driving is an expressive act as much as, if not more so than, a pragmatic one. As we have noted, the extensive national and international audience for the ecstatic posturing of Jeremy Clarkson and his pseudo-religious celebration of the car in *Top Gear* provides one insight into the power of this dynamic. Thus, being 'cut up' is not merely an impediment to your fluid progression from one place to another, it is perceived as a form of personal insult, even an assault – and perhaps more so if the perpetrator of this offence is someone you already have reason to quickly, perhaps automatically, constitute as a particular type of person/identity. Being cut up, then, is not just a unique personally distressing experience, it becomes 'typical of *them!*' They could be an attractive young woman in an expensive car, an older person in a 'suburban pram' or a young man in a 'pimped out' car. In social-psychological terms, this is not so much an interpersonal encounter as an *inter-group* encounter (Tajfel and Turner, 1979; Abrams and Hogg, 1999). The response may be directed to the individual driver, but the text for the encounter is framed by the perception of their category membership and reinforces the associated stereotype of the typical behaviour of all the category members.

It is the case that there is a subculture of driving style among some unfathomable proportion of the Pakistani population of Bradford that is a fusion of elan, speed and assertiveness. It can take the form of: rapid acceleration and late breaking in urban traffic; what might be called inconsiderate overtaking manoeuvres; and the unambiguously assertive/aggressive cutting up of other drivers. To that, we might also add the phenomenon of parking driver-to-driver in narrow inner-city streets in order to facilitate a conversation, where the claiming of space, and time, for a conversation is a provocative challenge to other drivers blocked by their self-indulgence. These behaviours seem unlikely to be unthinking expressions of automotive *joie de vivre*, since the offending drivers and their passengers are routinely palpably interested in the reaction they have generated in the other drivers they have discomforted. One of the researchers had a glorious example of this process when sitting as the first car at the traffic lights, waiting from them to change. Suddenly, a car with a young Asian driver came past at speed and immaculately cut in front. What might be described as an example of superb, yet highly provocative, driving was given a further dimension of projection when the art work in the rear windscreen of the offending car was registered. It read, quite simply, *'HATE ME NOW'*. Some outraged drivers would have been only too willing to comply with the invitation.

The taint of tint

It would, however, be a considerable mistake to regard the 'offence' caused in particular exchanges with young Asian drivers in Bradford as being solely related to their driving behaviour alone. It is possible to argue that, in certain circumstances, their presence on the road per se causes offence. Here, we are speaking not so much of driving behaviour itself, but of the performative possibilities of the car as a means of presentation of self, and as a setting for personal and shared engagement with a public. As we saw earlier, the car itself is literally a vehicle for self-expression. It is a means through which an individual may mark out their personal claim to individuality, or proudly assert their membership of a specific collectivity through using customised elements that are *de rigueur* for their in-group. Thus, for example, the presence of tinted windows is one of the stylistic options favoured by a subset of young drivers in general, and young Pakistanis in particular.

In speaking of the significance of tinted windows, Katz notes that their presence radically changes the dynamics between those in the car and those outside. Just as wearing sunglasses shifts the dynamics of interpersonal interaction if only one person is wearing them, so too:

> the windows of a car can be outfitted to put virtually the whole vehicle in 'shades'. The result in both cases is to create an aura of mystery rooted in a practical problem of interpretation: the reading of whether and where attentions may be directed becomes a unique problem for the person not sporting shades.... Because the person in shades does not as readily give off indications of his or her disposition but is presumably unimpaired in detecting the direction of others' gazes, an emotionally provocative potential for an asymmetrical uncertainty is built into street transactions. (Katz, 1999: 29)

It is exactly this asymmetrical uncertainty that constitutes the basis of a differential in power in the on-road interaction of the drivers involved. Those behind the tinted windows have the 'upper hand': they can see without being seen. Additionally, this reality does not exist in a neutral context. The possession of tinted windows has, *in itself*, already triggered a potent, culturally powerful set of expectations about 'the sort of person' who has tinted windows. In Knightsbridge in London, it may throw up a stereotypical expectation of some affluent yuppie or a 'celeb' going *incognito*, but in some parts of Bradford, a likely available stereotype is more probably that of drug dealer or assertive young male. The content of such a stereotype then provides the cognitive schema for interpreting the interaction. Selective perception is routinely in play independently of the actual intentions and behaviour of the occupants of the car with tinted windows. If their behaviour does violate the normal code of the road or is unambiguously challenging, then the response will be mediated through this already-activated sense of hostility and anxiety.

'Anxiety' is a good word here, for we are again in need of recognising the role of symbolic threat (Stephan and Stephan, 1996a). In inter-group relations, a sense of threat may not only be sensed in relation to the concrete and material interests of the in-group, but may also be experienced in terms of a threat to the cultural integrity of the in-group: *our* values, *our* ways of doing things, *our* sense of propriety are being mocked and undermined. In this way, taken-for-granted notions of privacy, and its complement – accessibility – have their own capacity to create a strong cultural aversion to perceived violations of the norm. Unlike the Netherlands, or perhaps parts of Scandinavia, Britain does not have a strong normative assumption that you have no need to draw the curtains in your living room when it gets dark, but we do seem to find tinted windows in cars to be problematic. Perhaps part of the origin of this sensibility lies in yet another expression of British class consciousness: traditionally, only the very affluent could afford to have tinted windows. However, it is reasonable to assert that heavily tinted windows are not 'normal'. Indeed, they continue to constitute and connote uniqueness and importance inasmuch as the driver/owner feels it necessary to protect their identity on the one hand, while conversely also projecting it on the other. Yet again, we can see the opportunity provided by individual owners' preferences for those who observe them, and their car, to produce meanings that can contribute to heightening inter-group sensitivities.

Cruising/gender/noise

Cruising can involve young men driving around in order to be seen and to see what is going on. As a young male–car interface, this is far from a unique facet of the inner-city, or urban, streetscape. Cruising has a long tradition (O'Connell, 1998; Best, 2006; Bengry-Howell and Griffin, 2007) and provides a congenial environment in which young men can rehearse the shibboleths of their particular shared identity. One distinctive element in this process is, of course, their gender and their sexual preference. Thus, one facet of cruising is an ability to observe, and assess, the female 'talent' on the street:

> For example, in a 1930 series on vice in Scottish cities, the Weekly Record painted a lurid picture of behaviour amongst young people in Dundee's dance halls and on the weekly 'monkey parades' in which young people promenaded the city's main thoroughfares in single-sex groups in the hope of pairing off with a member of the opposite sex. As the Weekly Record noted with considerable alarm, young men had taken to using cars in order to lure prospective sexual partners away from the public arena of the parades. These 'car-ghouls' drove about the thoroughfares ogling and smiling at young girls parading the pavements. (O'Connell, 1998: 105)

The finite social context of the car provides young men with a particular site from which to collectively play off each other in rehearsing their masculinity and sexual assertiveness. One form this takes is in shouting comments to the young women they pass on the street. This action contributes significantly to the sexualisation of social space that we encountered in Chapter Five, and creates a phenomenon that has a variety of potential respondents. For the young women so targeted, it is an uninvited engagement with strangers that they may find intensely offensive. For some, it may constitute an acceptable, if unsophisticated, recognition of their attractiveness. However, for all women, it is a clear statement of power relations on the street. It is significant that this behaviour is not exclusively confined to targeting young white women and, consequently, widens the range of observers who may have particular objections to this behaviour. For white males, this behaviour addressed to white women walking on the street is likely to provoke a racialised patriarchal response as they take offence on behalf of *THEIR* women. For members of the Pakistani-heritage (Muslim) community, both male and female, this behaviour is likely to be seen as a serious violation of norms of gendered decency. Again, we have an instance of a form of social interaction in which the actions of a hyper-visible few may have wide-ranging effects in stigmatising the large group who they are perceived to represent.

Of course, the social process of 'cruising' places the car and its occupants on the street, and, usually quite deliberately, on streets that are likely to have significant pedestrian as well vehicular traffic, since being observed is a core feature of cruising. Consequently, public responses to features of the customised car become a correlate of this activity. If at one time Chicanos/as 'drove "slow and low", then it could be asserted that a visible feature of young Bradfordian/Pakistani driving is a preference for rapid acceleration from being stationary, or from driving at a low speed' (Best, 2006: 33-42). Often associated with ill-advised overtaking in traffic, the ego-burst of rapid acceleration may say something about the technical capacity of the car, but it is also routinely accompanied by the howling of tyres and the roar of the engine. Additionally, where the car has been fitted with a customised exhaust system, the cumulative aural assault upon the pedestrian will be fully orchestrated. The deliberate creation of such aural celebrations of their machismo is not only an established feature of the urban driving style of a section of young Bradfordian/Pakistani men, it is of appeal to a much wider cohort of car modification enthusiasts. Nevertheless, a car's aural emission draws attention to both the driver/occupant and the car in a situation where, for some observers, both in interaction are highly charged sources of irritation and resentment. There appear to be, for example, young men who have a routine of driving their quad bikes through the town centre in the early evening. Whatever adjustments have been made to their exhaust systems has been truly impressive in the decibels they have been able to create as the exhaust system roars and explodes, spectacularly announcing their presence. Again, any fascination with the various flatulent possibilities of exhaust systems is, of course, not confined to a relatively small proportion of Bradford's Pakistanis; there is an extensive industry in supplying such enhancements to a wide a range of users across regional and national markets. Indeed, we have to be mindful to ensure that the reader is aware that our broader discussion remains firmly located within a general context of demographics, and while ethnicity is, of course, one highly cogent feature, masculinity and age are also key in influencing preferences and behaviours.

Similarly, the fusion of musical taste with expensively fitted sound systems[24] in cars provides instances where ethnic identity and taste, explicitly publicly displayed, may prove to be intrusive to both the musical aesthetics and eardrums of a range of pedestrians who become unwilling audience members. In the soundscape of multi-ethnic Bradford and Manningham, the eruption of sounds associated with the cultural pleasure in the possibilities of car ownership shared by some members of the Bradfordian/Pakistani community provide a basis for making highly salient the inter-ethnic nature of urban encounters, and for shaping these in a hostile inter-group mode. Each car defines its own ethnic/gender and class terrain, which may find itself in contestation with a car defined by different ownership criteria. Furthermore, each area and street may be claimed as an ethnic/racialised territory through which the passage of a declamatory motorised *Other* may stimulate resentment and the rehearsal of stereotyped inter-group sentiments.

Conclusion

On any given day and especially on particular inner-city Bradford roads, you will encounter a vibrant and, at times, overpowering car presence. The large four-wheel-drive Range Rovers, Audi Q7s and BMW X5s appear across the country. The Porsches, Ferraris, Lamborghinis and Audi RS8s are much more thinly spread, but an hour on a Bradford

---

[24] A growing, initially underground, complement to the custom ICE systems are 'bass-test' compositions: pieces of music that are purposefully constructed with beats that stretch and test speaker bass reflex and, more generally, the aural capacity of sound systems – volume and clarity of sound being important elements.

road will seem to suggest otherwise. The car traders we talked to, ranging from a 'one-man band' who sold 'anything and everything' to a family-owned business that specialised in 'sports and exotics', strongly suggested that Bradford's car-buying market appears to be healthy, the explanations for which are varied and complex: some want to be seen to be successful, some simply like cars, some enjoy the attention and some enjoy the experience of driving, speed and even freedom.

While some confer status – sports, executive and 'exotics', for example – others allow drivers to float along within a sea of anonymity: the Model T Ford along with Volkswagen's original Beetle variants were the early functional cars, which said very little about their drivers and owners other than that they were a part of the mass at whom these objects were aimed. More recently, Toyota Corollas and Ford Mondeos have come to be known as the 'everyman' and 'everywoman' car – functional, reliable and efficient – and although there are, of course, 'high-spec' variants (eg the ST Mondeo), they are principally defined as cars with very little appeal beyond the utilitarian. That said, cars – whatever their shape, size or cost – represent some sense of personal freedom inasmuch as they allow us to move distances that even a hundred years ago might have taken days, rather than hours, to complete (Sheller and Urry, 2003: 115).

The reality of automobility is simply this: cars and their associated infrastructure (ranging from discovering and refining fuel to building, maintaining and policing roads) are one of the most important facts of contemporary urban life. The car not only has a deepening economic and environmental impact on the world, but also 'reconfigures the relation between place, space and the mobility of people and objects' (Sheller and Urry, 2003: 115). The car remains more than an object with the specific utility of travel; it has a growing sense of variety not only in terms of design and size, but also in terms of purpose, 'symbolic' power and meaning. Not only have cars sprawled a huge infrastructure that sustains their existence, but there continues to develop an embodied relationship between driver and car. The 'car–driver' hybrid (Dant, 2004) and the 'car-system' (Urry, 2004) are interdependent elements of the same car hegemony within which there sit relations of dependence, collaboration and interaction in order to sustain the existence of both humans and cars. Perhaps more importantly, cars have the capacity to represent so much more than the sum of their parts. They are brands that, through decades' worth of image making and advertising, have their own associations and meanings; they yield the capacity to elicit emotions from us as individual consumers and group owners. In the world of advertising, cars are quite consciously developed as objects that have certain traits that we, as consumers, can identify with: a Volvo is safe, a Toyota is reliable and an Alfa Romeo continues to build on the notion of being a 'true' driver's car. The messages we have encoded, although mediated through advertising, remain subtle and indirect:

> For example, do you think the typical owner of a Volvo would be more or less conservative than the owner of a Ford? More or less affluent? Most people would agree that the Volvo owner is likely to be more conservative and more affluent than the Ford owner. Yet they have not acquired those pieces of information through any direct message. (Sutherland, 2008: 63)

Yet, this is only part of the story. The images and ideas that manufacturers use and exploit are only meaningful if the audience buys into them. If that audience is somehow fractured, be it through forms of class- or ethnic-based alienation, differentiation or even resistance, then there is a likelihood that they will create their own meanings through their own cultures, tastes and sensibilities, which, in turn, suggests that marginality does not have to mean passivity, or acceptance. At the same time, there is a confluence of car cultures in Bradford that clearly illustrates variety and change in structure among what is often purported to be a homogeneous ethnic bloc.

Whether we like to admit it or not, cars are integral elements of the social world and they offer us an opportunity to gain insights into human behaviours and attitudes. This chapter, therefore, has tried to dissect some of the complex, intersecting and, at times, even conflicting aspects of a city's car culture and reputation; in various ways, the car is a fascinating means through which individual and collective human identity can and ought to be explored. In the context of Bradford, the car becomes a highly flexible signifier of identity and difference, and while it plays a significant role in the manufacture of banal and not-so-banal multi-ethnic coexistence, it enables the performance of race thinking to become embodied and for further processes of racialisation to take place.

CHAPTER SEVEN

Conclusion: recognising diversity and planning for coexistence

In this final chapter, we briefly reflect upon some of the themes that have emerged through our data. It will be apparent that this research constitutes a further contribution to the necessary task of engaging with the unique physical and social infrastructure of a multi-ethnic urban space, and with the very distinctive histories and embedded discourses that animate people's understandings of their life there. The reality that then emerges stands in stark contrast to the distorting, broad-brush declamations about inner-city ghettos. It challenges a reduction of urban areas to a detailed demographic mapping of the population, and to the physical characteristics of the area. The discussion of the streetscape of Manningham in Chapters Two and Three provided a clear insight into the inherent social construction of the meanings of the physical characteristics of an area. Manningham clearly exists within a multiply nuanced web of histories that are known and owned by specific constituencies of interest and identity within, and beyond, the area.

The account we have offered has pragmatically drawn upon the very extensive social-psychological literature that has widened and deepened our understanding of the nature and operation of social identities. It is a clear theme within this data that space, place and identity are woven together in a very particular flux. The ready availability of heavily over-rehearsed collective identities recurs as a marked feature of the manner in which individuals make sense of their lives in Manningham through the lens of specific collective identities. Identities grounded in ethnicity, gender, class, faith or age do not provide rigid frameworks through which our residents must inexorably experience their everyday interactions. However, they do exist as an available repertoire of means of categorising self and others, which when made salient in a specific context, can radically change the social significance of the interaction, and its long-term implications. The shift from an interpersonal to an inter-group reading of a situation is a social-psychological dynamic that feeds off and reinforces, in the momentary interactions on the street, the polarised depictions of inter-group conflict that are so evident in the accounts of inner-city urban areas in the media and in academe. Where these encounters, and their construal in inter-group terms, become regularised in the local patterns of routine interaction, then we have a situation in which stereotypes become not only ossified, but also seemingly legitimated. The politicisation of such stereotypes in the flaccid theorisation, and assimilationist ethos, of the governmental rhetoric around social cohesion (Cheong et al, 2007; Husband and Alam, 2011) has provided no adequate conceptual framework from which to engage with the reality of the lived diversity of places such as Manningham, and we will seek to address this issue in the latter part of this chapter.

Diversity, identity and perceptions

The dynamics of life on the streets of Manningham are an *in vivo* demonstration of the complex intersectionality of contemporary lived identities. Each interaction is experienced through a cognitive filter that takes into consideration the multiple signs that each person presents to the viewer. The multiple modes of categorising any one individual provide a rich conceptual framework within which any individual may be located. However, this image of an extensive range of discrete pigeonholes into which an individual may be slotted is deeply misleading, for the essence of the social reading of other persons in our social field is to read them as a complex algebraic interaction of a number of salient features. Individuals, for example, are not seen as male or female, old or young, Pakistani or 'English', 'coloured' or 'white', respectable or disreputable, or safe or dangerous, but as a complex fusion of some of these characteristics. A person who is male, affluent and young may form a particular gestalt; add to that the additional characteristic 'Pakistani', and the gestalt may change radically. Change the gender to female and, again, the resultant whole may be radically different. Thus, in seeking to talk of the nature of interpersonal interaction on the streets of Bradford, we have to be careful about the conception of the perceptual processes in play that we bring to our account of this situation.

We are familiar with the easy use of the notion of *hybrid* identities and of the imagery of multiple social statuses and complex biographic realities that are invoked by the use of this term, but what we need to be certain to place at the forefront of our sensibility in using this term is the reality that, in every instance, this one person may engage with the multiple options of these characteristics in a unique, even if well-rehearsed, combination. Turner et al (1987), for example, in their theory of *self-categorisation*, point to the central importance of the ways in which individuals construe their identity, and seek to defend it, for any understanding of inter-group behaviour (see also Abrams and Hogg, 1999). The salient categories that we use to make sense of ourselves are also often the social categories through which we see ourselves as members of social groups, and it is the legitimacy and prestige of these groups that reciprocally help to sustain our sense of personal worth. It is for this reason that interpersonal interaction on the street can often be legitimately understood as being, in fact, an *inter-group* interaction.

When the unique human being we encounter on the street is perceptually reduced to being a member of an out-group (one of *them*), the dynamics of the resultant interaction are likely to be changed dramatically. *Their* complex hybridity can be reduced to a stereotypical assertion of their essential nature as an immigrant, a Roma beggar, a Pakistani youth or even, in this day and age, a banker. In so labelling someone, not only do we stereotype them in relation to a few over-rehearsed essential characteristics, but we also simultaneously render our own complexity void by, in this moment, seeing ourselves primarily as a member of a distinct group, defined in relation to this other. Where such a neighbourhood oppositional reading of relations is made in the context of national and local discourses that have both repetitively reproduced strong stereotypes and provided a legitimating account for the veracity of this perception, then the inter-group dynamics in place are very likely to reproduce rather than challenge this interpersonal (inter-group) positioning.

Interpersonal perception on the street is, therefore, always a very dynamic and contextual process. Consequently, in our analysis here, we must remain sensitive to the fact that the experiences recorded in the preceding chapters represent distinct readings of a social environment that are true for the observer, and we must be cautious not to render them as summary statements of an unambiguous reality. This is particularly so when interactions with individuals become translated in recall as experiences of categories of people.

The data presented earlier very richly demonstrate the often stark distinction between the inclusive, essentialising nature of the categorical attributions made of specific others, and the internal distinctions heavily policed by the members of this same category. Thus, for example, reference to recent East European migrants by established residents, white and Pakistani, typically show no appreciation of the multiple nuanced distinctions made within the Polish population of Bradford, as revealed in Chapter Five. Similarly, age and gender distinctions render common ethnic membership an ambiguous and dangerous basis for making predictive statements about the common characteristics of 'this group'. The racialisation of space and place can be seen as a theme running across our data. It is associated with the laying of racial characteristics upon specific persons who are encountered on the street, and is related to the territorialisation of place as an expression of claimed collective lived histories in the area. The streetscape of Manningham is not a fixed and given objective physical environment. It is, at all times, a social environment in which the physical properties of the streetscape are available as signs of presence, to be invoked and interpreted through the particular lens of each resident.

Similarity across difference

In the data presented in the previous chapters, there is a, perhaps necessary, recognition of the unique ways in which different individuals experience their life in Manningham. However, across this personal diversity, threads of commonality can be seen woven through the accounts of interaction. There are shared routines and social expectations held in common that frame the possibility for coexistence in such a diverse area. As we shall see, Smith et al (2010) helpfully point out that interaction in urban areas is shaped by patterns of flows as individuals pass in transit between destinations. One basis for the experience of similarity across social categories within Manningham is a recognition of the common motives for being mobile: a need to bring food into the home, a need to go to work or a need to seek recreation. Common needs also bring into a play the provision of common destinations that service these needs: parents take their children to local schools and playgrounds, and people go to the same shops or use the same public transport. In this process, there is not only a spatial mapping of shared activity, but also a temporal structure to shared lives as individuals do similar things at the same time. Thus, mobility within Manningham is not random; nor is it motiveless. A recognition of common daily routines provides the basis for a mapping of shared social expectations and the laying down of local norms as individuals daily negotiate their familiar routines. The streetscape becomes a familiar home ground for those who live there. In the previous chapters, we have seen the affective connection people have with living in Manningham. Across age, gender and ethnic categories, we have noted individuals' commitment to living in the area. They may experience life there differently, and they may draw upon different biographical narratives in explaining their satisfactions in living within the area, but many do have a shared commitment to Manningham. This terrain, then, with its familiar narratives, destinations, resources and activities, provides the common context of material attachments, where, in Amin's (2010: 23) words, 'In all these vignettes, things and relationships with them return as the stuff of social ties and affects. The entanglements make for ties with known and unknown others, always without straightforward civic and political connotations.'

Consistently with other contemporary literature, the significance of place and space for the residents of Manningham is not a given, but an ongoing negotiation of historicity, identity and the opportunity structure of their lives there. People of different class and ethnicity show an appreciation of the 19th-century housing they occupy, or the possibilities of shopping locally. They share common material attachments to the area, and they pursue common human aspirations in their shared urban environment.

We have seen how the reputation of the area affects individuals' social constructions of the rationale for their presence in Manningham. Additionally, we have seen the role of common forces of exclusion and opportunity as individuals chose to stay or exit from Manningham. At the same time, we have also noted the quite different dynamics of settlement and movement that have been a feature of the Polish, rather than the Pakistani community, where the absence of colour-based racism and an easier mobility into more affluent incomes provided the basis for a more rapid dispersal of the population from Manningham.

The importance of the particular character of a local area within Manningham for individuals' sense of attachment and satisfaction recurs across the data. Collective claims of legitimate territorial sensibilities provide one basis for mapping ethnicity over the area. However, as we saw with the data on gendered experience, ethnicity is a highly fluid and contingent category. The creation of meaningful lives through an active engagement with available collective identities, which are often defined in oppositional terms, provides one of the defining features of life in the area.

Gendered space reconsidered

Unsurprisingly, the data presented earlier have revealed the significance of gender in patterning the social relations of Manningham. Gender, as a marker, is pervasive in its penetration into the interstices of the social world. Furthermore, its impact becomes all the more salient when gender is melded with cultural difference, where differing normative conceptions of gender-appropriate behaviour become one of the most sensitive of boundary markers between communities. Too often in the inter-group posturing of men, women become the terrain over which contested claims to territory and prestige are fought. The policing of female modesty and clothing is but one element in this regulation of women as an expression of dominant ideology (Dwyer, 1998; Yuval-Davis, 2000).

For women, being stared at, commented on and made to feel uncomfortable while wandering around the city results in a restriction of women's freedom, as the feelings of insecurity that are generated by such unwanted public harassment directly impact on women's use of space (see, for example, Koskela, 1999; MacMillan et al, 2000). Unwanted public attention from men causes women to adopt a variety of strategies, routines and rituals for safety. As Stanko's (1990) research showed, women reported practising a wider variety, as well as a higher number, of safety rituals than men. Stanko (1990) described how women who live in the inner-city areas develop skills involved in reading the street. The skills include the ability to judge the behaviour of those around you, as well as constantly assessing your physical environment for signs of danger. These strategies and skills of safety vary, depending upon age, race, physical ability, living situation and where in the city the home is located. Avoiding certain neighbourhoods at various times of the evening is one such strategy for safety, and people usually develop a mental map of safety: which streets are bad, which streets are safe to walk, where the bad people are, where it is crowded and so on. Our data here, for example, revealed that women of a different age might experience the locale differently, and being known in an area may grant you a degree of privileged protection from male attention that a 'stranger' might not expect to avoid.

Fenster (2005a) claims that the issues of fear and safety cause gendered exclusions from the right to the city. In her study, the right to fully use the urban space is measured in relation to three notions: comfort, belonging and commitment. The women interviewed by Fenster (2005a) identified comfort with being in control and freedom, which often appeared to be restricted by patriarchal power relations. Moreover, the perception of comfort and freedom in public spaces was very much affected by the nature of power relations in the private domain of the home. For instance, women who felt controlled at home identified the public space of the city with their personal freedom. Another finding was that women defined the sentiment of belonging as resulting from the continuous use of the space. Using the urban space gave a sense of familiarity and belonging to women; thus, for example, the increased visibility of Pakistani/Muslim women in Lister Park has changed the perception of that terrain over time, so that it is now most definitely within their familiar domain – even though norms of propriety and safety continue to shape their use of it.

In examining the daily experiences of public harassment and how it affects women's position in society, Gardner (1995) claims that the regular subjection of women to public harassment and the fact that such unwanted attention is usually not given much attention, often being considered as a trivial reality of everyday life, is part of a general dynamic through which public order and social control is maintained. She sees women in public places as situationally disadvantaged: irrespective of their status or advantage in other contexts, women are subject to public harassment.

To prevent harassment or crime, women are most often advised not to walk alone when it gets dark, to have a male to escort them in public places, to dress in a way that does not attract men's attention and, in case they are harassed by strange men, to ignore it or put the best face on a harassing incident. These recommendations strongly suggest that women should take the responsibility for their own safety and they only have themselves to blame if they do not follow these rules of personal safety, whereas the behaviour of the harasser is taken for granted as being the reality of everyday life to which women should accommodate. As Koskela (1999: 121) has noted:

> Much of the power which modifies women's behaviour can be regarded as being control through 'consent' rather than through 'coercion' (Green et al, 1987, p 91). This power is often taken for granted, and thus remains unnoticed. The notion that 'exclusions take place routinely, without most people noticing' is an important aspect of the problem.

In many instances, this consent is encoded into a shared cultural understanding of behavioural proprieties that provides a cultural legitimation for male expressions of power. In other instances, it is better understood as an acceptance of the need to accommodate to the power of patriarchy: it is submission, rather than acceptance. In recognising the power of patriarchy embedded in cultural practice, there immediately occurs the fraught question of insider versus outsider perspectives on the acceptability of behaviours. Thus, for example, white feminist critiques of the oppression of women within minority communities have not always been appreciated by their minority sisters (see Phillips, 2007). The gendered nature of harassment signals a form of disenfranchisement of women, which takes on a particular sensitivity when examined in the context of issues concerning the group boundaries and spatial divisions between Asian and white communities, and within these communities.

This draws attention to the power hierarchies in public places that, in the case of Bradford, are intertwined with a variety of identity markers that position women and men of different 'race', ethnicity, age, class and sexual preference differently in relation to each other. These identity markers of both women and men create a variety of perceived hierarchies of power, status and belonging that may heighten the possibility of public harassment or crime. In this respect, normative cultural socialisation significantly shapes our attitudes and behaviour when encountering difference in public places. The nature of the culture(s) in which we are brought up can be considered a source of our initial assumptions about differences: their value, their level of acceptability, the threat they may pose and how we can or should react to them. Thus, in terms of the culture of different groups, it may be useful to try to distinguish the patterns of responding to difference that exist and are enacted by individuals belonging to various and mostly intersecting groups.

Another side of the issue of power hierarchies in public places is the established ways of expressing one's power in specific contexts, which directs us back to different expressions and styles of masculinities, and can be linked to normative cultural socialisation. The different ways in which men perform their masculinity affects their personal sense of power and the expressions of it that they see as appropriate, or required, in specific contexts in public places. Nor is the gendered environment in which men seek to negotiate their identity a stable one.

Women, too, are continually in a process of contesting the intrusions of patriarchy into their lives, and in expressing other salient aspects of their identity, are adopting new styles of behaviour and dress. Thus, in a city like Bradford, the relative success of young Asian women in education and employment vis-a-vis their brothers has produced an existentially based foundation for new forms of female self-expression. Entry into education and the labour market has provided many young Asian women with access to degrees of freedom that their mothers would not have experienced, located as they were more significantly within the domestic sphere. Their own generational changes and the accumulated successes of feminism have provided a context in which young Asian women are articulating new behavioural expressions of self-confidence and independence, which constitute a potential provocation to their brothers and male elders (Dwyer, 1998). Women's bodies are an ever-present element in the streetscape, which become 'sites of contested cultural representations' (Fenster, 2005b: 27).

There is, therefore, an issue here regarding whether the historical experience of settlement in Britain, with the multiple intersections of the dynamics of dislocation, diaspora and engagement with racism and marginalisation, has in any way produced a distinctive South Asian/British/Pakistani form of masculinity. The immediate naive observer's account of the young male Pakistani population of Bradford might well be to conclude that, indeed, yes, there is a distinctive mode of Pakistani machismo that can be seen as a striking feature of their public presence in Bradford. They would sustain such a claim by referring to the not-infrequent observation of young Pakistani Bradfordian men walking across major urban through-roads with a theatrical disdain for traffic lights or the consternation of drivers. They might refer to the distinctive assertiveness of their driving, noted earlier in Chapter Six, or to their confident disregard for double yellow lines, or to their loudly expressed sexist comments to young women, white and Asian. In doing so, they would have the confidence of being able to assert that such behaviours may not infrequently be observed on the streets of Bradford, and, in that, they would be right.

However, these instances need to be placed within a wider sensibility to the statistical prevalence of such behaviours across the whole population of young, and older, Pakistani-Bradfordian men. All of the previously mentioned indicators of the hypothesised machismo share a common property, in that they violate the dominant norm. Consequently, they have a much higher propensity for being noted and recorded in memory than the many banal 'acceptable' normative actions of their peers. Particularly once such behaviours have become identified as being typical of the category of 'young Pakistani men', they become a salient stereotype that has the propensity to be self-perpetuating through selective perception. Additionally, as we have already noted, male harassment and control of women is not a phenomenon unique to the British Pakistani communities. International research shows this to be an endemic condition in urban life.

Furthermore, the visibility of intrusive difference does not eradicate the multiple expressions of shared values and kindly behavioural proprieties that go unremarked, precisely because of their efficiency in lubricating everyday inter-ethnic interaction. Nor does the routine 'virtue' of individual minority ethnic individuals mobilise the same affective response as the negative instances noted earlier. The public presence of virtue lacks the impact, and fit with dominant stereotypes, of instances of intrusive incivility, and will have less travel through the discursive networks of reported experience.

Problematic Islam and gendered identities?

The linkage of British Muslim culture with their marginalised structural position within the majority society has been associated with a *racialised* perspective on their identity, which rather than addressing the forces that reproduce the exclusion and denigration of minority communities, instead produces an analysis that focuses upon the dysfunctional cultural adaptation of the minority individuals to their circumstances. Thus, in Alexander's (2000: 17) words: 'the concern over "Islamic fundamentalism" is usually understood as a reaction to racial hostility and a loss of patriarchal authority, a way of gaining self-esteem and a sense of individual and group control'.

Since the 1960s, Muslim communities in Britain have been associated in the white popular and academic gaze with the suppression of women within a patriarchal culture that has been nurtured by the continuing transnational affiliations of the settled Muslim communities in Britain. This perspective is itself nurtured by the long-established, and recently heavily rehearsed, Orientalist perspective of Islam as being locked in a traditional and anti-modernist world view, which has ossified values, beliefs and practices that stand in direct opposition to the claimed liberality of contemporary European values (Huntington, 1996). The Pakistani or Bangladeshi ethnicity of Manningham's Muslim communities facilitates a framing of these citizens within a discourse that provide a multilayered account of their *Otherness*. Their continuing affiliation to 'traditional' modes of dress and cuisine is seen as evidence of the veracity and legitimacy of this perspective. That this traditionalism can now also be understood in relation to their Muslim faith, made redolent of threat and divisiveness through the ubiquity of Islamophobic sentiments in contemporary British life (Poole, 2002; Poole and Richardson, 2006; Morey and Yaqin, 2011), provides additional and potent undertows to the perception of this community's potential threat and foundational difference. Finally, the fact that these same individuals can be framed within the colour-coded racism of British cultural sensibilities attaches to this difference a racial fixity that underlines the permanent stain of *their difference*. The current majority concern with the lives of Muslim women is reflected in the debates around the wearing of the veil, which rehearses the tenacity of their ethno-religious difference, and with their subjugation as women within their own communities, where their limited participation in the labour market, their lack of autonomy in relation to arranged and forced marriages, and their vulnerability to sexual predation are foci for rehearsing the patriarchal character of their domestic and communal life.

The emergence of the young Muslim male as a highly salient expression of the threat and difference of Muslim communities in our cities has been defined in terms that resonate in a complementary manner with this portrayal of the life of Muslim women. The invocation of a somehow alien manifestation of masculinity as routinely characteristic of the male members of these communities is the necessary complement to the perceived subjugation of their womenfolk. The association of the Bradfordian Muslim male with a 'traditional' sexist behavioural repertoire has been given a more abrasive and threatening edge for the majority white society through their association with the drug industry, crime, riot and terror. The media, nationally and locally, have had a routine practice of associating Islam with crime and terror, and the specificity of the Bradford riots with their locus around Manningham has given a local grounding to this reportage. Writing in 2000, Alexander provided a resume of this state of affairs, which was all the more telling since it pre-dated the riots of 2001 and the London bombings of 2005. She argued that:

> Muslim masculinities are then positioned as outside, and in opposition to, hegemonic norms of male behaviour, defined through deviance and subject to increasingly stringent forms of social control. There is, of course, the added specificity of an assumed religio-cultural anachronism which underscores the attribution of misogyny and patriarchal oppression, and which marks out rigid boundaries for the performance of male identities. The racialization of black young men, on the one hand, and the religio-ethnicization of Asian young men on the other, leaves Muslim youth visioned as twice disadvantaged and doubly dysfunctional, with apparently no space for difference, contestation or reimagination. (Alexander, 2000: 236–7)

In the dynamics of stereotyping and inter-group perception, it is precisely this drawing of rigid boundaries and the delineation of the key characteristics of the *other*, upon which the definitive rehearsal of their difference will be drawn, that makes the localised rehearsal of the disruptive presence of strangers so potent. The manner of perception of the young male Asian presence on the streets of Manningham and Bradford is permeated by a framing of their nature and significance that was constructed well beyond the terrain on which this understanding is mapped.

The demonisation of Islam within British popular and governmental discourse over the last two decades provides a very particular framework for the external grafting on of explanatory accounts of the lives of members of the Muslim communities living in Bradford and Manningham. The ubiquity of this generic 'othering' provides an ideological framework within which the particularities of specific sub-segments of this population may have their distinctive variant on this otherness defined for them. In this external imposition of the defining features of young Muslim men and women, there is little space for the 'more nuanced, local and historically situated account of identity formation, which encapsulates often contradictory processes of continuity and change, constraint and agency, solidarity and diffusion, representation and re-imagination' that Alexander (2000: 28) advocated for approaching any attempt to make sense of young Muslims' lives in urban Britain.

In the literature on the role of Islam in the formation of young Asian masculinities, there is a body of literature that, in its cultural determinism, reflects Alexander's (2000) concern with the attribution of misogyny and patriarchal oppression, 'and the marking out of rigid boundaries for the performance of male identities'. Alexander (2000), Archer (2001) and Ramji (2007) point to the often conflictual and conflicted engagement with Islam that young people may experience. Ramji (2007: 1185–6), for example, in employing Bourdieu's language of *social field* and *habitus*, concluded that:

> the mobilization of religion is reflective of the type of Islam these young men and women perceived as most useful and valuable as capital in the social field they occupied as a result of their gendered positioning ... we can conceive of religiously legitimated gender identities as a type of cultural capital sought after by young Muslim men and women ... the mobilization of religion is often ambivalent, contradictory and intersected with other social differences, particularly class.

From this perspective, an Islamic faith is not an ossified dogma that unilaterally determines the character and behaviour of young people; rather, it can be seen as a resource that young people seek to deploy on their own terms to facilitate their negotiation of the specificity of their structured location in society. For example, Ramji (2007) points to the ways in which young women utilise an active engagement with their Muslim identity as a means of contesting patriarchy and 'restrictive cultural practices'.

The young Muslim people whose lives are reflected in Chapter Five are British and predominantly self-defined Bradfordians. In negotiating their lives in Manningham, young Muslim women have been creating lives in which they have simultaneously sought to resist being seen through their wearing of the hijab and niqab as an intolerable iconic statement of Islamic non-assimilability to 'English' culture, and, through their same sartorial practices, being embraced by liberal British concern because of their perceived subjugation to traditional patriarchal Muslim pressures. Their agency as being actively engaged in constructing their own lives, within the social terrain in which they live, is thus, in both cases, being denied.

At the same time, many young Muslim men find themselves being represented as a quintessential expression of oversexed and over-assertive Asian machismo. Alexander (2000) provides a valuable account of the emergence of the popular imagery of the alienated and troublingly anti-social young Asian male in the latter part of the 1990s. She points to the carrying over of the well-established tropes of racial alienation and social breakdown that were integral to the prior social construction of early problematic youth: in the moral panics over Rastafarian drug dealers, black rioters, muggers and Yardies. Importantly, in her account of the creation of the new problem of 'Asian youth', she notes the central placement of Islam as a defining feature of this new pariah group, and, importantly for our argument here, she also cites the riots in Bradford of 1995 as one of the critical events that fed and legitimated this perception. Nothing that has happened in the subsequent two decades has done anything to attenuate the power of this demonisation of young Muslim men. The riots of 2001 and the visceral shock of the random violence of the home-grown bombers of 2005 have made young Muslim men the routine focus of a state that has become inured to the routine securitisation of everyday life (Huysmans, 2009). In recent years, the policies of community cohesion and counter-terrorism have both explicitly targeted young Muslim men as a high-risk category who must be *legitimately* regarded as targets for state intervention (Husband and Alam, 2011).

In both the representation of young Muslim women and of young Muslim men, the continuity of Orientalist constructions of the *other* are potently present. The gendered behaviour recorded in Chapter Five is significant both to the experience of people living in Manningham and for the stereotypical perception of the Muslim community as a whole. The high visibility of uncivil, assertive and sexually offensive behaviour by *some proportion* of the Muslim Pakistani population is high-octane fuel to the engine of British Islamophobia. Such behaviour is simultaneously a challenge to both the Muslim population and to other co-residents of Manningham. We have seen that the international research literature demonstrates that offensive patriarchal behaviour is the monopoly of no one culture. Manningham provides a context wherein the current transformation of gendered/ethnic/religious/aged identities is currently being actively negotiated in the flux of individuals going about their daily business.

Multicultural coexistence in Manningham

The lives of people living together in Manningham are too easily seen through the lens of contemporary political nostrums about the loss of civility, the threat of Islam and the crisis of security. The evidence we have presented in the previous chapters is of a de facto working multicultural neighbourhood. People live lives where they pursue common human aspirations, expressed through differing biographic cultural values and norms, with a remarkable efficiency. They track their daily routines through shared familiar routes between life's necessary daily destinations, and, in doing so, rehearse their unique sense of belonging to the area. There are conflicts of interest and there are acts of incivility and hostility, but this is not a maelstrom of nastiness. The overwhelming sameness of needs and aspirations, and a sense of the specific identity of the area that they share, facilitate an intercultural competence that enables them to effectively rub along together.

It would be wrong to seek to marginalise the conflicts of interest and the uncivil petty hostilities informed by neighbourhood and racially informed claims to a proprietary presence in an area. Nor should we play down the significance of the avoidance behaviours and tactical silences in public places as individuals negotiate, in their own way, the inter-group anxieties that keep ethnic difference a highly salient part of their perception of the streetscapes they inhabit (see Stephan and Stephan, 1996a; 1996b; Stephan et al, 1999). It is the case that a good part of ethnic interaction on the street and in the shops may include a tactical reserve of non-engagement. In avoiding anticipated social awkwardness or hostility, individuals merely rehearse their anxiety, rather than test its validity.

It is apparent that much of the daily flux of people going about their daily business on the streets of Manningham can be sustained by mutual non-engagement. Individuals shopping do not have to greet strangers with friendly 'hallos' and 'good-days' as though time-locked in some

1960s' Ealing comedy. Respect for personal space and a willingness not to express hostile or resentful sentiments may be sufficient to facilitate a viable civility. Where friends and acquaintances do exchange greetings and stop to chat, their sociability provides an expression of positive coexistence that contributes to the shared social environment of all. Christ et al's (2014: 3997) meta-analysis of research indicates that 'living in a place where fellow ingroup members interact positively with outgroup members has a benign impact on prejudice, beyond one's own contact experiences, via social norms that value diversity'. In basic terms, even if you have no positive interaction with members of an out-group yourself, living in a locale where members of your in-group do mix with the out-group has a capacity to positively improve your inter-group orientation.

Observing local residents sitting in their front gardens or sitting on the front step of their doorway presents a statement of pacific pleasure that, no matter how unintentionally, speaks of domestic security and a leisured pleasure in their space, which, again, transforms the perceived social character of the immediate area. From such little acts, a fabric of routine social interaction can be built that can be sufficient to contain the personally held inter-group sentiments that may, in other contexts, be the basis for expressions of inter-group resentments and hostility. Observing the people using Lister Park on a warm summer's day, it is apparent that the majority of social groups are mono-ethnic as families and friends enjoy its facilities for *their* shared enjoyment. The usage of the park on such occasions is visibly very multi-ethnic, even if much of the interpersonal interaction is not. However, should we expect more active interaction here than we would expect of the bourgeois groupings in the cafes of Ilkley, who share the cafe environment and studiously avoid chatting to strangers?

For the cosmopolitans in the data presented earlier, living in Manningham has a relish precisely because it does provide the opportunity for inter-ethnic engagement. For sections of the Pakistani community, it is apparent that living in Manningham provides a context where they feel secure and comfortable within the dominant presence they constitute in the area. For young aspirational Polish migrants, Manningham may be just a fortuitous location that will act as a platform for their future social mobility. For other unskilled 'East European' settlers, this may be a place where they feel that their street-based sociability attracts unreasonable criticism from their established Pakistani neighbours, who may not appreciate the lack of social and cultural capital they possess as recent arrivals in the area. The lived diversity of collective and individual experiences of negotiating a shared life in Manningham is shaped by the very considerable differences in economic, social and political power that frame individual and collective aspirations and interests. These imbalances of power and resources, experienced through specific narratives of settlement and belonging, provide a substantive basis for inter-group competition and resentments. It is through the construction of shared normative expectations, and behavioural routines, of civility that these different biographies can come to sustain a viable coexistence within their shared neighbourhood.

The capacity for clearly expressed, and even virulent, inter-group conflicts in Manningham cannot be dismissed as fictive inventions of malicious outsiders. They do have a realistic basis. We have seen that people may leave Manningham because of recurrent male harassment, and that others may seek to leave to find a 'better' area. We have seen the territorialisation of space in relation to identifications with Manningham as a whole, and specific neighbourhoods within it, and the attitudinal and behavioural consequences that follow from this as individuals pass judgement on new incomers. However, this remains an area that sustains wide-ranging lifestyles and great diversity in wealth and opportunity. It is a place where people can, and do, construct viable lives and seek to sustain a norm of practical civility that makes coexistence viable for many, and positively enriching for some. In the final section, we shall examine a potential model for the management of this coexistence on a local and national basis.

Developing a model for equitable coexistence

In a book such as this, it is possible to regard the presentation and analysis of the data as a sufficient ambition. However, given the current international retreat from a politics of multiculturalism, the preceding chapters are a provocation to consider their implications for the equitable management of multi-ethnic societies, and communities. Thus, in this final segment of the book, Charles Husband provides his response to this challenge. Such is the contested nature of the politics of diversity, and the wide range of intellectual and political positions available, that it is important to state clearly that the following argument represents his analysis, and, as such, would not find unqualified acceptance among all of his fellow authors.

Establishing a context

The question raised by our consideration of everyday multicultural encounters in Manningham can be reduced to a simple issue: 'What do we believe to be the necessary basis of equalitarian coexistence?' If racism and inequity are accepted as morally repugnant, what is it, then, that we believe should form the minimal basis of inter-ethnic interaction in our diverse urban environments? This question, like many of its kind, requires us to have a pre-existing conception of the problematic that this new order is to challenge and replace. In the context of contemporary Britain, this forces us to accept that there is no political consensus on the problems that underpin the reproduction of inequality and inter-group hostility. We have seen that, across Europe, there is a strident assertion that multiculturalism has failed, and more than that, that multiculturalism as a philosophy and political practice has actively contributed to the breakdown of social relations within British society (see, eg, David Cameron's Munich speech; Cameron, 2011).

The political struggles of the 1960s, 1970s and 1980s to force the British state to recognise the nature and extent of racism in society had a significant effect. They provided the political context in which the successive Race Relations Acts of Parliament cumulatively shaped an understanding of the modes of expression of racist intolerance and discrimination: through noting and sanctioning discrimination in public places; through legislating against the creative expressions of hate speech; through defining and acting against the 'non-intentional' basis of institutional racism; and through the wider shift from equating racism with individual 'prejudice' to combating its normative organisational practice. This forced public bodies and commercial organisations to recognise their complicity in facilitating the cultures of exclusion and denigration that reproduced racist practice in the routine operation of their organisation and businesses, and required local authorities to engage in introducing policies that would seek to make visible and problematic the normative manifestations of racist ideologies expressed in 'professional' practice. The introduction of Need and Impact Assessments in local authorities was one practical expression of this national engagement with the challenge of racism in our everyday life. The increasing fetid anxiety of xenophobes and racists expressed in their distraught elaboration of 'counter-narratives to multiculturalism' (Hewitt, 2005; Husband, 2010) was but one of the indications that these policies were effectively challenging the previous support enjoyed by routine racist thought and practice.

Additionally, over the last four decades, the social sciences have become increasingly sophisticated in revealing the internal dynamics of racist discourse and the psychosocial motors that give racism its ego-involving grip on individual consciousness and behaviour (Dovidio et al, 2005; Dixon and Levine, 2012). Racism was no longer the non-problematic pervasive cultural heritage of an ex-colonial society. It became a stain on the body politic of a society that, in significant ways, had entered into an interrogation of its history and current place in a post-colonial world. Along with the naming and shaming of male patriarchy and the assertive politics of feminism, the international reach of the bloody struggle to free South Africa from Apartheid, the transatlantic eddies of the black struggle in the US and the later struggles of Gay Pride in the public sphere in Britain all contributed to a major transition in the popular engagement with human rights and a shared concern with equity in our society.

Any attempt to address the question of where we should look for a model of coexistence in contemporary Britain must explicitly look at the recent, and long past, history of Britain's attempt to develop an anti-racist equitable society. For anyone who can remember the normative confident racism of the 1950s and early 1960s – 'No coloureds need apply' – or the strident assertive racism that surrounded Powellism and the introduction of the Immigration Act 1968, the transition in public discourse in the late 1990s and 2000s was striking. Racist discourse has not been eliminated from British life, but its expression has become increasingly sophisticated, in what Barker (1981) called *discursive de-racialisation*, namely, an ability to express racist sentiments in appropriately sanitised terms. We should recognise the extent of the political assault upon the claim of racists to 'Speak for England'. As Gilroy (2012: 282) has observed:

> 30 plus years of anti-racist struggle have rendered spontaneous and reckless outbursts of racist commentary deeply shameful. Nobody wants to be associated with them – not even the murderers of Stephen Lawrence and the precarious leaderships of openly xenophobic and ultranationalist groups like the BNP [British Nationalist Party] and the EDL [English Defence League].

At the same time, we should note that in comparison with other European countries, the routinised infrastructure of anti-discriminatory administrative policies and practice stood out as a major commitment to systemically seeking to challenge racism in British society.

The fact that racism is still a pervasive part of the experience of many minority ethnic persons in this country should not allow us to obliterate this reality from our current history; just as the persistence of racism should forcefully remind us of the multiple locales in which racist ideologies and unthinking racist behaviours remain deeply embedded in British culture and institutional structures. We are not short of sources of insight into the cumulative historical bases of these racisms in British life (Jordan, 1969; Walvin, 1971; Kiernan, 1972; Overy, 2009). The deep resonance of racist belief within the ideologies of nationalism (Goldberg, 2002) and the quietly rehearsed contemporary imaginings of 'nice' British citizens (Kundani, 2007) is a key element in the framing of the problematic of coexistence in contemporary Britain.

In 2014, we are a society that has demonstrated a capacity both to challenge racism at the level of public policy and collective consciousness, and to extensively reconfigure our collective imagining of the place of common human rights in shaping our understanding of our mutual coexistence as neighbours and citizens. We have demonstrably shown a capacity to engage with widening our vision of the necessary acceptance of diversity, and of the mutual pleasures that follow from this. From the 1950s until the present day, the demography of Britain has changed dramatically, permanently and in ways that would have seemed entirely improbable in 1950. For very large parts of the population, everyday inter-ethnic interaction has become an unremarkable and non-problematic aspect of their life in contemporary Britain (see, for example, Watson and Saha, 2013).

At the same time, however, we must accept the unfortunate inherent imbalance in this scenario. For every white majority person who happily interacts within a multi-ethnic environment in their workplace or neighbourhood, there is a real possibility of believing that the transition from normative racism to equitable coexistence has become a reality; their cosmopolitan life-space is positively valued and comfortably negotiated. However, for the members of the minority ethnic population with whom they interact, this sanguine view of mutual respect and conviviality may well be fractured by the sharp incisions of the racism that they experience. It may be that some of these barbs are delivered by the very white majority 'friends and colleagues' with whom they 'successfully' interact. The social psychology of aversive racism offers one insight into why this may be so (Dovidio, 2001). The everyday experience of minority ethnic persons reveals the extensive subtleties, and gross nastiness, of racist behaviour that robs them of the possibility of celebrating this vision of post-racial cosmopolitanism. To these assaults can be added the repetitive political discourse of mainstream politicians, who comfortably and confidently reiterate their view that the presence of *such people* in Britain constitutes a security threat, that they are a drain on the public purse and that the entry of more people like these into Britain is a catastrophe that must be avoided by all means. This routinised anti-immigrant discourse of mainstream political parties then, of course, provides the legitimating frame within which extremist right-wing groups promulgate their ideologies of hate, and the everyday person on the street feels legitimated in judiciously, or assertively, airing their racist views (Gilroy, 2012).

What is particularly relevant in seeking to make sense of these historical transitions and current realities in framing the context from which to seek to develop a model of multi-ethnic coexistence is the necessary recognition of the dramatic political retreat from commitments to common human rights and multicultural pluralism that has characterised the last decade in Britain and Europe. One implication of this recent political transformation in political life is that it is no longer easy to assume that there is a consensus that racism and inequity are morally repugnant. The resurgence of what Fekete (2009) has called 'Xeno-racism', as a central thematic of a newly self-conscious British nationalism, has underpinned an assertive rejection of any political commitment to a philosophy and practice of multiculturalism. What a decade or so ago might have been regarded as the reasonable concerns of marginalised minorities are now frequently dismissed as part of a cynical 'victim culture' deployed by minority ethnic communities who, in invoking their cultural rights, seek to deny the majority population their rights and 'naturally acquired' privileges. Thus, if human rights are permitted to be invoked in a discussion of inter-ethnic coexistence, from this perspective, it is to underpin an assertion of the 'victimisation of the majority' (Wodak and Matouscheck, 1993) at the hands of a rapacious minority and their lefty fellow travellers. The apparently self-evident verity touted from those holding this perspective is that tolerant Britons have gone too far in recognising the cultural heritage of minorities and that, consequently, it is now the case that it is the majority whose rights and values are being subjugated to the whims of alien minorities. Through wrapping their neoliberal-informed 'new-racism' (Barker, 1981) in a self-assured declaration of British tolerance, these distressed members of the white majority articulate their sense of outrage in a language of the 'limits of tolerance' (Blommaert and Verschueren, 1998). They bitterly declare that their profound capacity for tolerance has been extensively exploited by the rapacious demands of minority ethnic groups and asylum seekers, and the feckless multiculturalism of their leftist supporters.

A parallel political transition of recent decades further exacerbates the implications of the dominant values just reviewed. The triumph of neoliberal political philosophy and the increased individualism of everyday life have effected a transition in everyday personal consciousness such that self-interest has become an increasingly normatively acceptable moral position in British life. The erosion of collectivist sensibilities associated with active trade unionism and the introduction of ubiquitous personal performance indicators in the workplace have aided this experiential sense of necessary self-sufficiency and self-advancement. Instability in the labour market and mobility in pursuit of employment also contribute to the experience of living in a 'risk society' (Beck, 1992) in which anxiety about yourself and your 'nearest and dearest' are given external validation. The structural conditions for a widespread sense of pervasive threat are widely in place and the party-political pursuit of the 'stressed middle classes' does nothing to address the fundamental causes of inequity and instability, but, rather, offers parables about the virtues of political quiescence and belief in jam tomorrow. The scapegoating of 'welfare scroungers' and the cynical opposition drawn between the 'strivers' and the 'skivers' only exacerbate and entrench the sense of embattled individuality. There is little in contemporary party-political rhetoric, besides 'Little Englander' nationalism, that rehearses the values of civility and equity. The 'Big Society', which might have had a potential to energise such sensibilities, is so evidently contaminated by the political opportunism that set this up as an expedient notional safety net for the savage impact of austerity that it mocks the necessary spontaneous generosity of spirit that infuses true civility.

Following 11 September 2001 and the British experience of 'home-grown bombers', there has been an erosion of commitment to fundamental human rights principles (Wilson, 2005; Gearty, 2007). We are familiar with British cabinet ministers actively facilitating 'extraordinary rendition' (kidnap and illegal removal) and justifying the use of 'enhanced' modes of interrogation (torture) to elicit information. The extensive enhancement of the rights of the 'new protective state' (Hennessey, 2007) has seen the progressive erosion of civil liberties and an insidious retreat from human rights principles.

Thus, the implication of this brief contextual account is that we must conclude that if we wish to develop a model for multi-ethnic coexistence, then we need to start by explicitly stating the principles that frame this perspective. It is also apparent that the current context is not ideally suited to be receptive to the range of humanitarian, equalitarian and human rights principles that may be invoked in the following pages.

First steps to a model

It is indisputably the case that Britain is a multi-ethnic society. That is, the demography of Britain already demonstrates a rich diversity of heritages, cultures and identities among its population. Not only is there such diversity present in the population, but the demographic distribution of this population results in the existence of distinct concentrations of persons with common ethnic, faith and/or sexual identities in specific neighbourhoods. This is a reality and it is not going to go away in the near future. Britain *is* multi-ethnic and diverse. The lazy, if prevalent, conflation of whiteness with Britishness is not objectively tenable. While we may speak of a white majority, and of minority ethnic groups, as demographic variables, this is not the same as being able to invoke a core British mainstream identity and culture around which ethnically defined populations rotate as satellites, held in orbit by the inexorable gravity of British civilisation and its expression in the obligations of citizenship. The syncretic intermingling of cultures and the interweaving of biographies and genes has made Britain a newly ambivalent entity (see, for example, Ali et al, 2006).

However, this is not the same as saying that Britain embraces and practices a coherent politics of multiculturalism. There is no single definition of multiculturalism, and there has been, and is, a protracted and bitter contestation over its viability and desirability. However, *it is the foundational starting point of this argument that a political willingness to actively engage with the reality of demographic multiculturalism is both necessary and unavoidable.* Additionally, *it is a foundational assumption that the sustained presence of cultural communities that effectively reproduce their identity over generations is no threat to national identities or national security.*

In this process of cultural resilience, it is typically the case that the culture changes over time, while being embraced and valued by the identity community that sustains it. This is the essence of Gilroy's (1991) notion of *the changing same.* Nationalisms that wish to assert a single legitimate core culture are always a denial of both history and current reality. One only has to look at the current curriculum for the British citizenship test to note the fictions that have to be aired in order to sustain such a view.

Thus, the question remains: where should we start to find the basis for coexistence? There is no space here for entering into an overview of the potential offerings from the whole range of political philosophy, but, pragmatically, we will echo the concerns of Amin (2012) in arguing that *a confident humanism must be found at the heart of any model of multi-ethnic coexistence.*

A helpful question in approaching an understanding of the end state that we are seeking to achieve is to ask: *what expectations do we have of banal interaction within multi-ethnic coexistence?* Is it necessary that we should all like each other? Do we have to wish to be capable of forming close friendships with the range of persons we encounter in our daily life? Should we all expect to become competent intercultural navigators, developing a close understanding of each culture's unique historical trajectory and current behavioural codes?

Why should these expectations be imposed on a prospective multi-ethnic ethos when they are not, and have not been, meaningfully expressed in the inter-class relations within the dominant white majority? *What we are surely looking for is some basis for effective civility as a dominant norm within a multicultural politics that accepts the legitimacy and value of continuing ethnic diversity within the population of the UK.*

The praxis of civility/incivility

In seeking to develop an account of the potential role of civility within a wider model of multicultural coexistence, it is useful to start by reflecting upon the nature of civility's absence. Smith et al's (2010) creative interrogation of the routine nature of *incivility* is very helpful in tracking the nature and context of violations of expectations of civility that usefully informs our analysis here. Following a critique of the criminological tendency to associate incivility with specific locales in the urban context, and with particular categories of anti-social persons, Smith et al reveal incivility to be widely spread across the urban landscape and to be distributed across all classes of people. Indeed, they find that in looking at the distribution of the *rude stranger*:

> With respect to age, young people (twenties and thirties) were far from alone as the primary agents of everyday incivility (43 percent). Middle-aged adults (forties and fifties) sat alongside them as the age group most likely to have been identified in the study as rude strangers (40 percent). (Smith et al, 2010: 32)

Their research not only does much to undermine the routine stereotypical association of incivility with certain categories of person and with certain areas, but also reveals that incivility is mapped against the temporal and spatial flows of urban life. In their words:

> We have seen that most incivility takes place where people go regularly, and its nature is patterned by the time–space choreography of daily life. The performance of tasks and movement around the city allocate risks of encounter. This vision of human circulation through the dimensions of time and space is one that offers a vivid alternative to the conventional approach to incivility which allocates the problem to neighbourhoods and their populations (see Phillips and Smith, 2006). (Smith et al, 2010: 55)

From this perspective, the daily interactions to be found in Manningham are shaped by social routines. People tend to go shopping at specific times; they go for lunch and evening meals within a range of time. Certain areas of Manningham provide specific *destinations*. The shops on Oak Lane or White Abbey Road provide foci for interaction where local norms and demography may interact in shaping expectations. Thus, the young female researcher's experience of being made unwelcome in certain shops may have partially been a consequence of the fact that she was not expected to be there. Her arrival was not usual, was marked as exceptional and, in consequence, attracted a gaze and scrutiny that was felt as being intrusive and unwelcoming. When this writer lived in Manningham, his routine custom in specific neighbourhood Asian shops gave him a familiarity that largely removed such a cool greeting, and, in other instances, provided him with the happy recognition of *being a regular*. Whether it is outside schools awaiting the release of their children, in shops, in places of entertainment or in petrol station forecourts, the urban landscape provides a topography of destinations where, routinely, residents of an area may be expected to gather and interact. The demography of the city, and the neighbourhood, will significantly shape the dominant claims to ownership of these terrains, and the attempted enforcement of normative expectations. Thus, the definition of incivility is not made against an agreed absolute standard, but rests as a negotiated exercise in localised social power between the perceived rude stranger and the self-defined victim. In Smith et al's (2010: 64) succinct terms: 'Most [incivility] takes place in locations where people go frequently, not from infrequent visits to bad locations.' It is precisely because people frequently experience incivility in places with which they feel familiar, and in which they believe they have a legitimate presence, that incivility can generate such strong responses.

Smith et al additionally note that most instances of incivility (83%) occur under conditions when one or both of the interactants are in motion. Indeed, their research indicated that the most typical context for encountering incivility was when both the victim and the rude stranger were in motion (amounting to 48% of cases of incivility) (Smith et al, 2010: 64). The centrality of movement from one place to another in shaping the experience of incivility is hardly surprising, since it is under such conditions that there is a necessary flux of interaction between strangers. There may be expectations of territorial primacy that inform the behaviour of individuals in transit, as, for example, in the interaction between the two researchers and the young Asian men on Oak Lane. There may also be a conflict in the anticipated normative behaviour for a space and route, as, for example, in seeing a car and a road as a fusion of the need to get from A to B as opposed to a locale for performative self-expression. Additionally, that incivility so often takes place between persons in motion may reflect the reality that the transitory nature of the encounter may make the offending party feel that they are unlikely to be effectively held accountable for their behaviour. Our young Asian women noted that they were less likely to experience sexual harassment on their own patch, where the offenders stood a significant chance of being made to account for their lack of respect to *members of the community*. Furthermore, one of the features of car-based incivilities is the probability that the flow of traffic will pre-empt any immediate sanction.

As the work of Katz (1999) revealed in Chapter Six in relation to being 'cut-up' while driving, there may be strong emotional responses to perceived acts of incivility, and these reactions may result in an escalation of hostile interaction. Or, as in the case of our interaction on Oak Lane, the 'victims' may decide to adopt a stance of indifference and offer no response, either because they regarded the offence as trivial, or because they sought to effect an efficient exit from a situation that was wrapped around with an incalculable potential for rapidly escalating threat. Whatever the nature of the offending incivility, and the response, such interactions constitute an addition to the learned repertoire of the individual's urban streetcraft. Where the intersection of destinations and routes provides the basis for repeated encounters with the same patterns of incivility, we my expect there to be a cumulatively robust cognitive mapping of the area in terms of expectations of civil and uncivil encounters, and of appropriate strategies for their negotiation. In this way, where there exist class-, gender- and ethnic-based criteria for triggering incivility, and class-, gender- and ethnically informed identities shaping the perceptions of interaction, we may see the ossification of experiences and perceptions that become de facto identity-based perceptions of an area and of modes of negotiating interaction in an area. Thus, for example, we have seen the ways in which gender is scripted across the experience of persons moving within Manningham, and we have seen age/gender/ethnic intersectionally informed modes of adaptation, ranging from a self-conscious awareness of dress codes, to exit from the area. Smith et al (2010), for example, report that women are more likely to employ avoidance strategies in the face of incivility than men.

The work of Smith et al (2010) and of Phillips and Smith (2006) is invaluably provocative in demanding that we interrogate the context in which incivilities occur within an open-minded conception of the urban environment as a complex interactive system within which there can be perceived well-established routine patterns of interaction. Reciprocally, their work informs any discussion of the role of civility in an urban context, for it clearly underlines the intersection between individual agency and structured patterns of the social environment. Fundamentally, in establishing the subjective nature of the perception of incivility, we are forced to engage with revealing the construction of the normative basis of codes of civility, which when linked to an acceptance of the distinctive demographic profile of urban environments, results in our having to accept the culturally relative nature of neighbourhood norms of behaviour. Thus, *if codes for acceptable behaviour may differ from neighbourhood to neighbourhood, depending upon their social history and current demography, then we must necessarily ask: what is the generic nature of a civility that may moderate **all** behaviour across a multi-ethnic urban landscape?* This we can begin to explore in the following section.

Identifying the elements of civility

Invoking the concept of civility is not an entirely unproblematic endeavour, given the contested nature of the definition and purported practical relevance of civility in political theory. It has been associated with a range of critiques which suggest that attempting to use it here may introduce more ambiguity and contestation than clarity and consensus. For some, contemporary usages of civility represent a lack of moral rigour (eg MacIntyre, 1988), while for others, civility has represented an ideological stratagem of the elite to exclude and control others (Keane, 1998; Elias, 2000). Depending upon how you frame your analysis, there is some merit in all of these critiques, but the position argued here reflects Boyd's (2006) positive appraisal of the contemporary utility and relevance of civility as a concept, moral disposition and behavioural repertoire.

Boyd distinguishes between two types of civility. The first conceives of civility as a behavioural code, where, quite simply, 'to be "civil" is to speak or interact with others in ways that are mannerly, respectful or sociable' (Boyd, 2006: 864). He notes that, typically, this form of civility is wrapped around with well-established norms that may vary from culture to culture and from situation to situation. This he calls *formal civility* in comparison to *substantive civility*, which he sees as residing in a 'sense of standing or membership in the political community with its attendant rights and responsibilities' (Boyd, 2006: 864).

His argument succinctly traces possible relationships between these two elements of civility. On the one hand, it can be argued that 'because we are all members of the same political community, interacting on the grounds of civic equality, we have an obligation to be polite in our interactions with our fellow citizens' (Boyd, 2006: 864). From this perspective, we are driven to make salient the societal conditions that render this expectation of mutual regard and consideration legitimate and feasible. *It assumes an inclusive polity in which all members of the population have equal status within the state, and that there is a moral framework that regards equality of regard and treatment as self-evident and an aspiration of state policy.* (That is a framing set of foundational conditions that would be hard to attribute to the current situation in the UK.)

In inverting the relationship between substantive and formal civility, Boyd also notes that it is reasonable to argue that the routine operation of formal civility is a shared experience of mutuality that, in practice, 'generates a sense of inclusivity and moral equality, in both ourselves and for others' (Boyd, 2006: 865), which provides the *moral* context in which the political expectations of substantive citizenship become practically operable. It is this moral engagement with the inherent equal worth of the other that enables coexistence to operate in diverse societies where there may be no consensus on what constitutes the good life, but there is an equitable negotiation of unresolved difference. Thus, Boyd's following assertion is of considerable significance:

> Rather than simply being a negative of aversive disposition like tolerance, moderation, or peacefulness – which ask nothing more from us than to leave other people alone – *civility presupposes an active and affirmative moral relationship between persons.* Being civil is a way of generating moral respect and democratic equality. (Boyd, 2006: 875, emphasis added)

A correlate of this assertion is that civility cannot be legislated into place: being civil only because of fear of sanctions would be a hollow masquerade that would lack the intrinsic affective engagement that makes it meaningful. We are talking here of something akin to Taylor's (1989) invocation of civility as a necessary moral virtue that must be actively nurtured, or Parekh's (2008) invocation of an ethos of common humanity.

Thus, the model of civility that is emerging here takes the form of a double helix in which the moral disposition of formal civility is tied to the political status of substantive civility by the many different routines and obligations that are invoked in specific contexts, and given relevance through particular cultural norms.

Differentiated citizenship

Before we can proceed any further, there remains a further necessary clarification regarding the conception of citizenship that must frame substantive civility. We have already noted the situational contingency of norms of civility and we have recognised the necessary role of a commitment to rights in framing our understanding of civil interaction. The question that has become very pointed within political analysis rests upon whether we frame the provision of universal citizenship through the language of universal individual rights or whether we must necessarily invoke an appreciation of group rights, and an acceptance of *differentiated citizenship* (see the debate between Kymlicka [1995, 2001] and Barry [2001]). (This is an area of political philosophy that is riven by large, and nuanced, differences that cannot be addressed here. Vitikainen [2013] has provided a valuable overview of the many fundamental, and subtle, areas of contestation across these many disputed perspectives.)

Young (1989) is among those who have argued persuasively that within a universalist provision of individual rights, it is the interests and priorities of the majority that come to define what are the normative needs and cultural practices that should be addressed through treating people *equally*. In essence, a model of universal equal provision for individual rights becomes a legal/political framework for the hegemonic expression of dominant interests, whether those are defined in terms of class, gender or ethnicity. Treating people equally does not necessarily mean treating them the same. Drawing upon Taylor's (1992) discussion of *the politics of difference* and Kymlicka's (1995) work on *multicultural citizenship*, we have argued elsewhere for the necessity of adopting a model of differentiated citizenship as a necessary framework for delivering equitable substantive citizenship in diverse societies (Downing and Husband, 2005: ch 9). In essence, universalist principles of rights must be delivered with a systematic sensitivity to the particularity of their expression in relation to the diverse values and needs present in the population. In other words, to quote the Western

Australian Substantive Equality Policy:*'if you want to treat me equally, you may have to be prepared to treat me differently'* (EOCWA, 2005).

A willingness to recognise the limitations of addressing minority ethnic experiences of inequality through an individual rights perspective, and a consequent willingness to adopt group-based differentiated citizenship, does not require a necessary rejection of the role of individual human rights. On the contrary, individual human rights principles are required to protect individuals from the potentially oppressive impact of group pressure. Thus, a necessary pragmatic practice must recognise both the strategic essentialism (Phillips, 2007) of groups seeking to define and protect their shared interests, and the need of individuals to assert their own view of the good life and the freedoms that should attend it. Since individuals experience racial and sexual discrimination as members of specific social categories, rather than because of their individual character, it is appropriate that the redress for such discrimination should also recognise shared group interests. Invoking hopeful nostrums, based upon the established tolerance of 'the British character', is no adequate basis for the construction of equity and civility. However fraught and uncomfortable, the theoretical challenge of differentiated citizenship must be addressed, as must the practical dilemmas of constructing a policy framework capable of negotiating the particularistic expression of shared universal rights. As Amin (2006: 1015) has argued:

> the good city has to be imagined as the socially just city, with strong obligations towards those marginalised from the means of survival and human fulfilment (Wacquant, 1999). These are obligations that should draw on a solidarity of human rights and recognise the constitutive role of the distant other in whatever counts as the social 'ours'.

Multicultural civility: as a disposition

In a variety of locales in Manningham, we have observed examples of the success of multicultural coexistence that stand in stark opposition to the political rejection of multiculturalism as formal policy. This ability 'to get along together' is what Watson (2009) means by her concept of 'rubbing along':

> as a form of limited encounter between social subjects where recognition of others through a glance or gaze, seeing and being seen, sharing embodied spaces, in talk or silence,

has the potential to militate against the withdrawal into self
or the private realm. (Watson, 2009: 1581)

In Watson's usage of this notion, there is something of the dynamics
of the contact hypothesis (Pettigrew and Tropp, 2005) being invoked,
where she sees the banal nature of these casual encounters as providing
a basis for undermining 'racist discourse and stereotypes of unknown
others' (Watson, 2009: 1582). However, as we have noted in our
discussion of civility, we need to go beyond the mere potential of
physical interaction as a sufficient basis for underpinning a viable multi-
ethnic civility. There needs to be present a disposition to be open to
the other: a worldview that is something beyond Kim's (1992) trans-
cultural competence, and more akin to Levinas's (1978) 'being for the
other'. To make it more explicit, there needs to be available a humanist
sensibility that counters the pervasive sense of threat to self, the inner-
directed myopia and xenophobia that is the nurturant existential basis
for racist ideologies and belief in the legitimate inequitable distribution
of worth and resources.

There is no lack of relevant thinking that might be drawn upon in
developing such a necessary *political* exercise. We emphasise the political
nature of this enquiry, for while much of the essential material for this
debate already exists in academe, it is in the act of re-engaging with the
politics of multiculturalism, and loudly asserting the announcement of
its demise as premature, that an ideological struggle must be fomented
in the public sphere. The research links between a positive commitment
to a multicultural philosophy, which sees diversity as a good in society,
and positive inter-group relations should not be ignored (see, eg,
Verkuyten, 2005; Wolsko et al, 2006). Indeed, as Gonzalez et al (2008:
680), for example, have argued:

> The endorsement of multiculturalism was indirectly
> associated with prejudice, namely through its associations
> with symbolic threat and stereotypes. Individuals who
> endorsed multiculturalism more strongly perceived
> less symbolic threat and had less negative stereotypes.
> Multiculturalism was also negatively related with realistic
> threat.

Therefore, in developing a model for multicultural coexistence, there is
a need for something equivalent to Parekh's (2008) ethos of common
humanity: a willingness to live together in a spirit of human solidarity.
This invokes a disposition of mutual respect, and, more than that, a

willingness to engage in seeking to understand the other: to recognise their '*right to be understood*' (Husband, 1996, 1998).

What is being invoked here is a shared politics of civility underpinned by personal dispositions, and a shared humanist philosophy that provides an empathetic sense of equivalence with, rather than superiority towards, others. This, of course, is entirely counter to the assimilationist ideology of contemporary British state rhetoric, and is why it is so necessary that civility should be assiduously pursued as a necessary element for framing a future coexistence defined by diversity and change.

Beyond a humanist disposition

If we are to develop a multi-ethnic coexistence, then personal dispositions and a capacity to rub along will not, of themselves, be sufficient to guarantee substantive equality within a social context framed by civility. Civility as a behavioural disposition and value system must operate within a national regulatory framework that provides the institutional context for interaction.

If good people wish to be good, what shall facilitate their goodness? This returns us to the earlier discussion about the role of human rights in framing interaction in a diverse society skewed by entrenched inequalities. Britain has a long history of seeing itself as a quintessentially tolerant society. However, an ideology of tolerance is a poisonous starting point for framing multi-ethnic interaction. As we have argued elsewhere, tolerance is an exercise of power by those who control resources of recognition and reward (Husband, 2000, 2003). Toleration requires the tolerated to be grateful for the largesse with which their betters have favoured them. Toleration is not a viable value base for multi-ethnic civility (see Brown, 2008). If civility is to be protected from becoming a key tool in the hegemonic exercise of power by the privileged – seeking the compliance of those they have marginalised through rendering civility as a pacific expression of self-negating obsequiousness by the excluded – then there must be a framing ideology of rights that asserts a fundamental equivalence of all. Multi-ethnic civility requires that there be a common framework of rights to which all may appeal and by which all may be judged. The current government's attempted retreat from the European Convention of Human Rights is a perverse indicator of just why such a framework is necessary. A common basket of rights provides the coherence to those state institutions and collective organisational structures that are necessary to inhibiting selfishness and exclusion, and to promoting equity, in society.

Virtuous intent, underpinned by consensual ethical humanism, still requires an institutional infrastructure that will provide the means and power for enabling a multi-ethnic coexistence that routinely challenges racism and inequity, rather than connives in its insidious reproduction through established networks of privilege and power. An expectation by the state that its populace will interact on the basis of liberal notions of civility requires that the state reciprocally establishes those conditions of equity, access to justice and equal recognition that are necessary to the expression of civility. A framework of legislation outlawing discrimination, state systems of health, education and welfare that are sensitive to cultural diversity, and a civic infrastructure that is reflective of the demography are necessary foundations for multi-ethnic civility.

The discourse of the 'Big Society' assumed the viability of a communitarian civility in the absence of egalitarian politics and a consensual discourse of fundamental rights. On the contrary, as we noted earlier, we have seen a substantial retreat from a state commitment to fundamental human rights, and the pursuit of policies that have exacerbated inequalities and sustained racisms. Civility, as defined here, is not nourished through the repetition of the mantras of 'social cohesion' and 'inclusion' in a political environment that wilfully widens inequalities in concrete material terms and nurtures dehumanising exclusionary sensibilities towards others, defined by ethnicity, faith, gender, sexual preference and class, through state and party-political discourses of generic xenophobia. Civility as a disposition and behavioural repertoire must be framed within a politics of rights that explicitly engages with the sensitivities required by principles of differentiated citizenship. An assertive protection of the interests of all citizens within a diverse society is an absolutely necessary adjunct to the nurturing of a disposition of civility, which can provide an affective openness to the interests of others. Lacking such a framework, civility becomes the fragile tool of dominant interests. *A political/legal intolerance of racism and inequity is a necessary element in any national commitment to civility.*

What do we expect of multicultural civility?

The picture of life in Manningham that has emerged through the preceding pages is of an inner-city area whose daily life of coexistence stands in some considerable contrast to the stereotype of urban malaise, and the collapse of social relations in a multi-ethnic area, which available stereotypes of the area would suggest. This is an area that has a distinctive history as a locale for migrant settlement and for accommodation to the subsequent demographic changes. The interviews have revealed a strong theme of a positive affective affiliation with the area to be found among a wide range of different residents. Differences in age, ethnicity, income and faith are levelled by this capacity of residents to experience a strong bond with the area. However, crucially, this bond is typically experienced through an individual, and possibly familial, biographic understanding of how they come to be in this part of Bradford. Often, this recognition of a personal location within the available stories of the history of the area is juxtaposed with a knowing awareness of how outsiders see their home patch. Similarly, their position on the viability of their continued commitment to, and residence within, Manningham is framed by a mapping of other potentially more attractive places of residence, and of others that are seen as unattractively inferior and to be avoided. Within Manningham itself, particular neighbourhoods provide the spatial context for individual lives lived in a framework of social and physical resources experienced within a typical spatio-temporal daily routine. People have meaningful lives as residents of Manningham.

For very many, this coherence is established in relation to a specific ethnic subset of the population of Manningham. However, as the chapter on the Polish population of Manningham revealed, it would be wrong to assume that a population with a common ethnic heritage constituted a unitary community. The different trajectories of migration and settlement, and different familial and personal stories of financial betterment or stasis, fragment the social dynamics of all the ethnic populations of Manningham. So, too, do differences in age, gender, class and faith provide the basis for unique intersectional biographies that feed a wide range of modes of accommodation to coexistence in Manningham. However, by and large, coexistence is real, and the experience of *walking Manningham* revealed a banal domestic civility of negotiated difference on the street.

What does this mean? It means that despite the very many real differences in lifestyle, cultural norms and personal biographic characteristics, there is a viable modus operandi of *rubbing along* that allows effective coexistence within this multi-ethnic inner-city area. It does not mean that everyone likes everyone else. It does not mean that there are no violations of personal dignity and collective *amour propre* through all-too-frequent expressions of sexism and racism in the behaviour of some individuals towards others. Manningham, just like exclusive golf clubs, is a social work in progress. There are de facto criteria for in-group affiliation that provide the boundary markers for claims of legitimate group membership. There are historically laid down collective myths and social imaginaries that animate the

g of past inter-group relations and inform current inter-
nics. There are real contemporary social stresses around
it, housing, security and health that provide the structural
for the emergence of inter-group perceptions of realistic
olic threat. There are tensions between different collectivities
Manningham. However, it is still not the conflict-ridden
om of antagonisms that the stereotype of inner-city ghettos
have us believe.

the example of Manningham, there is a positive case study of
potential viability of the model of multi-ethnic civility that has
n sketched earlier. Despite the diversity of individual and collective
pirations and values, there is a prevailing expectation of civility that
ames the negotiation of these differences. Despite the very different
norms for correct behaviour, there is evidence of an ability to allow
for the coexistence of difference. Where there are instances of inter-
group resentment at the intrusive behaviours of others, we have seen
the possibility of a self-reflexive awareness that 'we too are somebody
else's source of irritation'.

Manningham has seen riot in the past, and there is nothing that
has been said here that precludes the possibility of rioting erupting in
Manningham again. The strong bonds of in-group identity, and a still-
viable repository of learned resentments in relation to specific repetitive
experiences of exclusion and abuse, provide a latent reservoir of well-
rehearsed grievance. For some members of the Asian communities,
this has generated an inter-group posture of social creativity where
they have found new means of establishing strong in-group self-regard
(see Turner, 1987; Simon et al, 2005). Thus, the car culture examined
earlier provides one means whereby members of the Asian communities
can create for themselves a social nexus and related behavioural
repertoire that can guarantee positive self-regard. For some residents
of Manningham, the creation of a strong multi-ethnic neighbourly
identity, expressed, for example, in constructing a common garden in
front of their houses, can provide a superordinate collective identity
that helps to attenuate the perceived inter-ethnic tension that may be
part of their environment (Gaertner et al, 1999). For others, various
forms of exit may be possible, as we have seen for some of the more
affluent members of the Asian communities and in the instance of the
distressed white female cosmopolitan.

However, for those whose circumstances pre-empt the possibility of
exit, and for whom the experience of marginalisation is recurrent, the
possibility of adopting a conflict model of inter-group relations remains
a real possibility. As an element of their shared collective *history*, the

Asian communities of Manningham have an established capacity for riot. They can realistically have a sense that this is a potential element in their available repertoire of responses to racism and sustained inequality. There is a degree of disinhibition in as much as there is a knowledge that they can do it: they have done it before on a spectacular scale. Furthermore, there may be a naïve sense that in the context of 20th-century British urban experience, riot has been an effective means of attracting central government's attention to local malaise. On the other hand, in Bradford, there is the still very salient memory of the draconian sentences that were handed down to the convicted rioters of 2001, which may act as a strong inhibition to civil disorder.

However, the reality of everyday successful multi-ethnic coexistence operates at the level of a routine local exercise of civility, in the face of diversity and of inequality. There is a local synergy of formal and substantive citizenship in the creation of an imagined community on the local terrain as a shared polity. Notably, this is not a polity defined through its expression in terms of participation in electoral politics, for which they is ambiguous regard, but a polity expressed through a sense of 'substantive civility' in the locale in which they live, where the daily rights and obligations of a shared citizenry are enacted in practice. Perhaps, particularly where people collectively create a viable coexistence in an area that is reputed to be undesirable and conflict-ridden, there is a shared capacity to celebrate the urban domain of sociability that they have established, and continue to maintain, through their collective self-regard for the area. This they have done despite the structural inequalities reproduced, and currently exacerbated, by central government policies. This they have done despite the lamentable discourses of racist and xenophobic self-interest that have so frequently been dominant elements in the public sphere of British political life. However, this rubbing along has a fragility that makes it vulnerable to the degradation of shared hope and collective aspiration that can follow from the failure of the state to facilitate equity, and to challenge ideologies of oppression and exclusion.

There is nothing in the use of the concept of rubbing along that implies the suppression of the awareness of, and attachment to, collective group identities. This is most definitely not a synonym for stealthy assimilationism. Indeed rubbing along can only take place when there is an awareness of the existence of difference. In the discussion of civility earlier (p 227) we spoke of the 'equitable negotiation of unresolved difference'. Thus within the constant flux of specific acts of rubbing along there is exactly this awareness of lives lived in the presence of diversity; and of the willing engagement with difference between self and others. But as we also noted (p 232) 'civility is not nourished through the repetition of mantras of "social cohesion" and inclusion'. Where the structural substantive basis for inequalities of respect, or rights or wealth are not addressed there will remain the possibility for the salience of these existing group identities to be made suddenly critically relevant through specific triggering events. The social virtues of rubbing along are not an alternative to addressing the reproduction of inequalities in society. Collective action by minorities remains a politically relevant intervention by the marginalised who are dissatisfied with, or disbelieving of, the political sleights of hand that offer prejudice reduction and social cohesion as policies whereby the dominant and privileged retain their advantage whilst asserting their tolerance.

As Wright and Baray (2012: 227) have asserted: 'A collective action perspective concerns itself with equality across groups, not harmony, and focuses on social justice, not social cohesion.' Being critical of the way in which prejudice reduction models of social intervention focus on the advantaged group as both the problem, and the agent of change, they remind us that collective action by excluded minorities requires that we consider the disadvantaged as causal agents who play a direct and decisive role in improving their status. Thus in addressing the model of coexistence that has been sketched earlier, it is imperative that we remember the historical, and current, struggles of marginalised groups who have taken responsibility for challenging the exclusion and oppression experienced at the hands of the more privileged and powerful. Shared memories of collective struggle for their current purchase on their place in society provide a common basis for mobilising new initiatives. (We might also note the current repertoire of extra-parliamentary actions, such as the Occupy movement (Gamson and Sifry, 2013; Rushkoff, 2013), which provide exemplars of collective action, and which point to the novel use of new social media. The presence of mundane, and laudable, practices of rubbing along provide no inoculation against the sustained awareness of inequalities, and their potential for mobilisation under the right circumstances.

We should also note that in the context of inter-ethnic relations, rubbing along applies just as much to intra-group relations as it does to inter-group relations. We saw earlier, for example, how gender, age or affluence, or their confluence, could produce quite different life experiences, and quite particular perceptions of individuals' situations in Manningham. The gendered politics of the streetscape in Manningham clearly provides the basis for women within ethnic communities to seek means of challenging their experience of exclusion and oppression by developing strategies of creative resistance, or direct confrontation, in relation to the patriarchal powers expressed within their community. These perceptions of intra-group discrimination based upon gender also provide the basis for women to identify with each other, across ethnic boundaries, and develop a 'one-group identity' (Dovidio et al, 2012) as women that would potentially facilitate common strategies aimed at improving their shared circumstances as women. Similarly, whilst both members of the Pakistani community and members of the majority white community have expressed negative views about the driving behaviour of young Pakistani drivers, from intra-group and inter-group perspectives respectively, as common citizens of Bradford and road users they also have the potential to identify themselves within a superordinate common group as 'responsible citizens of Bradford', and agree on shared responses to their common 'problem'. Whilst there is not the time here to develop this analysis, such cross-cutting webs of identity and experience point to the necessary complexity of understanding the nature and implications of 'rubbing along'.

Additionally, recent analyses of intergroup contact, and the development of more positive intergroup attitudes, point to the complex psychological dynamics that may be related to 'rubbing along'. Specifically, the development of common in-group identities that provide a superordinate order of affiliation between existing groups, such as, for example, Manningham resident, rather than second-generation Pakistani, or young Polish migrant, or working-class white resident, may indeed reduce prejudice between these groups, but identification with this common in-group may induce the minority residents to see the existing inequities as less serious, and reduce their inclination to collective action. For the more privileged majority participant in this change of salient identity, and intergroup perspective, it may lessen their prejudice but may not significantly change their willingness to support social policies aimed at reducing inequalities. Clearly the development of new common in-group identities may be both a consequence of, and facilitation to, rubbing along, and there are grounds in social psychological research to believe that this may well contribute to a diminution of inter-group prejudice. But the strong evidence of the complex linkage of this to changes in a willingness to challenge established inequalities must result in a concerned caution in greeting such developments as an unalloyed source of optimism (see Dixon and Levine, 2012, particularly Part II for a valuable introduction to this literature).

The framework of rights, and the espousal of values of being for the other, outlined above, would not be likely to inhibit collective mobilisation. On the contrary, social psychology has indicated that the key elements necessary for collective action are that status differences between disadvantaged groups and advantaged groups are seen as being illegitimate, and that collective identities are both salient and valued. Thus a robust framework of rights and an assertive commitment to equality in the public sphere would facilitate an awareness of inequalities, and provide a clear legal and moral framework for naming identified inequalities as illegitimate. In other words, rubbing along is not antithetical to the recognition of inequalities, and to the mobilisation of inter-group competition, and conflict around specific issues. The model briefly sketched above offers a means of facilitating viable multi-ethnic coexistence, whilst recognising the possibility, and in some circumstances the legitimacy, of inter-group conflict.

The data presented in this book has hopefully provided a useful insight into the many factors that shape lived diversity in a contemporary multi-ethnic inner city area. Bradford may have many different ethnic identities represented within its boundaries, but Manningham as a specific inner-city area does not have the superdiversity that may be found in, for example, Hackney in London. Thus there are fewer ethnic identities in play, and some identities in particular have developed within a shared history of intergroup relations which continue to give them real salience. We have quite deliberately taken the time to show something of the historical background to the development of Bradford and Manningham, and of the communities within them, for we are convinced of the continuing power of history and of the necessary relevance of historicity to any adequate understanding of urban inter-group dynamics. In the context of Manningham, the interplay of enduring stereotypes of the area against the reality of the physical streetscape and residents' own perceptions has emerged as a powerful theme in our analysis. Whilst this book in essence hopes to reveal the dynamics to be found in one inner-city area of multi-ethnic coexistence, we hope that it will stir fruitful insights that may be applied in quite different contexts. The model developed in the latter part of the book, in particular, hopes to provoke considerations beyond the descriptive, and to generate a concern with a politics that goes beyond the limited aspirations of urban 'social cohesion'.

APPENDIX

Data collection

All research requires the collaboration of a whole range of different people, and the richness of the data is often a consequence of the quite distinct personal and professional competences that each individual brings to a project. This research is no different and the individual competences and specialisms are multiple. One of the particular differences to be found across the individuals who have been involved in the data collection is their degree of familiarity with Bradford, and Manningham in particular. Dr Yunis Alam is of Pakistani heritage and is Bradford born and bred, and Manningham has been a part of his social terrain throughout his life. Charles Husband had lived in Manningham for almost 10 years and his role in the fieldwork involved him walking the streets of Manningham once more after a lapse of 11 years. For both, there was a familiarity with the area, but with differing experiential connections to the area, where the differences in their age and ethnicity would inevitably shape the perceptions of the current scene there. On the other hand, Rūta Kazlauskaitė-Gürbüz was deliberately recruited to the team because not only was she not familiar with Manningham, but, indeed, had no prior knowledge of Bradford. Both she and Charles Husband were responsible for the observational fieldwork carried out in Manningham, and it was felt that there was a definite need for a male and female perspective to be available for the collection of the data on the lived streetscape of 'Walking Manningham'. Additionally, the fact that Rūta was not British, and had not lived in Britain, meant that she brought an outsider's perspective to the inter-ethnic relations she observed. Dr Joanna Fomina, on the other hand, had lived in Bradford for a year as a Marie Curie Doctoral Fellow, and as a Polish-speaking resident of Warsaw, she brought a dual and complementary sensibility to interviews, and analysis, for the chapter on the Polish community of Bradford. Dr Jörg Huttermann has visited Bradford on a number of occasions and has a view of Manningham shaped by his complementary research on the inter-ethnic dynamics in Marxloh near Duisberg. His sustained theoretical engagement with the development of this research, and his acute awareness of the similarities and differences between Marxloh and Manningham, has provided an invaluable critical voice to the continuing dialogue within this project.

Different elements of the project have involved different actors as the key players in data collection. For Chapter Three, 'Walking Manningham', the main fieldwork took place over 2011/12 and was carried out by Charles Husband and Rūta Kazlauskaitė-Gürbüz. Husband's work was carried out over this period with multiple visits to Manningham at different times of the day and in different seasons, while Rūta's work was carried out over an intensive three-month period. This fieldwork was based upon observation and note taking as a means of building up confidence that the description of interactions being offered were not momentary aberrations or individual idiosyncrasies, but reflective of modes of behaviour that could be routinely encountered in the area. However, revealing but nonetheless unusual 'one-offs', such as Charles and Jörg's encounter on Oak Lane, also have a place in telling the story of Manningham.

The interviews for Chapter Four, 'Migratory waves and negotiated identities: the Polish population of Bradford', was carried out entirely by Dr Joanna Fomina. (This element of the project was funded independently by the Academy of Finland project: 'Bilingualism, Identity and the Media in Inter- and Intra-Cultural Comparisons' [BIM].) In the context of this project, two distinct cohorts of Poles resident in Bradford were identified, from which a sample was created of individuals who then took part in qualitative interviews. Sixty semi-structured interviews were carried out with functionally bilingual people. The first cohort was constructed from the post-war community of Poles in Bradford, and the sample was devised in order to provide a diverse cross-section of this population. Thus, it included second-generation Poles whose parents were both Polish, as well as those who had only one Polish parent. It also included children of second-generation Poles who were now adults themselves, as well as three respondents who were migrants from the 1960s–1970s. The total sample number of this cohort was 30 persons; the youngest was 22 and the oldest was 59 years old, with a predominance of people in their 40s and 50s.

The second cohort was made up of recent migrants into Bradford, most of whom were in their 30s. The majority of this sample have higher education and come from small- and middle-sized towns in Poland. A third of the participants had children. As noted elsewhere in this analysis, this sample represents a particular cross-section of the recent economic migrants entering Britain and is skewed towards those who have social and cultural capital that will enable them to accommodate to life in Britain with relative ease. In the sample, there were also several people with very limited knowledge of English. This sample also contained 30 interviewees, with the youngest being 18 and the oldest 55, but the majority were in their late 20s and early 30s.

The data for Chapter Five, 'Manningham: lived diversity', were derived from semi-structured qualitative interviews that allowed the respondents to develop their own perspective on living in Manningham, and to identify their own priorities about the aspects of life there that most engaged them. These interviews were carried out by Dr Yunis Alam, Dr Tom Cockburn and Professor Charles Husband, were predominantly carried out in individuals' homes or in their place of work, and were tape-recorded. The majority of the interviews lasted about an hour, but some ran well past this and a few were as brief as 35 minutes. Fifty interviews were carried out in total (24 with white residents and 26 with minority ethnic residents) and ages ranged from the early 20s to pensioners. Respondents were guaranteed absolute confidentiality and there was a strong sense that the responses that were obtained were spontaneous and uncontrived. In addition to these arranged interviews, innumerable ad hoc conversations that occurred in shops, on the street or in taxis in the context of the fieldwork for Chapter Three provided further grist to this ethnographic mill.

The final data collection took place in the context of developing the insights for Chapter Six, 'The car, the streetscape and inter-ethnic dynamics'. Data collection here was conducted by Dr Yunis Alam. His role as interviewer in this context was by no means that of the disinterested outsider. On the contrary, Yunis, in his own right, is something of a car enthusiast and his ability to talk the talk and emote the appropriate enthusiasms was no professional artifice. Yunis's depth of knowledge about this subject, and of the subcultural resonances it has in Bradford, was key to the quality of the data that was obtained. The interviews here varied considerably, but were predominantly carried out al fresco as individuals were in garages, standing by their cars or even driving their cars. Some were tape-recorded, others, because of the context, were recorded as written records of the meeting. In all, over 60 persons were interviewed for this chapter, and, yet again, innumerable casual conversations contributed to the author's confidence in the emergent analysis.

This project has drawn on a range of social science competences, and has been heavily dependent upon the willingness of individuals to be interviewed. The zest with which many of the interviewees have engaged in the process has been both helpful and gratifying. In going from data to analysis, there is an erratic dance between periods of sustained analysis and moments of electric insight. Some of this is the product of the labours of individual members of the team, but all of it is affected by the persistent flow of conversation, critique and collaboration that makes teamwork so valuable.

Bibliography

Abrams, D. and Hogg, M.A. (eds) (1999) *Social identity and social cognition*, Oxford: Blackwell.

Adeney, M. (1988) *The motor makers: the turbulent history of Britain's car industry*, London: Collins.

Ahmad, W.I.U. and Walker, R. (1997) 'Asian older people: housing, health and access to services', *Ageing and Society*, vol 17, pp 141–65.

Akhtar, S. (1989) *Be careful with Muhammad!: The Salman Rushdie Affair*, Bellew Pub.

Alam, M.Y. (2006) *Made in Bradford*, Pontefract: Route.

Alam, M.Y. (2011) *The invisible village: small world, big society*, Pontefract: Route.

Alam, M.Y. and Husband, C. (2006) *British-Pakistani men from Bradford: linking narratives to policy*, York: Joseph Rowtree Foundation.

Albrow, M. (1997) 'Travelling beyond local cultures' in J. Eade (ed) *Living the global*, London: Routledge, pp 37–55.

Alderman, D. (2008) 'Place, naming, and the interpretation of cultural landscapes', in B. Graham and P. Howard (eds) *The Ashgate research companion to heritage and identity*, Aldershot: Ashgate Press, pp 195–213.

Alexander, C. (1996) *The art of being black: the creation of black British youth identities*, Oxford: Oxford University Press.

Alexander, C. (2000) *The Asian gang: ethnicity, identity, masculinity*, Oxford: Berg.

Alexander, C. (2004) 'Imagining the Asian gang: ethnicity, masculinity and youth after "the riots"', *Critical Social Policy*, vol 24, no 4, pp 526–49.

Ali, N., Kalra, V.S. and Sayid, S. (eds) (2006) *A postcolonial people: South Asians in Britain*, London: Hurst and Co.

Allen, K. and Sturcke, J. (2010) 'Timeline: Toyota's recall woes', 23 February. www.guardian.co.uk/business/2010/jan/29/timeline-toyota-recall-accelerator-pedal

Amin, A. (2003) 'Unruly strangers? The 2001 urban riots in Britain', *International Journal of Urban and Regional Studies*, vol 27, no 2, pp 460–63.

Amin, A. (2006) 'The good city', *Urban Studies*, vol 43, nos 5/6, pp 1009–23.

Amin, A. (2008) 'Collective culture and urban public space', *City*, vol 27, no 1, pp 1–23.

Amin, A. (2010) 'The remainders of race', *Theory, Culture and Society*, vol 27, no 1, pp 1–23.

Amin, A. (2012) *Land of strangers*, Cambridge: Polity.

Anthias, F. and Yuval-Davis, N. (1993) *Racialized boundaries*, London: Routledge.

Anwar, M. (1979) *The myth of return: Pakistanis in Britain*, London: Heinemann Educational.

Appadurai, A. (2005) *Modernity at large: Cultural dimensions of globalization*, Minneapolis, MN: University of Minnesota Press.

Appiah, K.A. (2007) *Cosmopolitanism: ethics in world of strangers*, London: Penguin Books.

Appiganesi, L. and Maitland, S. (eds) (1989) *The Rushdie file*, London: ICA/Fourth Estate.

Archer, L. (2001) '"Muslim brothers, black lads, traditional Asians": British muslim young men's constructions of race, religion and masculinity', *Feminism and Psychology*, vol 11, no 1, pp 79–105.

Azaryahu, M. (1996) 'The power of commemorative street names', *Environment and Planning D: Society and Space*, vol 14, pp 311–30.

Back, L. (1996) *New ethnicities and urban culture*, London: UCL Press.

Back, L. (2007) *The art of listening*, Oxford: Berg.

Back, L., Keith, M., Khan, A., Shukra, K. and Solomos, J. (2002) 'New Labour's white heart: politics, multiculturalism and the return of assimilation', *Political Quarterly*, vol 73, no 4, pp 445–54.

Bagguley, P. and Hussain, Y. (2008) *Riotous citizens: ethnic conflict in multicultural Britain*, Aldershot: Ashgate.

Bailey, P. (1987) *Leisure and class in Victorian England: rational recreation and the contest for control*, London: Methuen.

Barker, M. (1981) *The new racism*, London: Junction Books.

Barry, B. (2001) *Culture and equality*, Cambridge: Polity.

Beck, U. (1992) *Risk society*, London: Sage.

Bengry-Howell, A. and Griffin, C. (2007) 'Self-made motormen: the material construction of working-class masculine identities through car modification', *Journal of Youth Studies*, vol 10, no 4, pp 439–58.

Benyon, J. (ed) (1984) *Scarman and after*, Oxford: Pergamon Press.

Benyon, J. and Solomos, J. (eds) (1987) *The roots of urban unrest*, Oxford: Pergamon Press.

Berg, L. and Vuolteenaho, J. (eds) (2009) *Critical toponymies: contested politics of place naming*, Aldershot: Ashgate.

Berking, H. (2006) 'Contested places and the politics of space', in H. Berking et al (eds) *Negotiating Urban Conflicts: Interaction, Space and Control*, Bielefeld: Transcript Verlag, pp 29–39.

Berry, J.W., Phinney, J.S., Sam, D.L. and Vedder, P. (2006) *Immigrant youth in cultural transition: acculturation, identity, and adaptation across national contexts*, New Jersey, NJ: Laurence Erlbaum.

Best, A. (2006) *Fast cars, cool rides: the accelerating world of youth and their cars*, New York, NY: New York University Press.

Blommaert, J. and Verschueren, J. (1998) *Debating diversity: analysing the discourse of tolerance*, London: Routledge.

Böhm, S., Jones, C., Land, C. and Paterson, M. (eds) (2006a) *Against automobility*, Oxford: Blackwell.

Böhm, S., Jones, C., Land, C. and Paterson, M. (2006b) 'Introduction: impossibilities of automobility', in S. Böhm, C. Jones, C. Land and M. Paterson (eds) *Against automobility*, Oxford: Blackwell, pp 3–16.

Booth, R., Weaver, M. and McCurry, J. (2010) 'Toyota recall: 250 UK cases reported, 20 stuck pedals found, and one accident injury claimed', 4 February. www.guardian.co.uk/business/2010/feb/04/toyota-recall-accelerator-fault

Bourdieu, P (1984 [1979]) *Distinction: a social critique of the judgment of taste* (trans R. Nice), Cambridge, MA: Harvard University Press.

Bowling, B. and Phillips, C. (2007) 'Disproportionate and discriminatory: reviewing the evidence on police stop and search', *The Modern Law Review*, vol 70, no 6, pp 936–61.

Boyd, R. (2006) 'The value of civility', *Urban Studies*, vol 43, nos 5/6, pp 863–78.

Bradford Commission (1996) *The Bradford Commission report: The report of an inquiry into the wider implications of public disorders in Bradford*, London: Bradford Commission.

Brewer, M.B. and Hewstone, R. (eds) (2004) *Self and social identity*, Oxford: Blackwell.

Brown, W. (2008) *Regulating aversion: tolerance in the age of identity and empire*, Princeton, NJ: Princeton University Press.

Browne, K.D. (2001) 'A review of car crime in England and Wales', *The British Journal of Social Work*, vol 31, no 3, pp 465–80.

Brubaker, R. (2004) *Ethnicity without groups*, Cambridge, MA: Harvard University Press.

Bujra, J. and Pearce, J. (2011) *Saturday night and Sunday morning*, Skipton: Vertical Editions.

Bull, M. (2000) *Sounding out the city*, New York, NY: Berg.

Bull, M. (2008) *Sound moves: iPod culture and urban experience*, New York, NY: Routledge.

Bull, M. and Back, L. (eds) (2003) *The auditory culture reader*, Oxford: Berg.

Burnley Task Force (2001) *Report of the Burnley Task Force. Chaired by Lord Clark*, Burnley: Burnley Task Force.

Burrell, K. (2008) 'Managing, learning and sending: the material lives and journeys of Polish women in Britain', *Journal of Material Culture*, vol 13, no 1, pp 63–83.

Burrell, K. (ed) (2009) *Polish migration to the UK in the 'new' European Union: after 2004*, Farnham: Ashgate.

Cameron, D. (2011) 'David Cameron speech on radicalistion amd Islamic extremism', Munich, 5 February. www.newstatesman.com/blogs/the-staggers/2011/02/terrorism-islam-ideology

Campbell, B. (1993) *Goliath: Britain's dangerous places*, London: Methuen.

Camuffo, A. and Weber, D.R. (2012) 'The Toyota way and the crisis: a new industrial divide?', in L. Ciravegna (ed) *Sustaining industrial competitiveness after the crisis: lessons from the automotive industry*, Houndmills: Palgrave Macmillan, pp 57–103.

Capozza, D. and Brown, R. (eds) (2000) *Social identity processes*, London: Sage Publications.

Carling, A. (2008) 'The curious case of the mis-claimed myth claims: ethnic segregation, polarization and the future of Bradford', *Urban Studies*, vol 45, no 3, pp 553–89.

Carrabine, E. and Longhurst, B. (2002) 'Consuming the car: anticipation, use and meaning in contemporary youth culture', *The Sociological Review*, vol 50, no 2, pp 181–96.

CCCS (Centre for Contemporary Cultural Studies) (1982) *The empire strikes back: race and racism in 70s' Britain*, London: Hutchinson.

Chamberlayne, P., Bornat, J. and Wengraf, T. (2000) *The turn to biographical methods in social science: comparative issues and examples*, London: Routledge.

Cheong, P.H., Edwards, R., Goulbourne, H. and Solomos, J. (2007) 'Immigration, social cohesion and social capital: a critical review', *Critical Social Policy*, vol 27, no 1, pp 24–49.

Choi, S.M. and Rifon, N.J. (2007) 'Who is the celebrity in advertising? Understanding dimensions of celebrity images', *The Journal of Popular Culture*, vol 40, no 2, pp 304–24.

Christ, O., Schmid, K., Lolliot, S., Swart, H., Stolle, D., Tausch, N., Al Ramiah, A., Wagner, U., Vertovec, S. and Hewstone, M. (2014) 'Contextual effect of positive contact on outgroup prejudice', *Proceedings of the National Academy of Sciences of the United States*, vol 111, no 11, pp 3996–4000.

Ciravegna, L. (ed) (2012) *Sustaining industrial competitiveness after the crisis: lessons from the automotive industry*, Houndmills: Palgrave Macmillan.

Clayton, J. (2009) 'Thinking spatially: towards an everyday understanding of inter-ethnic relations', *Social and Cultural Geography*, vol 10, no 4, pp 481–98.

Cleaver, E. (1969) *Soul on ice*, London: Jonathan Cape.

Cohen, R. (1997) *Global diasporas: an introduction*, London: University College London Press.

Community Cohesion Independent Review Team (2001) *Community cohesion: A report of the Independent Review Team, Chaired by Ted Cantle* (The Cantle Report), London: Home Office.

Corbett, C. (2003) *Car crime*, Cullompton: Willan.

Cormack, M. and Hourigan, N. (eds) (2007) *Minority language media: concepts, critiques and case studies*, Clevedon: Multilingual Matters Ltd.

Creswell, T. (2006) *On the move: mobility in the modern Western world*, London: Routledge.

Crimp, D. and Rolston, A. (1997) 'Aids activists graphics: a demonstration', in K. Gelder and S. Thornton (eds) *The subcultures reader*, London: Routledge, pp 436–44.

Cropley, A. (2004) 'Creativity as a social phenomenon', in M. Fryer (ed) *Creativity and cultural diversity*, Leeds: The Creativity Educational Centre, pp 13–24.

Curtis, L.P. (1971) *Apes and angels: the Irishman in Victorian caricature*, Newton Abbot: David & Charles.

Dabydeen, D. and Gilmore, J. (2007) *The Oxford companion to Black history*, Oxford: Oxford University Press.

Dant, T. (2004) 'The driver-car', *Theory, Culture and Society*, vol 21, nos 4/5, pp 61–79.

DCLG (Department of Communities and Local Government) (2010) *Evaluation of the National Strategy for Neighbourhood Renewal, final report*, London: Communities and Local Government Online. www. communities.gov.uk

Deakin, N., Cohen, B. and McNeal, J. (1970) *Colour and citizenship and British Society*, London: Panther Books.

De Certeau, M. (1984) *The practice of everyday life* (trans S. Rendall), Berkeley, CA: University of California Press.

Dench, G., Gavron, K. and Young, M. (2006) *The new East End: kinship, race and conflict*, London: Profile Books.

Denham Report (2001) *Building cohesive communities: A report of the ministerial group on public disorder and community cohesion*, London: Home office.

Dennis, K. and Urry, J. (2009) *After the car*, Cambridge: Polity.

DeWitt, J. (2002) *Cool cars, high art: the rise of kustomkulture*, Mississippi, MS: University Press of Mississippi.

Dixon, J. and Levine, M. (2012) *Beyond prejudice*, Cambridge: Cambridge University Press.

Dobbs, J., Green, H. and Zealey, L. (2006) *Office for National Statistics focus on ethnicity and religion*, Basingstoke: Palgrave Macmillan.

Dorling, D. (2009) 'From housing to health – to whom are the white working class losing out? Frequently asked questions', in K.P. Sveinsson (ed) *Who cares about the white working class? Runnymede perspectives*, London: Runnymede Trust, pp 59–65.

Dorling, D. (2010) *Injustice: why social inequality persists*, Bristol: The Policy Press.

Dovidio, J.F. (2001) 'On the nature of contemporary prejudice: the third wave', *Journal of Social Issues*, vol 57, no 4, pp 829–49.

Dovidio, J.F. and Gaertner, S.L. (2004) 'Aversive racism', in M.P. Zanna (ed) *Advances in experimental social psychology (volume 36)*, San Diego, CA: Academic Press, pp 1–51.

Dovidio, J.F., Glick, P. and Rudman, L.A. (2005) *On the nature of prejudice: fifty years after Allport*, Oxford: Blackwell.

Dovidio, J.F., Saguy, T., Gaertner, S.L. and Thomas, E.L. (2012) 'From attitudes to (in)action: the darker side of 'we', in Dion and Levine (eds) (op cit) pp 248–68.

Downing, J. and Husband, C. (2005) *Representing 'race': racisms, ethnicities and the media*, London: Sage.

Drissel, D. (2011) 'Hybridizing hip-hop in diaspora: young British South Asian men negotiating black-inflected identities', *The International Journal of Diversity in Organizations, Communities & Nations*, vol 10, no 5, pp 199–222.

Durrschimdt, J. (1997) 'The delinking of locale and milieu: on the situatedness of extended milieux in a global environment', in J. Eade (ed) *Living the global city*, London: Routledge, pp 56–72.

Duvell, F. (2004) 'Highly skilled, self-employed and illegal immigrants from Poland in United Kingdom', Working Paper, Centre for Migration Studies, Warsaw, Poland.

Dwyer, C. (1998) 'Contested identities: challenging dominant representations of young British Muslim women', in T. Skelton and G. Valentine (eds) *Cool places*, London: Routledge.

Eade, J. (1997) *Living the global city*, London: Routledge.

Eade, J., Garapich, M. and Drinkwater, S. (2006) *Class and ethnicity: Polish migrants in London*, London: CRONEM University of Roehampton.

Edensor, T. (2004) 'Automobilty and national identity: representation, geography and driving practice', *Theory, Culture and Society*, vol 21, nos 4/5, pp 101–20.

Elias, N. (2000) *The civilizing process*, Oxford: Blackwell.

Elias, N. and Scotson, J.L. (1965) *The established and the outsiders*, London: Cass.

Ellemers, N., Spears, R. and Doosje, B. (eds) (1999) *Social identity: context, commitment, content*, Blackwell: Oxford.

EOCWA (Equal Opportunity Commission of Western Australia) (2005) *The policy framework for substantive equality*, Perth: EOCWA.

Featherstone, M. (2004) 'Automobilities: an introduction', *Theory, Culture and Society*, vol 21, nos 4/5, pp 1–24.

Fekete, L. (2009) *A suitable enemy*, London: Pluto Press.

Fenster, T. (2005a) 'The right to the gendered city: different formations of belonging in everyday life', *Journal of Gender Studies*, vol 14, no 3, pp 217–31.

Fenster, T. (2005b) 'Identity issues and local governance: women's everyday life in the city', *Social Identities*, vol 11, no 1, pp 21–36.

Fieldhouse, J. (1978) *Bradford*, Bradford: Watmoughs Financial Print.

Finney, N. and Simpson, L. (2009) *'Sleepwalking to segregation'? Challenging myths about race and migration*, Bristol: The Policy Press.

Firth, G. (1997) *A history of Bradford*, Chichester: Phillimore.

Fiske, J. (1989) *Understanding popular culture*, London: Routledge.

Fogelson, R.M. (1971) *Violence as protest: a study of riots and ghettos*, Garden City, NY: Anchor Books.

Forgacs, D. (ed) (1989) *An Antonio Gramsci reader: selected writings, 1916–1935*, New York, NY: Schocken Books.

Fryer, M. (ed) (2004) *Creativity and cultural diversity*, Leeds: The Creativity Educational Centre.

Fyfe, N., Bannister, J. and Kearns, A. (2006) '(In)Civility and the city', *Urban Studies*, vol 43, nos 5/6, pp 853–61.

Gade, D.W. (2003) 'Language, identity and the scriptorial landscape in Quebec and Catalonia', *The Geographical Review*, vol 93, no 4, pp 429–48.

Gaertner, A.L., Dovidio, J.F., Nier, J.A., Ward, C.M. and Banker, B.S. (1999) 'Across cultural divides: the value of a superordinate identity', in D.A. Pentice and D.T. Miller (eds) *Cultural divides: understanding and overcoming group conflict*, New York, NY: Russell Sage Foundation.

Gamson, W. A. and Sifry, M. L. (2013) 'The #Occupy movement: an introduction', *The Sociological Quarterly*, vol 54, no 2, pp 159–63.

Garapich, M. (2007) 'Odyssean refugees, migrants and power – construction of "other" within the Polish "community" in the UK', in D. Reed-Danahay and C. Brettell (eds) *Citizenship, political engagement and immigration in Europe and citizenship in Europe and the United States S. Anthropological Perspectives*, Rutgers: Rutgers UP, pp 124–37 [preprint: www.surrey.ac.uk/cronem/files/Odyssean_Reffuges_Migrants_and_Power.pdf]

Garapich, M. (2008) 'The migration industry and civil society: Polish immigrants in the United Kingdom before and after EU enlargement', *Journal of Ethnic and Migration Studies*, vol 34, no 5, pp 735–52.

Garapich, M. (2009a) 'Migracje, społeczeństwo obywatelskie i władza. Uwarunkowania stowarzyszeniowości etnicznej i rozwoju społeczeństwa obywatelskiego wśród polskich emigrantów w Wielkiej Brytanii', in M. Duszczyk and M. Lesińska (eds) *Współczesne migracje: dylematy Europy i Polski*, Warsaw: Ośrodka Badań nad Migracjami UW, Petit.

Garapich, M. (2009b) 'Migracje, społeczeństwo obywatelskie i władza. Kulturowe uwarunkowania tworzenia stowarzyszeń etnicznych', in M. Duszczyk and M. Lesińska (eds) *Współczesne migracje: dylematy Europy i Polski*, Warsaw: Ośrodka Badań nad Migracjami UW, Petit, pp 39–69.

Gardner, C.B. (1995) *Passing by: gender and public harassment*, Berkeley and Los Angeles, CA: University of California Press.

Garner, S. (2009) 'Home truths: the white working class and the racialization of social housing', in K.P. Sveinsson (ed) *Who cares about the white working class*, London: The Runnymede Trust.

Gartman, D. (2004) 'Three ages of the automobile: the cultural logics of the car', *Theory, Culture & Society*, vol 21, nos 4/5, pp 169–95.

Gearty, C. (2007) 'Terrorism and human rights', *Government and Opposition*, vol 42, no 3, pp 340–62.

Gelder, K. (1997) 'Introduction to Part Two', in K. Gelder and S. Thornton (eds) *The subcultures reader*, London: Routledge, pp 83–9.

Gelder, K. and Thornton, S. (eds) (1997) *The subcultures reader*, London: Routledge.

Giddens, A. (1984) *The constitution of society: outline of the theory of structuration*, Cambridge: Polity.

Giddens, A. (1991) *Modernity and self-identity*, Cambridge: Polity Press.

Gill, R. (2008) 'Empowerment/sexism: figuring female sexual agency in contemporary advertising', *Feminism and Psychology*, vol 18, no 1, pp 35–60.

Gilroy, P. (1987) *There ain't no black in the Union Jack*, London: Hutchinson.

Gilroy, P. (1991) 'Sounds authentic: black music, ethnicity, and the challenge of a "changing same"', *Black Music Research Journal*, vol 11, no 2, pp 111–36.

Gilroy, P. (2001) 'Driving while black', in D. Miller (ed) *Car cultures*, Oxford: Berg, pp 81–104.

Gilroy, P. (2012) '"My Britain is fuck all": zombie multiculturalism and the race politics of citizenship', *Identities: Global Studies in Culture and Power*, vol 19, no 4, pp 380–97.

Glick Schiller, N., Caglar, A. and Guldbrandsen, T.C. (2006) 'Beyond the ethnic lens: locality, globality, and born-again incorporation', *American Ethnologist*, vol 33, no 4, pp 612–33.

Goffman, E. (1969) *The presentation of self in everyday life*, London: Allen Lane.

Goffman, E. (1972) *Interaction ritual: Essays on face-to-face behavior*, London: Allen Lane.

Goldberg, D. (2002) *The racial state*, Malden, MA: Blackwell Publishing.

Goldberg, D. (2009) *The threat of race: reflections on racial neoliberalism*, Oxford: Wiley-Blackwell.

Goldman, R. and Papson, S. (1998) *Nike culture*, London: Sage.

Gonzalez, K.V., Verkuyten, M., Weesie, J. and Poppe, E. (2008) 'Prejudice towards Muslims in the Netherlands: testing integrated threat theory', *British Journal of Social Psychology*, vol 47, pp 667–85.

Gordon, P. (1983) *White law: racism in the police, courts and prisons*, London: Pluto Press.

Gordon, P. and Klug, F. (1986) *New Right, new racism*, London: Searchlight Publications.

Gorter, D., Marten, H.F. and Van Mansel, L. (eds) (2012) *Minority languages in the linguistic landscape*, Basingstoke: Palgrave Macmillan.

Goulbourne, H. (1990) *Black politics in Britain*, Aldershot: Avebury.

Goulbourne, H. (1990) *The contribution of West Indian groups to British politics*, Aldershot Avebury.

Gramsci, A. (1977) *Selections from political writings 1910–1920*, London: Lawrence and Wishart.

Hall, S. and Datta, A. (2010) 'The translocal street: shop signs and local multi-culture along the Walworth Road, South London', *City, Culture and Society*, vol 1, no 2, pp 69–77.

Hall, S., Critcher, C., Jefferson, T., Clarke, J. and Roberts, B. (1978) *Policing the crisis: mugging, the state and law and order*, London: Hutchinson.

Halstead, M. (1988) *Justice and cultural diversity: An examination of the Honeyford Affair*, London: Falmer Press.

Hammond, R.G. (2012) 'Sudden unintended used-price deceleration? The 2009–2010 Toyota recalls', Raleigh, NC: North Carolina State University.

harry4lyf (2011) 'Toyota Corolla GT coupe AE86 donuts – Bradford' (online video), www.youtube.com/watch?v=IBH33QZT1cY

Harvey, D. (1990) *The condition of postmodernity: an enquiry into the origins of cultural change*, London: Blackwell.

Harvey, D. (1996) *Justice, nature and the geography of difference*, Oxford: Blackwell.

Harvey, D. (2000) *Spaces of hope*, Berkeley, CA: University of California Press.

Hebdige, D. (1979) *Subculture: the meaning of style*, London: Methuen.

Hennessy, P. (ed) (2007) *The new protective state: government, intelligence and terrorism*, London: Continuum.

Herbert, J. (2008) *Negotiating boundaries in the city*, Aldershot: Ashgate.

Hesmondhalgh, D.J. and Melville, C. (2002) 'Urban breakbeat culture – repercussions of hip-hop in the United Kingdom', in T. Mitchell (ed) *Global noise: rap and hip hop outside the USA*, Middletown, CT: Wesleyan University Press, pp 86–110.

Hewitt, R. (2005) *White backlash and the politics of multiculturalism*, Cambridge: Cambridge University Press.

Hills, J. (2007) *Ends and means: the future roles of social housing in England*, CASE Report 34, London: LSE. http://sticerd.lse.ac.uk./dps/case/cr/CASEreport34.pdf

Hills, J., Sefton, T. and Steward, K. (2009) *Towards a more equal society? Poverty, inequality and policy since 1997*, Bristol: The Policy Press.

Hillyard, P. and Percy-Smith, J. (1988) *The coercive state: The decline of democracy in Britain*, Glasgow: Fontana/Collins.

Hiro, D. (1973) *Black British, White British*, Harmondsworth: Penguin.

Hitch, P.J. and Rack, P.H. (1980) 'Mental illness among Polish and Russian refugees in Bradford', *British Journal of Psychiatry*, vol 137, no 3, pp 206–11.

Hjarvard, S. (2008) 'The mediatization of society. A theory of the media as agents of social and cultural change', *Nordicom Review*, no 2, pp 105–34.

Hoggart, R. (1957) *The uses of literacy: aspects of working class life*, London: Chatto and Windus.

Hollway, W. and Jefferson, T. (2000) *Doing qualitative research differently: free association, narrative and the interview method*, London: Sage.

Humphrey, D. (1972) *Police power and black people*, London: Panther.

Humphrey, D. and John, G. (1971) *Because they're black*, Harmondsworth: Penguin Classic.

Humphrey, J., Lecler, Y. and Salerno, M.S. (eds) (2000) *Global strategies and local realities: the auto industry in emerging markets*, London: Macmillan.

Huntington, S.P. (1996) *The clash of civilizations and the remaking of world order*, New York, NY: Simon and Schuster.

Husband, C. (1994a) *'Race' and nation: the British experience*, Perth, Australia: Paradigm.

Husband, C. (1994b) 'The political context of Muslim communities' participation in British society', in B. Lewis and D. Schnapper (eds) *Muslims in Europe*, London: Pinter Publishers, pp 79–97.

Husband, C. (1996) 'The right to be understood: conceiving the multi-ethnic public sphere', *Innovation*, vol 9, pp 205–15.

Husband, C. (1998) 'Differentiated citizenship and the multi-ethnic public sphere', *Journal of International Communication*, vol 1, nos 1/2, pp 134–48.

Husband, C. (2000) '"Recognizing diversity and developing skills": the proper role of transcultural communication', *The European Journal of Social Work*, vol 3, no 3, pp 225–34.

Husband, C. (2003) 'Una Buena Practica Sigilosa, Aungue Flirteando Con El Racismo', *Migraciones*, vol 14, no 203, pp 145–80.

Husband, C. (2010) 'Counter narratives to multiculturalism and the assimilationist drift in British policy: lessons from the era of New Labour', *Translocations*, vol 6, no 2, pp 1–23.

Husband, C. and Alam, Y. (2011) *Social cohesion and counter-terrorism: a policy contradiction?*, Bristol: The Policy Press.

Husband, C. and Alam, Y. (2012) 'Ethnic diversity and creative urban practice: the case of Bradford's Mughal Garden', *COLLeGIUM: Studies Across Disciplines in the Humanities and Social Sciences*, vol 13, pp 93–114.

Husband, C. and Fomina, J. (2011) 'Inhabiting heteroglossic media spaces: intra-group transitions, identity construction and the language–media interface of "Bradfordian Poles"', in C. Husband and T. Moring (eds) *Living languages in bilingual media environments*, Helsinki: NORDICOM.

Hussain, Y. and Bagguley, P. (2005) 'Citizenship, Ethnicity and Identity: British Pakistanis after the 2001 'riots'', *Sociology*, vol 39, no 3, pp 407–25.

Hüttermann, J. (2003) 'Policing an ethnically divided neighborhood in Germany: day-to-day strategies and habitus', *Policing and Society*, vol 13, pp 381–97.

Huysmans, J. (2006) *The politics of insecurity: fear, migration and asylum in the EU*, London: Routledge.

Huysmans, J. (2009) 'Conclusion: Insecurity and the everyday', in P. Noxolo and J. Huysmans (eds) (2009) *Community, Citizenship and the 'War On Terror': Security and Insecurity*, Houndmills, Basingstoke: Palgrave MacMillan, pp 196–207.

Illich, I. (1973) *Deschooling society*, Harmondsworth: Penguin.

James, D. (1990) *Bradford*, Halifax: Ryburn Publishing.

Janowski, M. (2004) 'Imagined Polands: notions of identity among the "first wave" of Polish migrants in the UK', paper presented at the fourth conference 'Imagining Diasporas: Space, Identity and Social Change', University of Windsor, Canada, 14–16 May.

Jeffreys, S. (2005) *Beauty and misogyny: harmful cultural practices in the West*, Hove: Routledge.

Jessop, B., Bonnet, K., Bromley, S. and Ling, T. (1988) *Thatcherism*, Oxford: Polity Press.

Jordan, W.D. (1969) *White over black*, Harmondsworth: Penguin.

Joshua, H., Wallace, T. with Booth, H. (1983) *To ride the storm: the 1980 Bristol riot and the state*, London: Heinemann.

Jost, J.T. and Hamilton, D.L. (2005) 'Stereotypes in our culture', in J.F. Dovidio, P. Glick and L.A. Rudman (eds) *On the nature of prejudice: fifty years on*, Oxford: Blackwell, pp 208–24.

Kaczmarczyk, P. (2008) *Współczesne migracje zagraniczne Polaków. Aspekty lokalne i regionalne*, Warszawa: O rodek Bada nad Migracjami, Uniwersytet Warszawski.

Kalra, V.S. (2009) 'Between emasculation and hypermasculinity: theorizing British South Asian masculinities', *South Asian Popular Culture*, vol 7, no 2, pp 113–25.

Kamata, S. (1982) *Japan in the passing lane: an insider's account of life in a Japanese auto factory*, T. Akimoto: translator and editor (1983), Boston, MA, London: Allen & Unwin.

Katz, J. (1999) *How emotions work*, Chicago, IL: University of Chicago Press.

Kay, D. and Miles, R. (1992) *Refugees or migrant workers? European voluntary workers in Britain 1946–51*, London: Routledge.

Keane, J. (1998) *Civil society: old images, new visions*, Stanford, CA: Stanford University Press.

Keith, M. and Pile, S. (eds) (1993) *Place and the politics of identity*, London: Routledge.

Kellet, S. and Gross, H. (2006) 'Addicted to joyriding? An exploration of young offenders' accounts of their car crime', *Psychology, Crime & Law*, vol 12, no 1, pp 39–59.

Kettle, M. and Hodges, L. (1982) *Uprising: the police, the people and the riots in Britain's cities*, London: Pan Books.

Khan, S. (2006) 'Muslims!', in N. Ali, V.S. Kalra and S. Sayyid (eds) *Postcolonial people: South Asians in Britain*, London: Hurst, pp 182–7.

Kiernan, V.G. (1972) *The lords of human kind*, Harmondsworth: Penguin.

Kim, Y.Y. (1992) 'Intercultural communication competence: a systems-theoretic view', in W.B. Gudykunst and Y.Y. Kim (eds) *Readings on communications with strangers*, New York, NY: McGraw-Hill.

Koskela, H. (1999) '"Gendered exclusions": women's fear of violence and changing relations to space', *Geografiska Annaler* (Series B, Human Geography), vol 81, no 2, pp 111–24.

Kundani, A. (2007) *The end of tolerance*, London: Pluto Press.

Kymlicka, W. (1995) *Multicultural citizenship*, Oxford: Oxford University Press.

Kymlicka, W. (2001) *Politics in the vernacular*, Oxford: Oxford University Press.

Lane, A.T. (2004) *Victims of Stalin and Hitler: the exodus of Poles and Balts to Britain*, London: Palgrave Macmillan.

Lane, R.L. (2006) *The postcolonial novel*, Cambridge: Polity.

Lantin, A. and Titley, G. (2011) *The crises of multiculturalism*, London: Zed Books.

Lelohe, M.J. (1966) 'Bradford', *Race & Class*, July, vol 8: pp 30–42.

Levinas, E. (1978) *Otherwise than being, or, beyond essence* (trans A. Lingis), Dordrecht and Boston, MA: Kluwer Academic Publishers.

Levitas, R. (1986) *The ideology of the New Right*, Oxford: Policy Press.

Levitas, R. (2005) *The inclusive society? Social exclusion and New Labour*, Basingstoke: Palgrave Macmillan.

Levitt, S.D. and Dubner, S.J. (2005) *Freakonomics: A rogue economist explores the hidden side of everything*, London: Penguin.

Lewis, G. (1985) 'From Deepest Kilburn' in L. Heron (ed) *Truth, dare, promise: Girls growing up in the fifties*, London: Virago, pp 213–36.

Lewis, L. and Schnapper, D. (1994) *Muslims in Europe*, London: Pinter Publishers.

Light, L., Nee, C. and Ingham, H. (1993) *Car theft: the offender's perspective*, London: HMSO.

Lofland, L. (1989) 'Social life in the public realm', *Journal of Contemporary Ethnography*, vol 17, no 4, pp 453–82.

MacIntyre, A. (1981) *After virtue*, Notre Dame: University of Notre Dame Press.

Macintyre, A. (1988) *Whose Justice? Which Rationality*, Notre Dame: Notre Dame University Press.

MacMillan, R., Nierobisz, A. and Welsh, S. (2000) 'Experiencing the streets: harassment and perceptions of safety among women', *Journal of Research in Crime and Delinquency*, vol 37, no 3, pp 300–22.

Madden, R. (2010) *Being ethnographic: a guide to the theory and practice of ethnography*, London: Sage.

Marzac, J. (1988) *The role of the Catholic Church in the Polish community of the UK*, Leeds: Leeds University Department of Theology and Religious Studies.

Mason, J. (1996) *Qualitative researching*, London: Sage.

McDonald, C. and Scott, J. (2007) 'A brief history of advertising', in G.J. Tellis and T. Ambler (eds) *The SAGE handbook of advertising*, Thousand Oaks, CA: Sage.

McLoughlin, S. (2005) 'Mosques and the public space: conflict and cooperation in Bradford', *Journal of Ethnic and Migration Studies*, vol 31, no 6, pp 1045–66.

McLoughlin, S. (2006) 'Writing British Asian Bradford', in N. Ali, V.S. Kalra and S. Sayid (eds) *A postcolonial people: South Asians in Britain*, London: Hurst and Co.

Michael, M. (2001) 'The invisible car: the cultural purification of road rage', in D. Miller (ed) *Car cultures*, Oxford: Berg, pp 59–80.

Middleton, J. (2010) 'Sense and the city: exploring the embodied geographies of urban walking', *Social and Cultural Geography*, vol 11, no 6, pp 576–96.

Miles, R. and Phizacklea, A. (1984) *White man's country: racism in British politics*, London: Pluto Press.

Miller, D. (2001a) 'Driven societies', in D. Miller (ed) *Car cultures*, Oxford: Berg, pp 1–34.

Miller, D. (ed) (2001b) *Car cultures*, Oxford: Berg.

Miller, D. (2012) *Consumption and its consequences*, Cambridge: Polity.

Miller, R.L. and Brewer, J.D. (2003) *The A–Z of social research*, London: Sage.

Morey, P. and Yaqin, A. (2011) *Framing Muslims: stereotyping and representation after 9/11*, Cambridge, MA: Harvard University Press.

Moring, T. (2007) 'Functional completeness in minority language media', in M. Cormack and N. Hourigan (eds) *Minority language media: concepts, critiques and case studies*, Clevedon: Multilingual Matters Ltd, pp 17–33.

Murji, K. and Solomos, J. (eds) (2005) *Racialization: studies in theory and practice*, Oxford: Oxford University Press.

Nasta, S. (2002) *Home truths: fictions of the South Asian diaspora in Britain*, Basingstoke: Palgrave.

Noble, G. (2009) '"Countless acts of recognition": young men, ethnicity and the messiness of identities in everyday life', *Social and Cultural Geography*, vol 10, no 8, pp 875–91.

O'Byrne, D. (1997) 'Working class culture: local community and global conditions', in J. Eade (ed) *Living the Global*, London: Routledge, pp 73–89,

O'Connell, S. (1998) *The car in British society: class, gender and motoring 1896–1939*, Manchester: Manchester University Press.

Oldham Independent Panel Review (2001) *One Oldham, one future*, Oldham: Oldham Metropolitan Borough Council.

ONS (Office for National Statistics) (2011) 'Migration statistics quarterly report statistical bulletin – May 2011'. www.statistics.gov.uk/statbase/Product.asp?vlnk=15230

Ouseley, H. (2001) *Community pride not prejudice (The Ouseley Report)*, Bradford: Bradford City Council.

Overy, R. (2009) *The twilight years: the paradox of Britain between the wars*, New York, NY: Viking.

Packard, V. (2007 [1957]) *The hidden persuaders (with an introduction by Mark Crispin Miller)*, Brooklyn, NY: Ig Publishing.

Parekh, B. (2008) *A new politics of identity*, Basingstoke: Palgrave.

Paterson, M. (2006) *Consumption and everyday life*, London: Routledge.

Paterson, M. (2007) *Automobile politics: ecology and cultural political economy*, Cambridge: Cambridge University Press.

Pearce, J. and Milne, E.-J. (2010) *Participation and community on Bradford's traditionally white estates*, York: Joseph Rowntree Foundation.

Pentice, D.A. and Miller, D.T. (eds) (1999) *Cultural divides: understanding and overcoming group conflict*, New York, NY: Russell Sage Foundation.

Pettigrew, T. and Tropp, L.R. (2005) 'Allport's intergroup contact hypothesis: its history and influence', in J.F. Dovidio, P. Glick and L.A. Rudman (eds) *On the nature of prejudice: fifty years on*, Oxford: Blackwell, pp 262–77.

Phillips, A. (2007) *Multiculturalism without culture*, Princeton, NJ: Princeton University Press.

Phillips, D. (2006) 'Parallel lives? Challenging discourses of British Muslim segregation', *Environment and Planning D: Society and Space*, vol 24, no 1, pp 25–40.

Phillips, D., Athwal, B., Harrison, M., Robinson, D., Bashir, N. and Atkinson, J. (2010) *Neighbourhood, Community and Housing in Bradford: building understanding between new and settled groups. Final report to the Joseph Rowntree Foundation*, York: Joseph Rowntree Foundation.

Phillips, D., Davis, C.M. and Butt, M.F.F. (2002) 'The racialisation of space in Bradford', *Yorkshire and Humber Regional Review*, vol 12, pp 9–10.

Phillips, D., Davis, C. and Ratcliffe, P. (2007) 'British Asian narratives of urban space', *Transactions of the Institute of British Geography*, vol 32, no 2, pp 217–34.

Phillips, T. and Smith, R.D. (2006) 'Rethinking urban incivility research: strangers, bodies and circulations', *Urban Studies*, vol 43, nos 5/6, pp 879–901.

Poole, E. (2002) *Reporting Islam: Media Representations of British Muslims*, London: I B Tauris.

Poole, E. and Richardson, J. (eds) (2006) *Muslims and the News Rhetoric of British Broadsheet Newspapers*, Amsterdam: John Benjamins.

Power, A. (2009) 'New Labour and unequal neighbourhood', in J. Hills, T. Sefton and K. Steward (eds) *Towards a more equal society? Poverty, inequality and policy since 1997*, Bristol: The Policy Press, pp 115–34.

Rabikowska, M. and Burrell, K. (2009) 'The material worlds of recent Polish migrants: transnationalism, food, shops and home', in K. Burrell (ed) *Polish migration to the UK in the 'new' European Union: after 2004*, Farnham: Ashgate.

Ramji, H. (2007) 'Dynamics of religion and gender amongst young British Muslims', *Sociology*, vol 41, no 6, pp 1171–89.

Ratcliffe, P. (1996) *'Race' and housing in Bradford: addressing the needs of the South Asian, African and Caribbean communities*, Bradford: Bradford Housing Forum.

Rattansi, A. (2005) 'The uses of racialization: the time-spaces and subject-objects of the raced body', in K. Murji and J. Solomos (eds) *Racialization: studies in theory and practice*, Oxford: Oxford University Press.

Rex, J. and Moore, R. (1967) *Race, community and conflict*, Oxford: Oxford University Press.

Robertson, R. (1992) *Globalization*, London: Sage

Robertson, R. (1995) 'Glocalization: time-space and homogeneity-heterogeneity', in M. Featherstone et al (eds) *Global modernities*, London: Sage, pp 25–44.

Rose-Redwood, R. and Alderman, D. (2011) 'Critical interventions in political toponymy', *ACME: An International E- Journal for Critical Geographies*, vol 10, no 1, pp 1–6.

Rose-Redwood, R., Alderman, D. and Azaryahu, M. (2010) 'Geographies of toponymic inscription: new directions in critical place-name studies', *Progress in Human Geography*, vol 34, no 4, pp 453–70.

Ruddick, S. (1996) 'Constructing difference in public spaces: race, class and gender as interlocking systems', *Urban Geography*, vol 17, pp 132–51.

Rushkoff, D. (2013) 'Permanent revolution: occupying democracy', *The Sociological Quarterly*, vol 54, no 2, pp 164–73.

Ruthven, M. (1991) *A satanic affair*, London: Hogarth Press.

Ryan, L., Sales, R., Tilki, M. and Siara, B. (2008) 'Social networks, social support and social capital: the experiences of recent Polish migrants in London', *Sociology*, vol 42, no 4, pp 672–90.

Samad, Y. (1992) 'Book burning and race relations: the political mobilisation of Bradford Muslims', *Journal of Ethnicity and Migration Studies*, vol 18, no 4, pp 507–19.

Sandberg, L. and Tollefsen, A. (2010) 'Talking about fear of violence in public space: female and male narratives about threatening situations in Umeå, Sweden', *Social and Cultural Geography*, vol 11, no 1, pp 1–15.

Sarantakos, S. (1998) *Social research* (2nd edn), Basingstoke: Macmillan.

Scarman, Lord. (1981) *The Brixton Disorders 10–12 April 1981. Report of an Inquiry by the Rt. Hon. Lord Scarman OBE*, London: HMSO.

Schafer, R.M. (1969) *The new sound,* Toronto: Bernadol Music.

Schafer, R.M. (1977) *The tuning,* New York: A. A. Knopf.

Schafer, R.M. (1993) *The soundscape: Our sonic environment and the tuning of the world,* Rochester, VT: Inner Traditions Bear and Company.

Schein, L. and Thoj, V. (2010) 'Gran Torino's boys and men with guns: Hmong perspectives', *Hmong Studies Journal*, vol 10, pp 1–52.

Seale, B. (1970) *Seize the time,* London: Arrow Books.

Secor, A. (2004) 'There is an Istanbul that belongs to me: citizenship, space and identity in the city', *Annals of the Association of American Geographers*, vol 94, pp 352–68.

Seidel, G. (1986) 'Culture, nation and "race" in the British and French New Right', in R. Levitas (ed) *The ideology of the New Right*, Oxford: Policy Press.

Shaw, A. (1988) *A Pakistani community in Britain*, Blackwell: Oxford.

Shaw, A. (2000) *Kinship and continuity: Pakistani families in Britain*, Amsterdam: Harwood Academic.

Sheller, M. (2004) 'Automotive emotions: feeling the car', *Theory, Culture & Society*, vol 21, nos 4/5, pp 221–42.

Sheller, M. and Urry, J. (2000) 'The city and the car', *International Journal of Urban and Regional Research*, vol 24, pp 737–57.

Sheller, M. and Urry, J. (2003) 'Mobile transformations of "public" and "private" life', *Theory, Culture & Society*, vol 20, no 3, pp 107–25.

Simmel, G. (1950 [1903]) 'The metropolis and mental life', in K. Wolff (ed) *The sociology of Georg Simmel*, New York, NY: Free Press, pp 409–24.

Simon, B., Aufderheide, B. and Kampmeier, C. (2005) 'The social psychology of minority–majority relations', in M.B. Brewer and M. Hewstone (eds) *Self and social identity*, Oxford: Blackwell.

Simpson, L. (2004) 'Statistics of racial segregation: measures, evidence and policy', *Urban Studies*, vol 41, no 3, pp 661–81.

Simpson, L. (2007) 'Ghettos of the mind: the empirical behaviour indices of segregation and diversity', *Journal of the Royal Statistical Society: Series A (Statistics in Society)*, vol 170, no 2, pp 405–24.

Simpson, L., Husband, C. and Alam, M.Y. (2009) 'Recognizing complexity, challenging pessimism: the case of Bradford's urban dynamics', *Urban Studies*, vol 46, no 9, pp 1995–2001.

Skelton, T. and Valentine, G. (eds) (1998) *Cool places*, London: Routledge.

Smith, G. and Jackson, P. (1999) 'Narrating the nation: the "imagined community" of Ukrainians in Bradford', *Journal of Historical Geography*, vol 25, no 3, pp 367–87.

Smith, M.P. (2005) 'Transnational urbanism revisited', *Journal of Ethnic and Migration Studies*, vol 31, no 2, pp 235–44.

Smith, P., Phillips, T.L. and King, R.D. (2010) *Incivility: the rude stranger in everyday life*, Cambridge: Cambridge University Press.

Smith, T. and Winslow, M. (2000) 'Keeping the faith: the Polish community in Britain', Bradford Heritage Recording Unit in association with the Migration & Ethnicity Research Centre at the University of Sheffield.

Snyder, B.R. (1971) *The hidden curriculum*, New York, NY: Knopf.

Soja, E.W. (1997) 'Six discourses on postmetropolis', in S. Westwood and J. Williams (ed) *Imagining cities: scripts, signs and memory*, London: Routledge, pp 19–30.

Solomos, J. (2003) *Race and racism in Britain*, Basingstoke: Palgrave Macmillan.

Solomos, J. and Back, L. (1995) *Race, politics and social change*, London: Routledge.

Springer, P. (2009) *Ads to icons: how advertising succeeds in a multimedia age* (2nd edn), London: Kogan Page.

Stachura, P.D. (2004) *Poles in Britain. From 1940–2000. From betrayal to assimilation*, London: Frank Cass.

Stanko, E.A. (1990) *Everyday violence: how women and men experience sexual and physical danger*, London: Pandora.

Stephan, W.G. and Stephan, C.W. (1996a) 'Predicting prejudice', *International Journal of Intercultural Relations*, vol 20, nos 3/4, pp 409–26.

Stephan, W.G. and Stephan, C.W. (1996b) *Intergroup relations*, Boulder, CO: Westview Press.

Stephan, W.G., Ybarra, O. and Bachman, G. (1999) 'Prejudice towards immigrants', *Journal of Applied Social Psychology*, vol 29, no 11, pp 2221–37.

Strinati, D. (1995) *An introduction to theories of popular culture*, London: Routledge.

Sumption, M. (2009) *Social networks and the Polish immigration to the UK*, Economics of Migration Working Paper no 5, London: IPPR.

Sutherland, M. (2008) *Advertising and the mind of the consumer: what works, what doesn't and why* (3rd edn), Crows Nest, New South Wales: Allen and Unwin.

Sveinsson, K.P. (ed) (2009) *Who cares about the white working class*, London: The Runnymede Trust.

Swanton, D. (2010) 'Flesh, metal, road: tracing the machinic geographies of race', *Environment and Planning D: Society and Space*, vol 28, no 3, pp 447–66.

Sword, K. (1996) 'Identity in flux', London School of Eastern and Slavonic Studies.

Tajfel, H. (1981) *Human groups and social categories*, Cambridge: Cambridge University Press.

Tajfel, H. and Turner, J.C. (1979) 'An integrative theory of intergroup conflict', in W.G. Austin and S. Worchel (eds) *The social psychology of intergroup relations*, Monterey, CA: Brooks/Cole.

Taylor, C. (1989) *Sources of the self: the making of the modern identity*, Cambridge, MA: Harvard University Press.

Taylor, C. (1992) *Multiculturalism and 'the politics of recognition'*, Princeton, NJ: Princeton University Press.

Taylor, C. (2004) *Modern social imaginaries*, Durham, NC: Duke University Press.

Taylor, S. and Gibson, K. (2010) *Manningham: character and diversity in a Bradford suburb*, Swindon: English Heritage.

Tellis, G.J. and Ambler, T. (2007) *The SAGE handbook of advertising*, Thousand Oaks, CA: Sage.

Thacker, A. (2006) 'Traffic, gender, modernism', in S. Böhm, C. Jones, C. Land and M. Paterson (eds) *Against automobility*, Oxford: Blackwell, pp 175–89.

Thomas, D., Holden, L. and Claydon, T. (1998) (eds) *The motor car and popular culture in the 20th century*, Aldershot: Ashgate.

Thrift, N. (2004) 'Driving in the city', *Theory, Culture and Society*, vol 21, nos 4/5, pp 41–59.

Tragos, P. (2009) 'Monster masculinity: honey, I'll be in the garage reasserting my manhood', *The Journal of Popular Culture*, vol 42, no 3, pp 541–53.

Triandafyllidou, A. (2006) *Contemporary Polish migration in Europe: complex patterns of movement and settlement*, Lampeter: Edwin Mellon Press.

Tung, M.P. (2000) *Chinese Americans and their immigrant parents: conflict, identity, and values*, Binghampton, NY: The Haworth Critical Practice Press.

Tunstall, R. and Coulter, A. (2006) *Twenty five years on twenty estates: turning the tide?*, York: Joseph Rowntree Trust.

Turner, J.C. (1987) *Rediscovering the Social Group*, Oxford: Basil Blackwell.

Turner, J.C. (1999) 'Some current issues in research on social identity and self-categorization theories', in N. Ellemers, R. Spears and B. Doosje (eds) *Social identity: context, commitment, content*, Blackwell: Oxford, pp 6–34.

Turner, J.C., Hogg, M.A., Oakes, P.J., Reicher, S.D. and Wetherall, M.S. (1987) *Rediscovering the social group*, Oxford: Basil Blackwell.

UKCrimeStatistics (2014) www.ukcrimestatistics.com/Neighbourhood/ West_Yorkshire_Police/Bradford_South_Manningham_and_Toller

Urry, J. (2000) *Sociology beyond societies: mobilities for the twenty-first century*, London: Routledge.

Urry, J. (2004) 'The "system" of automobility', *Theory, Culture and Society*, vol 21, nos 4/5, pp 25–39.

Urry, J. (2006) 'Inhabiting the car', in S. Böhm, C. Jones, C. Land and M. Paterson (eds) *Against automobility*, Oxford: Blackwell, pp 17–31.

Urry, J. (2007) *Mobilities*, Cambridge: Polity.

Verkuyten, M. (2005) 'Ethnic group identification and group evaluation among minority and majority groups: testing the multicultural hypothesis', *Journal of Personality and Social psychology*, vol 88, pp 121–38.

Verkuyten, M. (2006) 'Multicultural recognition and ethnic minority rights: a social identity perspective', in W. Stroebe and M. Hewstone (eds) *European review of social psychology (volume 17)*, London: Psychology Press, pp 148–84.

Vitikainen, A. (2013) *Limits of liberal multiculturalism*, Philosophical Studies from the University of Helsinki, 38, Helsinki: University of Helsinki.

Wacquant, L. (2008) *Urban outcasts*, Cambridge: Polity Press.

Walvin, J. (1971) *The black presence*, London: Orback and Chambers.

Warren, A. and Gibson, C. (2011) 'Blue-collar creativity: reframing custom-car culture in the imperilled industrial city', *Environment and Planning A*, vol 43, no 11, pp 2705–22.

Watson, S. (2006) *City publics: the (dis)enchantments of urban encounter*, London: Routledge.

Watson, S. (2009) 'The magic of the marketplace: sociality in a neglected public space', *Urban Studies*, vol 46, no 8, pp 1577–91.

Watson, S. and Saha, A. (2013) 'Suburban Drifts: mundane multiculturalism in outer London', *Ethnic and Racial Studies*, vol 36, no 12 pp 2016–34.

Werbner, P. (1990) *The migration process: capital, gifts, and offerings among British Pakistanis*, New York, NY: Berg.

Westbrook, M.H. (2001) *The electric car: development and future of battery, hybrid and fuel-cell cars*, London: Institution of Electrical Engineers.

Westwood, S. and Williams, J. (eds) (1997) *Imagining cities: scripts, signs and memory*, London: Routledge.

West Yorkshire Policing and Community Research Partnership (2011) *Manningham and Toller policing and wellbeing evaluation*, Bradford: Bradford Law School.

Whisler, T.R. (1999) *The British motor industry, 1945-1994: a case study in industrial decline*, Oxford: Oxford University Press.

White, A. (2011) *Polish families and migration since EU accession*, Bristol: The Policy Press.

Williams, R. (1958) *Culture and Society: 1780-1950*, London: Chatto and Windus.

Wilson, R.A. (ed) (2005) *Human rights in the 'war on terror'*, Cambridge: Cambridge University Press.

Wodak, R. and Matouscheck, B. (1993) '"We are dealing with people whose origins one can clearly tell just by looking": critical discourse analysis and the study of neo-racism in contemporary Austria', *Discourse and Society*, vol 4, no 2, pp 225–48.

Wollen, P. and Kerr, J. (2002) (eds) *Autopia: Cars And Culture*, London: Reaktion Books.

Wolsko, C., Park, B., Judd, C.M. and Wittenbrink, B. (2006) 'Considering the Tower of Babel: correlates of assimilation and multiculturalism among ethnic minority and majority groups in the United States', *Social Justice Research*, vol 19, pp 277–306.

Wood, J. (1988) *Wheels of misfortune: the rise and fall of the British motor industry*, London: Sidgwick & Jackson.

Wright, S.C. and Baray, G. (2012) 'Models of social change in social psychology: collective action or prejudice reduction? Conflict or harmony?' in J. Dixon and M. Levine (eds) *Beyond prejudice*, Cambridge: Cambridge University Press, pp 225–47.

Young, I.M. (1989) 'Polity and group difference: a critique of the idea of universal citizenship', *Ethics*, vol 99, no 2, pp 250–74.

Yuval- Davis, N. (2000) 'Citizenship, territoriality and gendered construction of difference', in E. Isin (ed) *Democracy, citizenship and the global city*, London: Routledge.

Yzerbyt, V. and Corneille, O. (2005) 'Cognitive processes: reality constraints and integrity concerns in social perception', in J.F. Dovidio, P. Glick and L.A. Rudman (eds) *On the nature of prejudice: fifty years on*, Oxford: Blackwell, pp 175–91.

Zanna, M.P. (ed) (2004) *Advances in experimental social psychology (volume 36)*, San Diego, CA: Academic Press.

Zubrzycki, J. (1956) *Polish immigrant in Britain: a study of adjustment*, Oxford: Oxford University Press.

Index